THINKING LIKE A LAWYER

THINKING LIKE A LAWYER

A NEW INTRODUCTION
TO LEGAL REASONING

Frederick Schauer

HARVARD UNIVERSITY PRESS

Cambridge, Massachusetts

London, England

First Harvard University Press paperback edition, 2012

Library of Congress Cataloging-in-Publication Data

Schauer, Frederick F., 1946–
  Thinking like a lawyer : a new introduction to legal reasoning / Frederick Schauer.
    p.   cm.
  Includes bibliographical references and index.
  ISBN 978-0-674-03270-5 (cloth: alk. paper)
  ISBN 978-0-674-06248-1 (pbk.)
  1. Law—Methodology.   I. Title.
  K212.S325 2009
  340′.1—dc22   2008035011

for Bobbie

CONTENTS

This is a book about thinking and reasoning. More particularly, it is about the thinking, reasoning, and argumentative methods of lawyers and judges, which may or may not be different from the thinking, reasoning, and argumentative methods of ordinary people. Whether lawyers think, reason, and argue differently from ordinary folk is a question and not an axiom, but it is nonetheless the case that certain techniques of reasoning are thought to be characteristic of legal decision-making. The focus of this book is on those techniques. Its aim is partly to make a serious academic contribution to thinking about various topics in legal reasoning, but mostly it is to introduce beginning and prospective law students to the nature of legal thinking. In the typical law school, especially in the United States, the faculty believes that it teaches legal thinking and reasoning by osmosis, or interstitially, in the process of providing instruction in substantive subjects such as torts, contracts, criminal law, property, civil procedure, and constitutional law. But less teaching of legal thinking and reasoning actually occurs than faculties typically believe, and even if it does take place, there may be a need to provide in one volume, abstracted from particular subjects, a description and analysis of much of what law students are supposed to glean from the typically indirect teaching of legal reasoning. Similarly, although most law teachers think that it is important that students know something about the major figures, themes, and examples in the canon of legal reasoning, much of this material also falls through the cracks in the modern law school, and again there appears good reason for presenting it in one place. This book seeks to address these needs, at the same time giving lawyers and legal scholars something to chew on—and disagree with—about most of the topics it takes on.

It is surprising but true that some of the most significant contributions to a deep understanding of law have been targeted at beginning law students. Oliver Wendell Holmes's enduring "The Path of the Law" was originally a lecture at the dedication of a building at the Boston University School of Law, where presumably most of those in attendance were law students. Karl Llewellyn's *The Bramble Bush* was intended as a guide to law study for those in their first year of such study. Edward Levi's *An Introduction to Legal Reasoning* had similar aspirations, and H. L. A. Hart explicitly intended *The Concept of Law* as an introduction for English undergraduates. Yet despite aiming in large part at beginners, each of these works, and many others like them, have made such an enduring impression on the scholarly study of law that academics still read, write, and argue about them, even as beginning students continue to learn from them.

It would be presumptuous to compare this book with those, but my goals are similar. On various topics, I seek not only to describe but also to explain and analyze the issues in a way that may prompt new insight or at least fruitful disagreement. And in general I want to present a sympathetic treatment of the formal side of legal thinking, and thus at least slightly to go against the grain of much of twentieth- and twenty-first-century American legal thought. My perspective may seem to slight the creative element in legal thought, but in emphasizing those aspects of legal reasoning that are somewhat formal, somewhat resistant to always doing the right thing in the particular case, and somewhat committed to taking law's written-down character seriously, this book aims to present a picture of legal thinking that accurately reflects the realities of lawyering and judging, while providing an explanation of law's unique contribution to social decision-making.

Some of the topics in this book—rules, precedent, authority, interpretation, and reason-giving, for example—are ones that I have been thinking and writing about for many years. But this book is not a collection of previously published articles, and it has been written anew so that the book will hang together as a coherent whole. Examples and themes will occasionally be repeated, on the assumption that books are often read in relevant chunks rather than from beginning to end, but every sentence and paragraph in this book has been written for this book alone and with the particular goals of this book in mind. Other topics—holding and dicta, law and fact, analogy, presumptions, and Legal Realism, for example—are ones that I have dealt with only in passing in previous writings, but this has seemed the right occasion both to say more about them and to recognize the way in which they are necessary components of a comprehensive account of legal reasoning.

Although it would be impossible to thank all of those from whom I have profited over the years in discussion of various topics about legal reasoning, or even those whose comments on previous written manuscripts have helped me immeasurably, it is important to thank them collectively. Some of the ideas in this book might properly be attributable to others in ways I cannot now disentangle, and others are simply better because they have been honed by the comments of generous friends and critics over the years. With respect to this book, however, acknowledging the immediate help of others is more of a pleasure than an obligation. Larry Alexander, friend and collaborator, offered useful written comments on the entire manuscript, as did an anonymous reviewer for the Harvard University Press. Chapter 1 emerged from a conference on "The Psychology of Judging" at the University of Virginia, and a later version formed the basis for a lecture at the Uehiro Centre for Practical Ethics at the University of Oxford. Chapter 2 was presented at a conference on "Defeasibility in Law" organized at Oxford by Jordi Ferrer and Richard Tur. Chapter 3 benefited from the challenging comments of Brian Bix, Jody Kraus, and Bill Swadling, and Swadling also helped considerably with his comments on Chapter 5. Chapter 4, which benefited greatly from the comments of Adrian Vermeule, was presented and discussed at a Faculty of Law Seminar at University College London, at the Harvard Law School Public Law Workshop, at the Cambridge University Forum on Legal and Political Philosophy, and at the remarkable institution of the Oxford Jurisprudence Discussion Group, where the audience was particularly engaged and incisive. Two members of that group, Jorge Oliveira and Noam Gur, also provided helpful written comments on that chapter, parts of which have appeared, in very different form, in the *Virginia Law Review*. The aforementioned Brian Bix, whose knowledge of jurisprudence is encyclopedic as well as deep, also provided valuable comments on Chapter 7, as did the audience at the annual Legal Research Conference and Lecture at Oxford University. Finally, Bobbie Spellman provided characteristically challenging comments on Chapters 1 through 7 and was the source of valuable discussion on almost every topic in this book. She is responsible not only for some of the words that are contained here but, perhaps more importantly, for many of the words that are not.

Most of this book was written while I had the remarkable privilege of serving as the George Eastman Visiting Professor at the University of Oxford, where I was also honored to be a Fellow of Balliol College. Oxford and Balliol provided enormous tangible and intangible support, a congenial and multidisciplinary academic environment, and a unique group of legal academics whose collective interest in legal theory and legal reasoning is unmatched anywhere in the world. This book is vastly better for their support and for their interest.

THINKING LIKE A LAWYER

1

INTRODUCTION:

IS THERE LEGAL REASONING?

Law schools the world over claim to instruct their students in how to "think like a lawyer." Studying law is not primarily about learning a bunch of legal rules, the law schools insist, for law has far more rules than can be taught in three years of legal education. Besides, many of the legal rules that might be learned in law school will have been changed by the time the students enter legal practice. Nor is legal education about being instructed in where to stand in the courtroom or how to write a will, for many of these skills are better learned once in practice than at a university. Now it is true that both knowing some legal rules and acquiring the skills of lawyering are important to success in the practice of law. And it is also true that some of this knowledge is usefully gained in law school. But what really distinguishes lawyers from other sorts of folk, so it is said, is mastery of an array of talents in argument and decision-making that are often collectively described as *legal reasoning*. So even though law schools do teach some legal rules and some practical professional skills, the law schools also maintain that their most important mission is to train students in the arts of legal argument, legal decision-making, and legal reasoning—in thinking like a lawyer.[1]

But *is* there a form of reasoning that is distinctively *legal* reasoning? *Is* there something that can be thought of as thinking like a lawyer? Of course some lawyers do think and reason better than others, but the same can be said for physicians, accountants, politicians, soldiers, and social workers. And many lawyers think more analytically, or more precisely, or

1. In the 1973 film *The Paper Chase,* the notorious Professor Kingsfield provides a dramatic illustration of the traditional claim, proclaiming in his Contracts class that "you teach yourself the law. I train your minds. You come in here with a skull full of mush, and if you survive, you'll leave thinking like a lawyer."

more rigorously, than many ordinary people, but so do many economists, scientists, and investment bankers. So the claims of law schools to teach legal reasoning must be other than just teaching students how to think more effectively, or more rationally, or more rigorously. And indeed they are. Law schools aspire to teach their students how to think *differently*—differently from ordinary people, and differently from members of other professions. Lord Coke maintained as long ago as 1628 that there was an "artificial" reason to law[2]—a distinction between simple rationality and the special methods of the law, and particularly of judges. Of course Lord Coke might have been wrong. Perhaps he was mistaken to suppose that legal reasoning is distinctive, and perhaps legal reasoning is simply reasoning. Sometimes good reasoning, sometimes bad reasoning, and mostly in between, but nevertheless simply reasoning. But then again, Lord Coke might have been right. After all, the idea that legal reasoning is different from ordinary reasoning, even from very good ordinary reasoning, has been the traditional belief of most lawyers, most judges, and most law schools for a very long time. So although the traditional belief in the distinctiveness of legal reasoning might be mistaken, it comes to us with a sufficiently distinguished provenance that the possibility that there *is* legal reasoning ought not to be dismissed out of hand.

That there might be something distinctive about legal reasoning does not flow inexorably from the existence of law as a discrete profession, for it is far from obvious that those who take up some specialized calling must necessarily think and reason differently from those outside that calling. Electricians know things that carpenters do not, and carpenters know things that plumbers do not. But it would be odd to talk of thinking like a carpenter or a plumber. Indeed, maybe it is just as odd to talk of thinking like a lawyer. Yet law schools do not think it odd, nor do most lawyers and judges. Law schools and the lawyers and judges they train suppose that lawyers are characterized by more than knowing things that nonlawyers do not. Knowledge of the law is important, as are skills of advocacy and drafting, but the traditional account of what makes lawyers distinctive is that they have something other than this.

What lawyers have other than their technical skills and their knowl-

2. Sir Edward Coke [pronounced "cook"], *Commentaries upon Littleton* 97b (Charles Butler ed., 1985) (1628). For a modern elaboration, see Charles Fried, "The Artificial Reason of the Law or: What Lawyers Know," 60 *Tex. L. Rev.* 35 (1981).

edge of the law is not so simple to pin down, however. It is relatively easy to say what thinking like a lawyer is not. It is rather more difficult to say what it is, and that difficulty may account for part of why there have been numerous skeptical challenges over the years to law's claim to distinctiveness. Legal Realists (about whom much more will be said in Chapter 7) such as Jerome Frank and (to a lesser extent) Karl Llewellyn insisted that lawyers and judges do not approach problems in any way that differs significantly from the approaches of other policymakers and public decision-makers. Many of the political scientists who study Supreme Court decision-making often make similar claims, arguing that the ideologies, attitudes, politics, and policy preferences of the Justices play a larger role in the Court's decisions than do any of the traditional methods of legal reasoning. Psychologists examining the reasoning processes of lawyers and judges focus less on the supposedly characteristic modes of legal reasoning than on those shortcomings of rationality that bedevil all decision-makers, whether lawyers or not.[4] And as far back as the acid critique of the legal profession ("Judge and Company," he called it) offered by Jeremy Bentham in the early part of the nineteenth century,[5] skeptical or deflationary accounts of legal reasoning have existed. Lawyers and judges may be lawyers and judges, so the common thread of these challenges to the traditional story about legal reasoning goes, but they are also human beings, with more or less the full array of human talents and human failings. And the fact that lawyers and judges are human beings explains far more about the methods of legal and judicial reasoning, it

3. See, e.g., Lawrence Baum, *The Puzzle of Judicial Behavior* (1997); Saul Brenner & Harold J. Spaeth, *Stare Indecisis: The Alteration of Precedent on the U.S. Supreme Court, 1946–1992* (1995); Lee Epstein & Jack Knight, *The Choices Justice Make* (1998); Jeffrey A. Segal & Harold J. Spaeth, *The Supreme Court and the Attitudinal Model Revisited* (2002); Harold J. Spaeth & Jeffrey A. Segal, *Majority Rule or Minority Will* (1999); Lawrence Baum, "Measuring Policy Change in the U.S. Supreme Court," 82 *Am. Pol. Sci. Rev.* 905 (1988).

4. See, e.g., Chris Guthrie, Jeffrey J. Rachlinski, & Andrew J. Wistrich, "Inside the Judicial Mind," 86 *Cornell L. Rev.* 777 (2001); Dan Simon, "A Third View of the Black Box: Cognitive Coherence in Legal Decision Making," 71 *U. Chi. L. Rev.* 511 (2004); Barbara A. Spellman, "On the Supposed Expertise of Judges in Evaluating Evidence," 155 *U. Penn L. Rev.* PENNumbra No. 1 (2007), http://www.pennumbra.com/issues/articles/155–1/Spellman.pdf.

5. Jeremy Bentham, "Introductory View of the Rationale of Evidence," *in* 6 *The Works of Jeremy Bentham* 22–24 (John Bowring ed., 1843).

is said, than anything that lawyers or judges may have learned in law school, mastered in legal practice, or picked up while serving as a judge.

The skeptics of legal reasoning do not generally believe that lawyers and judges are lying. They do believe, however, that what lawyers and judges think they are doing—their internal view of their own activities—often masks a deeper reality, one in which policy choices and various other nonlegal attributes play a much larger role in explaining legal arguments and legal outcomes than even the participants themselves believe or understand. Insofar as this more skeptical picture accurately reflects reality, legal reasoning may be less distinctive and consequently less important than many have thought. But if instead the traditional account is largely sound, and if lawyers and judges, even though they admittedly share many reasoning characteristics with their fellow humans, possess methods of thinking that are distinctively legal, then it is important to explore just what those special characteristics and methods might be. Consequently, one way of approaching the alleged distinctiveness of legal reasoning is to consider just how much of the reasoning of lawyers and judges is explained by their specialized training and roles, on the one hand, and just how much is explained simply by the fact that they are human, on the other.[6]

The claim that there *is* such a thing as legal reasoning is thus a (contested) hypothesis that lawyers have ways of approaching problems and making decisions that others do not. But just what are these ways? Sometimes people argue that the special skill of the lawyer is a facility in dealing with facts and evidence, coupled with the related ability to understand the full context of a particular event, dispute, or decision.[7] Yet although these are important skills for good lawyers to have, it is not so clear that successful lawyers have or need them to a greater extent than successful police detectives, historians, psychiatrists, and anthropologists. Similarly, others have sought to characterize legal reasoning in

6. See Frederick Schauer, "Is There a Psychology of Judging?," *in* David E. Klein & Gregory Mitchell, *The Psychology of Judicial Decision Making* (forthcoming 2009).

7. See, e.g., Steven Burton, *An Introduction to Law and Legal Reasoning* (3d ed., 2005); Richard A. Bandstra, "Looking Toward Lansing: Could You Be a Lawyer/Legislator?," 89 *Mich. B.J.* 28 (2005); Martha Minow & Elizabeth Spelman, "In Context," 63 *S. Cal. L. Rev.* 1597 (1990).

terms of a heightened ability to see the other side of an argument,[8] or, relatedly, of being empathetic to individuals and putting one's self in the shoes of another,[9] but these too are attributes we expect to see in good thinkers and good people of all stripes. Indeed, even the oft-touted legal talent for reasoning by analogy[10] is hardly distinctive to lawyers and judges, for using analogies effectively may well be what distinguishes experts from novices in almost any field of endeavor.[11] So yes, we would like lawyers and judges to be smart, sympathetic, analytic, rigorous, precise, open-minded, and sensitive to factual nuance, among other things, but because these are also the traits we wish to have in our politicians, social workers, physicians, and investment bankers, it is not yet so clear what skills or characteristics, if any, lawyers are supposed to have that others do not.

The chapters in this book are dedicated to exploring the various forms of reasoning that have traditionally been especially associated with the legal system, such as making decisions according to rules, treating certain sources as authoritative, respecting precedent even when it appears to dictate the wrong outcome, being sensitive to burdens of proof, and being attuned to questions of decision-making jurisdiction—understanding that it is one thing to recognize a correct outcome but another to realize that some institutions might be empowered to reach that outcome while others are not. But we should not at the outset set up unrealistic aspirations for legal reasoning's claim to distinctiveness. In the first place, law cannot plausibly be seen as a closed system, in the way that games like chess might be. All of the moves of a game of chess can be found in the rules of chess, but not all of the moves in legal argument and

8. See Suzanna Sherry, "Democracy and the Death of Knowledge," 75 *U. Cinc. L. Rev.* 1053 (2007).

9. See Katherine Bartlett, "Feminist Legal Methods," 103 *Harv. L. Rev.* 829 (1990).

10. E.g., Edward Levi, *An Introduction to Legal Reasoning* (1949); Cass R. Sunstein, *Legal Reasoning and Political Conflict* (1996); Lloyd Weinreb, *Legal Reason: The Use of Analogy in Legal Argument* (2005).

11. See, e.g., Kenneth D. Forbus, "Exploring Analogy in the Large," *in The Analogical Mind: Perspectives from Cognitive Science* 23 (Kenneth D. Forbus, Keith J. Holyoak, & Boris N. Kokinov eds., 2001); Keith J. Holyoak, "Analogy," *in The Cambridge Handbook of Thinking and Reasoning* 117 (Keith J. Holyoak & Robert J. Morrison eds., 2005).

legal decision-making can be found in the rules of law.[12] Not only does law of necessity depend on numerous skills other than those explicitly understood to be legal, but law is inevitably and especially subject to the unforeseeable complexity of the human condition. We can at best imperfectly predict the future, just as we continue to be uncertain about what we will do with that future once we get there. As the world continues to throw the unexpected at us, law will find itself repeatedly forced to go outside of the existing rules in order to serve the society in which it exists. Law may well contain within its arsenal of argument and decision-making the resources it needs to adapt to a changing world, but insofar as that is the case, it is even less likely that the image of a totally closed system in which existing rules of law—and maybe even the existing practices of legal argument—will be an accurate picture of what law does and how it does it.

Not only is law not a closed system, but its characteristic methods of reasoning, if indeed there are such methods, are also not ones that are completely unique to law. Perhaps there is little overlap between Estonian and English, or between literary criticism and multivariate calculus, but it is not plausible to deny that even the most characteristic forms of legal reasoning are found outside the legal system. It is true that lawyers and judges frequently make arguments and decisions based on the dictates of written-down rules, but so do bureaucrats, bankers, and every one of us when we observe the speed limit written on a sign. The legal system also seems particularly concerned with precedent—with doing the same thing that has been done before just because it has been done before. But this form of thinking is again hardly unique to law, as is well known to parents when dealing with the argument by a younger child that he or she should be allowed to do something at a certain age only because an older sibling was allowed to do the same thing at that age. And although law is also an institution characterized by authority-based reasoning—taking the source of a directive rather than the reasons behind it as a justification for following it—this too is hardly unknown outside of the legal system. The family is again a good example, and every parent who has ever in exasperation exclaimed "Because I said so!" to a stub-

---

12. For a well-known denial that law can possibly be seen as a closed and deductive system, see H.L.A. Hart, "Positivism and the Separation of Law and Morals," 71 *Harv. L. Rev.* 593, 608 (1958).

born child recognizes that appeals to authority rather than reason have their place throughout human existence.

Yet although the characteristic modes of legal reasoning are all frequently found outside the law, it might still be that these forms of reasoning and decision-making are particularly concentrated in the legal system. For however much these various forms of reasoning do exist throughout our decision-making lives, it is important not to forget that they are odd, and odd in a special way. And this special oddness is that every one of the dominant characteristics of legal reasoning and legal argument can be seen as a route toward reaching a decision *other than* the best all-things-considered decision for the matter at hand. Often when we obey a speed limit we are driving at a speed that is not the same as what we think is the best speed given the traffic, the driving conditions, and our own driving skills. Consequently, to obey a speed limit is to do something we do not think best. Similarly, making a decision just because the same decision has been made before—following precedent—gets interesting primarily when we would otherwise have made a different decision. The parent who gives the younger child the same privileges at the same age as an older child feels the pull of precedent only when he or she otherwise thinks there is a good reason for treating the two differently, and so being constrained by precedent is again a path *away* from what had otherwise seemed to be the right decision. And we say we are *obeying* or *following* an authority only if what we are doing because of what the authority has said is not the same as what we would have done if left to our own devices to make the decision we thought best. The soldier who follows an order might well do something else if allowed to make his or her own unguided (or uncommanded) decision, just as the obedient student or child is one who suppresses his or her own desires to do something else.

Once we understand that these admittedly common forms of reasoning and decision-making are nevertheless somewhat peculiar—that they often dictate outcomes other than those the decision-maker would otherwise have chosen—we can understand as well that the substantial presence of these forms of reasoning in the legal system—more substantial, proportionately, than in the totality of our decision-making lives—can provide the foundation for a plausible claim that there is such a thing as legal reasoning. If these somewhat counterintuitive forms of reasoning— forms of reasoning that often lead to results other than what would otherwise seem to be the best all-things-considered outcome for the case at hand—are dominant in law but somewhat more exceptional elsewhere, then we might be able to conclude that there *is* such a thing as legal reasoning, that there *is* something we might label "thinking like a lawyer," and that there *is* accordingly something that it is vitally important that lawyers and judges know how to do well and that law schools must teach their students. To repeat, this array of reasoning methods is not unique to the legal system, and these are not the only methods that the law uses. The modes of legal reasoning are found elsewhere, and the modes of what we might call "ordinary" reasoning have a large place in legal argument and legal decision-making. But if it turns out that there are indeed methods of reasoning that are found everywhere but that are particularly concentrated and dominant in legal argument and decision-making, then the claim that there is something called legal reasoning will turn out to be justified.

Law's seemingly counterintuitive methods are not simply a historical peculiarity. Rather, they are a function of law's inherent *generality*. Although disputes, in court and out, involve particular people with particular problems engaged in particular controversies, the law tends to treat the particulars it confronts as members of larger categories. Rather than attempting to reach the best result for each controversy in a wholly particularistic and contextual way, law's goal is often to make sure that the outcome for *all* or at least most of the particulars in a given category is the right one. Once again Lord Coke is illuminating: "It is better saith the Law to suffer a mischiefe (that is particular to one) than an inconvenience that may prejudice many."[13] In other words, for Coke it was better to reach the wrong result in the particular controversy than to adopt a rule that would produce what would seem to be the correct result for this case but at the cost of producing the wrong result in many others.

Coke's lesson can be observed in the traditional ritual of Socratic dialogue[14] that takes place between student and teacher in the first year

13. Sir Edward Coke, as quoted in J.R. Stoner, *Common Law and Liberal Theory: Coke, Hobbes, and the Origins of American Constitutionalism* 25 (1992).

14. There is scant connection between the question-centered methods of teaching employed by Socrates in the Platonic dialogues and the type of questioning that has traditionally taken place in the law school classroom. Even apart from the enormous advantage that Plato had over the rest of us in being able to write the answers as well as the questions, Socrates' goal was to extract from his interlocutors some latent but nonspecialized insight, rather than to inculcate in them a special-

thinking like a lawyer

of law school. After eventually being coaxed into accurately reciting the facts of some reported case, the student is asked what she thinks should be the correct result for the present case. Typically, the student then responds by announcing what she believes to be the fairest or most just outcome between the opposing positions of the particular parties. At this point the student is asked by her interrogator to give the rule or principle that would support this outcome, and here the characteristic pattern of Socratic inquiry begins. By a series of patterned and well-planned (and often well-worn) hypothetical examples, the professor challenges the student's initially offered rule, with the aim of demonstrating that the rule that would generate a just or fair or efficient outcome in the present case would generate less just, less fair, or otherwise less satisfactory results in other cases. And in taking the chosen victim through this series of uncomfortable applications of her initially selected rule, the professor attempts to get all the students in the class to understand, just as Coke argued, that the best legal rule may at times be one which will produce an unjust result in the present case but which will produce better results in a larger number of cases, the result in the present case notwithstanding.

results

This form of Socratic inquiry is not restricted to the law school classroom, and it is noteworthy that it is the common form of judicial questioning in appellate argument. Because appellate courts often see themselves as pronouncing rules that will control other and future factual situations, and as writing opinions that will serve as precedents in subsequent cases, appellate judges are often concerned as much with the effect of their immediate ruling on future cases as with reaching the best result in the present case. As a consequence, appellate advocates frequently find themselves asked in oral argument how the rule or result they are advocating will play out in various hypothetical situations. Just as in the law school classroom, judges pose these hypothetical scenarios to the lawyers who argue before them because of the belief that what seems initially to be the right result in the particular dispute before the court will wind up

---

ized skill that they hitherto did not possess. Now it may be that the ability to engage in reasoning focused not simply on this case or this dispute is latent in virtually everyone, but if it is sufficiently latent that it takes a squadron of law professors and three years of law school to extract it for most people, then there is no difference of consequence between what we might label the inculcation and the extraction models of legal education. In either case, the purpose of legal education is to develop in the student an ability actually to *do* something he or she could not do before.

as the actual outcome only if it can be justified in a way that will not produce the wrong outcomes in too many expected future cases.

In seeking to demonstrate to the hapless student or the struggling advocate how the best legal outcome may be something other than the best outcome for the immediate controversy, the prototypical Socratic interrogation embodies law's pervasive willingness to reach a result differing from the one that is optimally fair or maximally wise, all things considered, in the particular case. In *United States v. Locke*,[15] for example, the Supreme Court dealt with a case in which a renewal of a land claim that had been filed on December 31, 1982, had been rejected by the Bureau of Land Management because the relevant statute required that such filings be lodged "prior to December 31" of any given year. Although it seemed obvious to the Court and to virtually everyone else that the language of the statute was defective, and that what Congress really meant to say was "on or prior to December 31," Justice Thurgood Marshall and five other Justices concluded that the particular rights and wrongs of Locke's own claim were less important than the larger question whether the Supreme Court should be in the business of rewriting even obviously mistaken federal statutes, especially ones dealing with deadlines and filing dates. Here and elsewhere, law is typically concerned with the full array of applications of some general rule and principle, and as a result the law often pursues that concern at the cost of being less worried than nonlegal decisionmakers might be with a possible error or injustice or unfairness in the particular case. When the Rule of Law is described, as it traditionally was, in contrast to the rule of men, the idea was that the Rule of Law was a principle that was wary of individual judgment and reluctant to rely too heavily on the unguided judgments and whims of particular people. So although it may sometimes seem unfair to take the existence of a clear rule or a clear precedent as commanding a result the judge herself thinks wrong, following even a rule or precedent perceived by the judge to be erroneous is what, under the traditional understanding, the law often expects its decision-makers to do.[16]

15. 471 U.S. 84 (1985).
16. Consider, for example, Justice Louis Brandeis's famous observation that "in most matters it is more important that the applicable rule of law be settled than that it be settled right." *Burnet v. Coronado Oil & Gas. Co.*, 285 U.S. 393, 412 (1932) (Brandeis, dissenting).

10

It is important to understand that the belief that there is a moderately distinct form of reasoning we can call "legal reasoning" is in the final analysis an empirical claim. Most people can describe a unicorn, but our ability to describe a unicorn is not inconsistent with the crucial fact that there are no actual unicorns in the world. Similarly, most of us can point to examples of genuine self-sacrificing heroism, but even as we do so we recognize that such behavior is highly unusual. And so the lesson we should draw from these examples is that our ability to describe legal reasoning, and even to point to actual examples of its use, says less than is commonly supposed about how often such reasoning is an important component of what lawyers and judges actually do. To point to one or a few instances of genuine constraint by precedent, for example, says almost nothing about the frequency of such constraint throughout the universe of legal decisions. And to identify real cases in which rules or authority have made a difference is itself not strong evidence that rules and authority make a difference very often. Still, if it turns out that we can identify large numbers of real-world examples of genuine legal reasoning, the burden of proof will shift to those who would say that such reasoning is rare or that it is all or mostly imaginary. The skeptical position that distinctively legal reasoning is unusual rather than typical in actual legal practice may in the final analysis be sound, but the premise of this book is not only that legal reasoning does exist, even if it is not all that lawyers and judges do, but also that its actual existence is sufficiently widespread to say that there is, descriptively, something we can accurately characterize as "thinking like a lawyer."

Even if we conclude that there *is* such a thing as legal reasoning, that is not necessarily to conclude that legal reasoning is a good thing. Indeed, maybe the Rule of Law is not such a good thing. Plato notoriously proposed a society that would be governed by philosopher-kings, and it is hardly self-evident that in such a society the wise and good philosopher-kings should be bound to follow rules that will lead them away from their own best judgment, or should be constrained by precedent to decide things the way they had been decided in the past when the previous decision seems mistaken, or should be commanded to obey authorities whose judgment may very well be flawed. In a society governed by the wise and the good, legal reasoning is likely simply to get in the way. And in such a society, were such a society ever to exist, the Rule of Law would be at least superfluous, and quite possibly pernicious.

11

Of course, we do not live in Plato's utopia,[17] and thus we understand that the values of legal reasoning and the Rule of Law may serve important goals in constraining the actions of leaders lacking the benign wisdom of Plato's hypothetical philosopher-kings. But even when we leave Plato's utopia and find ourselves in the real world with real leaders and their real flaws, the same dilemma persists. Legal reasoning in particular and the Rule of Law in general will often serve as an impediment to wise policies and to the sound discretion of enlightened, even if not perfect, leaders.[18] When and where the Rule of Law might turn out to serve the wrong interests, or simply to be so concerned with preventing abuses of individual discretion that it impedes sound discretion, is not the focus of this book. Evaluating law and assessing the Rule of Law is the work of a lifetime, and indeed not just the lifetime of any one person. The far more modest goal of this book, therefore, is to identify, describe, analyze, and at times evaluate the characteristic modes of legal reasoning. Determining, in the aggregate, whether and when those modes are worth having, a question whose answer is far from self-evident, is best left for other occasions.

17. Nor did Plato, as he well recognized.
18. See Morton J. Horwitz, "The Rule of Law: An Unqualified Human Good?," 86 *Yale L.J.* 561 (1977) (book review).

2

RULES—IN LAW AND ELSEWHERE

2.1 Of Rules in General

Reasoning with *rules* is perhaps the most common image of what lawyers and judges do. A widespread popular conception has it that lawyers argue their cases by appealing to abstruse rules not understandable by ordinary people, and that judges make their decisions by consulting books full of such rules. Having found the right rule, so it is thought, the judge proceeds to apply it mechanically to the case at hand, and that is the end of the matter.

Legal sophisticates commonly mock this image, which strikes insiders to the law as being far removed from the realities of actual practice. And for a host of reasons it is, not least being that most controversies or events involving a straightforward application of existing rules will not wind up in court at all.[1] But for all the inaccuracies and exaggerations built into this ubiquitous caricature of what lawyers and judges do, it nevertheless captures a genuinely important part of law. Rules actually do occupy a large part of law and legal reasoning. Lawyers frequently consult them, and judges often make decisions by following them. Law may not be all about rules, but it is certainly a lot about rules, from the

---

1. Because straightforward or easy applications of legal rules are rarely litigated, the cases that come to a court are predominantly and disproportionately ones that are in some way hard. The litigated hard cases thus represent a biased sample of all legal events, a phenomenon typically referred to as the *selection effect*. See George L. Priest & William Klein, "The Selection of Disputes for Litigation," 13 *J. Legal Stud.* 1 (1984). We will take up the selection effect and its consequences in the next section of this chapter, and return to it in Chapters 7 and 8.

Rule Against Perpetuities in property to the "mailbox rule" in contracts to the felony murder rule in criminal law to the Federal Rules of Civil Procedure to innumerable others. And because rules loom so large in what law does and how it does it, figuring out in a noncaricatured way what rules are and how they work will take us some distance toward understanding legal reasoning, legal argument, and legal decision-making.

Consider the typical speed limit, which is a rather uncomplicated example of a rule. The sign says SPEED LIMIT 55, and our first reaction is that the speed limit is 55 miles per hour.[2] But why 55? Presumably the speed limit was set at 55 because someone in authority—possibly the legislature, but more likely the highway department, the county commissioners, or the state police—believed that driving faster than 55 on this road would be unsafe. All well and good, and probably right for most circumstances, but an important feature of the speed limit sign is that it is there *all* the time. And equally important is that the speed limit applies to virtually everyone.[3] The speed limit is 55 when it is raining and 55 when it is clear. It is 55 when there is heavy traffic and 55 when there is none. It is 55 for cars designed to go up to120 and 55 for cars that start to shake at 50. And although 55 is the speed limit for safe drivers, it is also the speed limit for the reckless and the inexperienced. The speed limit of 55 is designed to achieve safety, but in some circumstances 55 might be too high to achieve that goal, and in others it might be unnecessarily low.

So suppose that you are out driving your new and carefully maintained car one clear, dry, traffic-free Sunday morning. And suppose that you are an experienced and cautious driver. Indeed, you have never been in an accident and have never been cited for a moving traffic violation. Because you are a good driver and because the conditions are ideal,

2. Some people will respond to this example by pointing out that when the posted speed limit is 55, the "real" speed limit is somewhat higher. For many drivers, perhaps even most drivers, SPEED LIMIT 55 means you should not drive over 64, because they know that typically the police will not stop you unless you have exceeded the speed limit by at least 10 miles per hour. The discussion of Legal Realism in Chapter 7 will address this issue, examining more carefully the implications of the fact that official practice often diverges from the literal meaning of a written rule. This divergence raises important and complex questions, but the typical speed limit is more straightforward. Most drivers know what the acceptable leeway is, and almost all of the point of the example in the text is preserved even when there is a widespread knowledge that the actual speed limit is the posted speed limit plus 9 miles per hour.

3. We need not worry for the moment about fire engines, ambulances, and police cars.

you decide to drive—perfectly safely—at 70. Having made that decision, however, you look in your rearview mirror and are disturbed to see the flashing lights of a police car signaling you to pull over. The next thing you know, the police officer is informing you that you have been clocked at 70 miles an hour in a 55-miles-per-hour zone. "I know," you say to the officer, "but let me explain. The fifty-five-miles-per-hour limit is designed to ensure safety, but actually I am driving very safely. There is no traffic. The weather is clear. The highway is dry. My car is in good condition. And I have a perfect driving record. You can check. You and I know that fifty-five is just an average for all drivers and all conditions, but the real goal of the speed limit is to make sure that people drive safely, and you can't deny that I was driving very safely."

We all know what would happen next. The officer would point to the speed limit sign, if one were visible, and then say something like, "The speed limit on this road is fifty-five. Fifty-five means fifty-five, not what *you* think is safe driving." And that would be the end of it. You would receive a speeding ticket, and you would get that ticket even though the goal of the speed limit rule was to make people drive safely, and, most importantly, you would get the ticket even though you *were* driving safely.

This example may seem trivial, even silly, yet it illustrates a larger and central point about the very idea of a rule. Every rule has a background justification—sometimes called a rationale—which is the goal that the rule is designed to serve.[4] Just as the typical speed limit is designed to promote safety on the highways, so the goal of the Rule Against Perpetuities is to limit to a plausible time the period of uncertainty in the possession and disposition of property. The goal of Rule 56 of the Federal Rules of Civil Procedure—the summary judgment rule—is to eliminate before trial those cases in which there is no legally serious and factually supportable claim. The goal of the parol evidence rule is to effectuate the intention of parties to reduce their agreement to writing. And so on. Every rule has a rationale or background justification of this variety, and thus every rule can be seen as an attempt to further its background justification.

In theory, it would often be possible for the rule simply to be a restatement of the background justification. A few years ago, for example,

4. For a lengthier discussion, see Frederick Schauer, *Playing by the Rules: A Philosophical Examination of Rule-Based Decision-Making in Law and in Life* (1991). See also Larry Alexander & Emily Sherwin, *The Rule of Rules: Morality, Rules, and the Dilemmas of Law* (2001).

the state of Montana eliminated all fixed speed limits, requiring instead only that driving should be "reasonable and prudent."[5] But drivers have widely divergent ideas of what is reasonable and what is prudent, and so do police officers and judges. As a result, there developed wide variations in speed limit enforcement, the consequence being that drivers became highly uncertain about just how fast they could go without running afoul of the law. This much uncertainty was too much for the Montana Supreme Court, which struck down the "reasonable and prudent" rule as excessively vague. Indeed, even had the rule not been declared unconstitutional under the Montana Constitution, it was likely that the legislature would itself have reinstituted numerical speed limits and eliminated the "reasonable and prudent" rule. In Montana, as elsewhere, people understand that the background justifications themselves are often too vague to be helpful, too fuzzy to give people the kind of guidance they expect from the law, and too subject to manipulation and varying interpretation to constrain the actions of those who exercise power. So although in theory a speed limit rule could simply restate these abstract rationales—Drive Safely, or Drive Prudently, or Drive with Care—in practice the abstract rationales or background justifications are typically reduced to concrete rules. These concrete rules are designed to serve the background justifications, but it is the rule itself that carries the force of law, and it is the rule itself that ordinarily dictates the legal outcome. That is why the safe driver gets a ticket when she is driving safely at 70 miles per hour, and this example is just one of many that illustrate the way in which it is the concrete manifestation of a rule and not the abstract justification lying behind it that normally represents what the law requires.

Consider, to take another example, the somewhat technical rule (Rule 16(b) of the Securities Exchange Act of 1934) in the American law of securities regulation that prohibits certain corporate insiders from buying and then selling (or selling and then buying) shares in their own company within a period of six months or less.[6] Lying behind this rule is the goal—the rationale—of preventing corporate insiders, who are presumed to have inside information typically unavailable to the public and unknown by those with whom insiders might trade, from trading on that inside information. But the rule itself says nothing about the actual possession of

5. Mont. Code Ann. 61–8–303 (1996), invalidated on grounds of excessive vagueness in State v. Stanko, 974 P.2d 1132 (1998). See Robert E. King & Cass R. Sunstein, "Doing Without Speed Limits," 79 *B.U. L. Rev.* 155 (1999).

6. 5 U.S.C. §78p(b) (2000).

inside information, and instead simply prohibits any officer, director, or holder of 10 percent or more of a company's shares from buying and then selling or selling and then buying the company's shares within a six-month period. The thinking that produced such a specific rule was that by prohibiting people from engaging in so-called short-swing transactions, the rule makes it that much more difficult for insiders to profit from the knowledge they have gained just because of their position as insiders. The rule does its work, therefore, by prohibiting short-swing transactions regardless of whether the person engaging in the transaction actually has insider knowledge, just as the speed limit rule prohibits driving at a speed in excess of the limit regardless of whether the driver is in fact driving unsafely. The short-swing purchaser or seller who qualifies as an insider under the highly precise definition of an insider has violated the rule and is required to "disgorge" his profits even if he has no inside information whatsoever. And although a person who trades on inside information without being an insider as defined by this rule may well find himself in trouble under some other rule,[7] it is noteworthy that he is not liable under *this* rule, just as the person driving unsafely but below the speed limit has not violated the speed limit rule.

Still another example comes from the laws in many jurisdictions prohibiting the possession of burglar tools.[8] The law does not *really* care about burglar tools—it cares about burglaries and about limiting their frequency. But although the rule serves the background justification of preventing burglaries, it puts that background justification into effect by prescribing something more specific. The rule prohibits possessing burglar tools rather than just anything that might increase the risk of burglary, just as the typical speed limit is an explicit numerical rule and not a mandate that everyone drive safely or prudently, and just as the short-swing transaction rule prohibits all transactions by defined insiders in a defined period of time and not all or only those transactions in which a person trades on inside information.

The lesson to be drawn from these examples is that one of the principal features of rules—and the feature that makes them rules—is that

---

7. In particular, Rule 10b-5 promulgated by the Securities and Exchange Commission, 17 C.F.R. §240.10b-5 (2007), which, among other things, makes it unlawful in many securities transactions to omit to state a material fact to other participants in the transaction.

8. E.g., Conn. Gen. Stat. Ann. 53A-106 (West, 1999); Cal. Penal Code 466 (West, 1999).

what the rule *says* really matters. That is why the police officer will give you a ticket if you are driving above the speed limit even when you are driving carefully and safely, and that is why corporate officials and major shareholders are liable for damages if they trade in their company's stock within a six-month period even when they have no inside information at all. Recall from Chapter 1 the discussion of *United States v. Locke,*[9] in which the Supreme Court enforced the "prior to December 31" Bureau of Land Management filing rule even though it was obvious that what Congress really meant to say was something like "on or prior to December 31." The decision in *Locke* seems to some commentators mistakenly to take the importance of the actual language of the rule to absurd extremes,[10] and perhaps it does, but the fact that six Supreme Court Justices were willing to enforce to the letter the literal language of the "prior to December 31" rule demonstrates the way in which a big part of a rule's "ruleness" is tied up with the language in which a rule is written. Central to what rules are and how they function is that what the rule *says* is the crucial factor, even if what the rule says seems wrong or inconsistent with the background justifications lying behind the rule, and even if following what the rule says produces a bad result on some particular occasion. When we take up statutory interpretation in Chapter 8, we will delve more deeply into these issues, including considering the circumstances under which what a statute literally says is not the last word in interpreting its meaning and application. But even when what a rule says is not the last word, it is almost always the first word, and understanding what rules are and how they work entails understanding that the rule, as written, is important in itself, rather than being merely a transparent window into the rule's background justification.

2.2 The Core and the Fringe

Although a large part of how rules work is a function of what the words of a rule say, it is often difficult for lawyers and judges, and even more for

9. 471 U.S. 84 (1985).

10. Richard A. Posner, "Legal Formalism, Legal Realism, and the Interpretation of Statutes and the Constitution," 37 *Case West. Res. L. Rev.* 179 (1986); Nicholas S. Zeppos, "Legislative History and the Interpretation of Statutes: Toward a Fact-Finding Model of Statutory Interpretation," 76 *Va. L. Rev.* 1295, 1314–16 (1990).

law students, to appreciate this feature of rules. This is because so much of what judges, lawyers, and law students do takes place at the edges of rules rather than at their centers. The English legal philosopher H. L. A. Hart famously drew a distinction between the clear center (he called it the "core") of a rule and its debatable edges (which Hart labeled the "penumbra"), and in the process offered a hypothetical example that has become legendary.[11] In his example, Hart asked us to imagine a rule prohibiting "vehicles" from a public park. This rule, Hart observed, would plainly prohibit automobiles, because automobiles clearly count as vehicles according to the widely accepted meaning of the word "vehicle." And Hart would undoubtedly have reached the same conclusion with respect to trucks, buses, and motorcycles, all of them being core examples of "vehicles" as well. But what, Hart asked, if we were considering whether bicycles, roller skates, or toy automobiles were also prohibited by the "no vehicles in park" rule? And what, he might have asked, about baby carriages? And, these days, what about skateboards or motorized wheelchairs? Now we are not so sure. We are no longer at the core of the rule, where things appeared pretty straightforward. Instead we have moved out to the fuzzy edge or penumbra of the rule, where we might be required to look to the purpose behind the rule to see whether some particular fringe application should be included or not. If the rule's background justification had been to promote safety for pedestrians, for example, then perhaps baby carriages but not bicycles or roller skates would be allowed in the park. But if instead the rule had been aimed at keeping down the noise level, then maybe there would be no reason to exclude bicycles, roller skates, or baby carriages, although there might be good grounds for wanting to keep out gas- or electric-powered toy cars.[12]

11. H. L. A. Hart, *The Concept of Law* 125–26 (Joseph Raz & Penelope Bulloch eds., 2d ed., 1994). The example first appeared in H. L. A. Hart, "Positivism and the Separation of Law and Morals," 71 *Harv. L. Rev.* 593, 608–15 (1958). For an extended analysis, see Frederick Schauer, "A Critical Guide to Vehicles in the Park," 83 *N.Y.U. L. Rev.* 1109 (2008). We will return to the example in Chapter 8 when taking up the subject of statutory interpretation.

12. In a memorable debate in the pages of the *Harvard Law Review*, Lon Fuller, Hart's American contemporary, challenged the idea that the plain meaning of words alone could *ever* produce a clear outcome without consultation of the purpose lying behind the rule. Lon L. Fuller, "Positivism and Fidelity to Law—A Reply to Professor Hart," 71 *Harv. L. Rev.* 630 (1958), *replying to* H. L. A. Hart, "Positivism and the Separation of Law and Morals," 71 *Harv. L. Rev.* 593 (1958). The

That rules have debatable fringes where there are good arguments on both sides of the question whether the rule apples or not is hardly news to lawyers. Indeed, such disputes are a large part of the lawyer's stock in trade. But the clear and undebatable core of a rule is often neglected by lawyers and law students because plain or easy applications of rules so rarely get to appellate courts. For that matter, they rarely get to court at all, or even to lawyers. If the driver of a pickup truck with family in tow and picnic aboard arrived at the park and observed the NO VEHI-CLES sign, we would expect him in the normal case simply to turn around and drive somewhere else, producing no controversy at all. Similarly, although there might be difficult and contested questions at the edges of even a rule specifying a precise time limit, in the ordinary course of things a defendant in federal court will answer a complaint or request an extension prior to the expiration of the twenty-day period specified in Rule 12(a)(1)(A)(i) of the Federal Rules of Civil Procedure. These straightforward applications of legal rules rarely appear in casebooks or law school classes, and as a result much that is important about legal rules tends to operate invisibly to law students, invisibly to lawyers, and especially invisibly to judges.[13]

The distinction between the clear core and the fuzzy edge of a rule can be illustrated by way of a real case decided by the United States Supreme Court a few years ago, a case intriguingly similar to Hart's hypothetical example of the vehicles in the park. In *Stewart v. Dutra Barge Company*,[14] the question before the Court was whether a large dredge called a Super Scoop was a "vessel" as that word is used in federal maritime law. In fact, the Super Scoop was the largest dredge in the world at the time, and was being used to excavate Boston Harbor as part of the project known as the Big Dig. Willard Stewart, a worker on the Super Scoop, was injured while on the job, and he sued the owners of the dredge, claiming that the company's negligence was the cause of his injuries. It turned out, however, that whether Stewart could bring such a suit depended on whether the Super Scoop was a "vessel." If it was, then a federal statute called the Jones Act[15] would allow and provide the basis

---

relationship between text and purpose is important and will be among the central themes we deal with in Chapter 8.

13. See Frederick Schauer, "Easy Cases," 58 *S. Cal. L. Rev.* 636 (1985).

14. 543 U.S. 481 (2005).

15. 46 U.S.C. App. §688(a)(2000).

for the suit. But if the Super Scoop was not a vessel, then another federal statute—the Longshore and Harbor Workers' Compensation Act[16]—would allow people like Stewart to claim the equivalent of workers' compensation payments but would preclude a suit against the company for negligence. So whether Stewart had a right to bring an action for negligence against the barge company turned on whether the Super Scoop was a vessel.

This was a hard case. Although the Super Scoop spent most of its time in a stationary position while dredging out the channel, and although its almost total lack of capacity for self-propulsion required that it be towed from one location to another, it did have a captain and crew, and it did float, both while dredging and while being moved from place to place. Consequently, Stewart made the plausible argument that the Super Scoop's normal floating position, combined with its captain and crew, made it a vessel, while the barge company offered the equally plausible argument that the Super Scoop's lack of self-propulsion and resemblance in appearance and function to a piece of stationary land-based construction equipment made it something other than a vessel. At the end of the day, the Supreme Court decided unanimously that the Super Scoop was indeed a vessel, but the actual outcome need not detain us. What is important here is that although the case before the Supreme Court was a hard one in which there were nonfrivolous arguments on both sides, the Supreme Court case is likely to paint a false picture of the routine and unlitigated operation of this particular set of legal rules. Unlike the question of the Super Scoop in Willard Stewart's lawsuit, most of the questions—virtually all of the questions, for that matter—about whether something is or is not a vessel would almost certainly never reach the Supreme Court, would probably not get to an appellate court, and likely would not even have been litigated. If the question had been whether a thousand-passenger cruise ship was a vessel, there would be no serious argument that it was not, and no competent lawyer would argue otherwise. There might be other good arguments available in the overall dispute, but it is unlikely that a court would be called on to adjudicate the question of whether the ocean liner was a vessel. The rule would be applied, but it would never see the inside of a courtroom. Similarly, if the edge of a harbor were being dug out by a land-based excavating machine that did not and could not enter the water, the machine's status as some-

16. 33 U.S.C. §902 (2000).

21

thing other than a vessel would in all likelihood not have been challenged and again would not have come before a court at all.

Because genuinely easy cases and straightforward applications of legal rules are so rarely disputed in court, the array of disputes that *do* wind up in court represents a skewed sample of legal events. The effect, known as the selection effect,[17] is such that the cases that wind up in court are only—or almost only—the ones in which two opposing parties holding mutually exclusive views about some legal question *both* believe they have a reasonable chance of winning. If one of the parties thought it had no reasonable likelihood of prevailing in the case as a whole, or even just prevailing on this particular issue, it would not, barring unusual circumstances,[18] contest the matter at all. It would follow the law, or pay the claim, or settle the case, or rely on some other argument in litigation. The cases and arguments that are seriously contested in court, therefore, are the ones in which both parties think they might win, and this situation typically occurs only when they both have plausible legal arguments. With respect to legal rules, therefore, both parties will reasonably think that they might win when, ordinarily, the relevant question lies at the edges and not at the core of the pertinent rule. And thus the selection effect is so called because the incentives of the legal system create a world in which only certain applications of law or rules are selected for litigation, and the ones selected have the special characteristic of be-

17. There is a large literature on the selection effect in law, but the seminal article is George L. Priest & William Klein, "The Selection of Disputes for Litigation," *supra* note 1. See also Richard A. Posner, *Economic Analysis of Law* §21 (3d ed., 1986); Frederick Schauer, "Judging in a Corner of the Law," 61 *S. Cal. L. Rev.* 1717 (1988). An excellent overview of the issues and the literature is Leandra Lederman, "Which Cases Go to Trial?: An Empirical Study of Predictions of Failure to Settle," 49 *Case West. Res. L. Rev.* 315 (1999). And it is worth noting Karl Llewellyn's much earlier observation that litigated cases bear the same relationship to the underlying pool of disputes "as does homicidal mania or sleeping sickness, to our normal life." Karl N. Llewellyn, *The Bramble Bush: On Our Law and Its Study* 58 (1930).

18. One such unusual circumstance occurs when a party litigates or threatens litigation even when it knows the law is contrary, simply for the purpose of wearing down an adversary by delay or expense. In theory the legal system has devices to prevent this—summary judgment, for example—but in practice parties do pursue losing causes for strategic reasons more than the pure theory of the selection effect would predict.

ing at the fringes of legal rules, or in some broader way at the edges of the law.

The selection effect is the major factor in determining which disputes or law-controlled events wind up in litigation, but the effect is even greater as we proceed up the appellate ladder. In its 2007 Term,[19] for example, the United States Supreme Court, which has almost total power to decide which cases it wants to hear, was asked to hear more than nine thousand cases from the federal courts of appeals and from the highest courts of the states, but agreed to take and decide, with full briefing and argument and opinions, only seventy-one.[20] These seventy-one cases were almost all ones in which there was no clear legal answer, and taking these seventy-one as representative of how law works or how rules work would be a major blunder.

Very much the same dynamic applies to the cases selected for law school casebooks. What makes those cases interesting and pedagogically valuable is, usually, that they are hard cases, ones in which the lawyers on both sides can make strong arguments and in which the students can analyze and evaluate the opposing positions. And because these are hard cases, the opinions of the deciding courts can almost always be questioned, which is a big part of what case-based law classes do. In itself, there is nothing wrong with this. Learning how to make good arguments on both sides is part of becoming a lawyer, and so is learning how to expose the weaknesses in a judicial opinion. But it is nevertheless an error to suppose that all or even most cases are hard, that most legal events are disputable, and that legal rules never or rarely give clear answers. Appellate courts and law school classrooms have good reasons for operating in the gray areas of rules—on the fuzzy edges. But it is a big mistake to assume that rules are nothing but gray areas and fuzzy edges.

19. The Supreme Court hears and decides cases in what is called a Term, traditionally starting on the first Monday of October and ending when the Court finishes deciding the cases it has heard, typically in June. The Term is designated by the year in which it starts, so sometimes it is called the October 2007 Term, for example, and sometimes just the 2007 Term.

20. The exact count for the 2006 Term, the most recent Term for which exact statistics were available at the time of publication, is that the Court received 8922 appeals or petitions for review, decided 278 of those by summary order without opinion, and agreed to hear and decide 77, of which 73 wound up actually being decided, after briefing and oral argument, with full opinions. "The Supreme Court, 2006 Term: The Statistics," 121 *Harv. L. Rev.* 436 (2007).

2.3 The Generality of Rules

Although the application of legal rules to the world is characterized by easy cases, adjudication is dominated, for the reasons just examined, by the hard ones. These hard cases, however, come in several varieties. One is the case at the fuzzy edge of a rule, of which *Stewart v. Dutra Barge Company* is a typical example. A very different type of hard case, however, resembles the speed limit scenario more than it does the Super Scoop case. When you are pleading to the police officer that you were not actually driving unsafely, you are not claiming that the rule is unclear in this application, as you might be if you were stopped for not having your lights on after dark if it were dusk or if you were stopped in Montana during the regime of the "reasonable and prudent" speed limit. Rather, the typical attempt by a driver to talk her way out of a ticket involves acknowledging that the rule according to its literal terms plainly applies to her—she really was going 70 in a 55-miles-per-hour zone—but she nevertheless claims that literal application of the rule's terms to *this* case would not serve the background justification lying behind the rule. She admits she was going more than 55, but she certainly wasn't driving unsafely. Or so she says.

Such conflicts between the outcome that the words of a rule indicate and the outcome indicated by the rationale behind the rule are ubiquitous. For example, the Seventh Amendment to the Constitution provides the right to a jury trial in any civil case at common law in a federal court in which the amount in controversy is "twenty dollars," and it is obvious that the purpose behind the twenty-dollar minimum was to limit jury trials to cases in which substantial sums were involved. But although twenty dollars was a substantial amount of money in 1791, when the Seventh Amendment was adopted, it is hardly substantial anymore. Much the same can be said about the requirement in Article II of the Constitution that the president have attained the "Age of thirty-five Years," a requirement created when the life expectancy at birth for a male (almost no one at the time contemplated that women could even vote, let alone be president) was under forty, as compared to the current average life expectancy at birth for American men and women combined of over seventy-five.[21] But as with the effect of inflation on the twenty-dollar threshold

21. Many children died from disease in the eighteenth century, so the raw figures can be a bit misleading, because most adult males did live into their fifties and

for jury trials, the fact that the literal meaning of the "Age of thirty-five Years" rule fails to serve the rule's background purpose does not change the meaning of the rule itself, a meaning that remains tethered to the meaning of the words in which the rule is written. If you are only thirty-two years old, you cannot be president, and it verges on the fantastic to imagine circumstances in which that would not be true, regardless of the underlying rationale for the rule.[22] So too with the more controversial requirement, also in Article II, that the president be a "natural born citizen." This rule, which has precluded secretaries of state such as Madeline Albright and Henry Kissinger and governors such as Arnold Schwarzenegger and Jennifer Granholm from seriously contemplating running for president, is almost certainly a poor embodiment of the original background justification of ensuring loyalty and commitment, but the words of the rule prevail nevertheless.

Although the words of a rule triumph over its purpose in these and many other instances, it is not always so. An often-cited example of purpose prevailing over literal meaning is *United States v. Church of the Holy Trinity.*[23] There, a church had been prosecuted for violating a federal law prohibiting any American employer from paying the passage of an alien employee from a foreign country to the United States for the purpose of taking up employment. The defendant church had done just that, the payment being part of the process of hiring a new pastor, and so the church was in literal violation of the statute. Nevertheless, the Supreme Court held that the statute should not be literally applied in this case. The law, Justice Brewer reasoned, was aimed at employers who were importing large quantities of cheap foreign labor into the United States. And because the church's payment of its new pastor's ocean passage was well removed from what the Court saw as Congress's purpose in enacting the

---

sixties. But even for those who reached adulthood, the differences between 1787 and now are still substantial.

22. It is not clear what age in 2009 would be equivalent to thirty-five in 1787. In an era in which it is possible—by virtue of television, the Internet, technological advances in publishing, and air travel, for example—to learn far more far earlier than was previously possible, it could be argued that the purpose behind the thirty-five-year rule would be served by lowering the minimum age. But if the framers of the Constitution wanted to ensure that the president was drawn from the older and more experienced segment of the population, then perhaps the underlying rationale would now counsel an age threshold substantially higher than thirty-five.

23. 143 U.S. 457 (1892).

law, the Court concluded that the literal meaning of the words of the statute should yield to the statute's actual rationale, and as a result the church was deemed not to have violated the rule at all.

In reaching this conclusion, Justice Brewer relied on an even earlier case to the same effect, *United States v. Kirby*.[24] In *Kirby*, the defendant was a Kentucky law enforcement officer who had been convicted under a federal law making it a crime to interfere with the delivery of the mail. And that was exactly what Kirby had done. He had unquestionably interfered with the delivery of the mail, but he had done so in the process of boarding a steamboat to arrest a mail carrier named Farris who had been validly indicted for murder by a Kentucky court. As in *Church of the Holy Trinity* twenty-four years later, the Supreme Court in *Kirby* held that the literal words of the statute should not be applied when, as here, applying those words would hardly serve the underlying purpose of the statute.

We will examine additional examples of the tension between language and purpose in Chapter 8, when we take up issues of statutory interpretation. For now, however, these few examples are sufficient to illustrate an important feature of rules—their generality. In contrast to specific *commands*—*you* take out *this* bag of trash *now*—rules do not speak merely to one individual engaging in one act at one time. Instead, rules typically address many people performing multiple acts over an extended period of time. The speed limit applies to all drivers on all days under all circumstances, just as the rule promulgated by the Occupational Safety and Health Administration (OSHA) requiring hearing protection for workers applies to all factories of a certain type and to all employees in those factories.

Rules are characterized by being general in just this way, but like most generalizations—even statistically sound ones—they might not get it right every time. It is a pretty good generalization that Swiss cheese has holes, but some of it does not. And few people would disagree with the generalization that it is cold in Chicago in January, but warm January days in Chicago are not unheard of. And so too with the generalizations that are part of all rules. But precisely because rules are general, there is always the risk that the generalization that a rule embodies will not apply in some particular case. Even if it is true in *most* instances that drivers should not drive at greater than 55 miles per hour, there will be some cases in which the generalization that driving at more than 55 is unsafe

24. 74 U.S. (7 Wall.) 482 (1868).

will not apply, and when that eventuality arises the rule can be said to be *overinclusive*. The rule includes or encompasses instances that the background justification behind the rule would not cover, as in the *Kirby* and *Church of the Holy Trinity* cases, as with the driver driving safely at 70, and as with an ambulance which might fall within the literal scope of the "no vehicles in the park" rule. In such cases the reach of a rule is broader than the reach of its background justification, and so we say that the rule is overinclusive.

At other times a rule's generalization will be *underinclusive,* failing to reach instances that the direct application of the background justification would encompass. If the purpose of the "no vehicles in the park" rule is to prevent noise, it will be overinclusive with respect to quiet electric cars (which are certainly vehicles) but underinclusive with respect to musical instruments, political rallies, and loud portable radios, all of which are noisy but none of which are vehicles. So too with the rule at issue in *Kirby,* for we can imagine all sorts of impediments to reliable postal service that would not count as an "obstruction" of the mails.

A modern example of both over- and underinclusiveness can be seen in the efforts of an increasing number of states to prohibit driving while talking on a cell phone.[25] The justification for these laws—a justification apparently well supported by the available evidence—is that people who are talking on their cellular phones while driving pay less attention to their driving than they would if they were not on the phone and that this practice is a significant cause of automobile accidents. But those who have objected to such laws say that the laws are overinclusive with respect to drivers who are talking on the phone but still paying attention, and thus the objectors insist that the reach of a "no cell phone" rule is broader than its "no distraction" justification. Moreover, the critics contend, the proposed bans are underinclusive with respect to other sources of distraction while driving, such as eating or listening to an exciting sporting event on the radio. These objections have sometimes prevailed, and sometimes they have not,[26] but it is important to recognize the way

25. See, e.g., Cal. Stat. Ch. 290 (2006), Cal. Vehicle Code § 23123 (2006); N.J. Stat. Ann. 39:4–97.3 (West 2004); N.Y. Vehicle & Traffic Law § 1225-c (Consol. Cum. Supp. 2004).

26. See Note, "The 411 on Cellular Phone Use: An Analysis of the Legislative Attempts to Regulate Cellular Phone Use By Drivers," 39 *Suffolk U.L. Rev.* 233 (2005); Note, "Driving While Distracted: How Should Legislators Regulate Cell Phone Use Behind the Wheel," 28 *J. Legis.* 185 (2002).

in which, as relatively uncontroversial examples like that of the speed limit illustrate, at least *some* degree of both over- and underinclusiveness is an inevitable part of governing human behavior by general rules.[27]

That rules, because of their intrinsic generality, could produce bad results in particular cases was noticed by Aristotle long before there were cell phones and long before the Supreme Court decided cases like *Kirby* and *Church of the Holy Trinity*. In explaining why there needed to be a way of avoiding the mistakes of under- and overinclusion, Aristotle pointed out that "all law is universal," and that "the law takes account of the majority of cases, though not unaware that in this way errors are made. And the law is none the less right; because the error lies not in the law nor in the legislator, but in the nature of the case; for the raw material of human behavior is essentially of this kind."[28]

Aristotle's solution for this problem—equity—will occupy some of our attention in Chapter 6, but for now what is important is only to understand that rules are inevitably general. Rules work as rules precisely because of their generality, and even if it were possible to anticipate every possible application of a rule and incorporate the right result for every application into the rule, such a rule would be too complex to provide the guidance we expect from rules. And even if we were willing to sacrifice intelligibility and useful guidance for precision, we would still be unable to predict the future perfectly. Just as we cannot fault the original drafters of the patent laws for being unable to anticipate in the late eighteenth century that living organisms could be created in the laboratory,[29] so must we recognize that even the most careful of drafters cannot possibly predict what will happen in the future, nor can they predict how we

27. An even more controversial example comes from the efforts of some municipalities to ban certain breeds of dogs—pit bulls, most commonly—on the grounds that some breeds tend to be more aggressive and dangerous than other breeds. Because most pit bulls are not dangerous, however, the ban would be overinclusive, and because dogs of other breeds can be dangerous, the ban would also be underinclusive. In this respect, pit bull bans are little different from rules of any kind, but the opponents of breed-specific bans have nevertheless had considerable success, often by borrowing the language of civil rights and objecting, for example, to "breedism" and "canine racism." For a more extensive discussion and analysis of the controversy, see Frederick Schauer, *Profiles, Probabilities, and Stereotypes* 55–78 (2003).

28. Aristotle, *Nicomachean Ethics* 1137a–b (J. A. K. Thomson trans., 1977).

29. See Diamond v. Chakrabarty, 447 U.S. 303 (1980).

will want to deal with that future when we get there. It is precisely in the inevitable generality of rules, therefore, that we are forced to confront the tension between what a rule says and what it might best be interpreted to do, a tension that pervades the use of rules both in law and outside of it.

2.4 The Formality of Law

There is no uniform answer to whether and when the language of a rule will or should yield to the goal of reaching the best result in the particular case. Nor does the law always give the same answer when there is a conflict between the outcome that would be produced by a rule's background justification and the outcome indicated by the literal meaning of the rule's words. Although cases like *United States v. Locke* show that taking the words at face value even at some sacrifice to reaching the best result for the particular case is common in American law (and even more common elsewhere),[30] so too is the opposite result. Yes, it would be a mistake to ignore the numerous instances such as *Locke* in which what the words most literally say carries the day in legal decision-making. But it is just as much of a mistake to ignore the descriptive importance, in the United States and even elsewhere, of the *Church of Holy Trinity* principle: that achieving a rule's purpose even at some sacrifice to literal meaning is the appropriate course of action.[31] Indeed, if we understand this characterization of the two positions as another way of describing the frequent tension between the letter and the spirit of the law, it is impossible to conclude, especially in the United States, that one approach is more dominant than the other.

Legal arguments for preferring the letter to the spirit of the law are often criticized as *formalistic,* and judicial decisions like *Locke* routinely attract charges of formalism. Yet although it is true that nowadays to call

---

30. In the United Kingdom, for example, courts are somewhat less likely to ignore the words of a legal rule even when doing so is necessary to serve the rule's background justification. See Patrick Atiyah & Robert S. Summers, *Form and Substance in Anglo-American Law: A Comparative Study in Legal Reasoning, Legal Theory and Legal Institutions* (1987). For a more comprehensive comparative analysis, see D. Neil MacCormick & Robert S. Summers, *Interpreting Statutes: A Comparative Study* (1991).

31. See generally Aharon Barak, *Purposive Interpretation in Law* (2005).

a judge or opinion or decision formalist is rarely a compliment, it is not entirely clear what it is to be a formalist or just what is wrong with it.[32]

Often the charge of formalism is leveled against those who appear to deny the degree of choice available to a judge in some legal controversy. Under this view, judges are being formalistic when they believe that they are operating in the core of a legal rule when in reality they are at the fringe. When Justice Peckham in *Lochner v. New York*,[33] for example, concluded that the word "liberty" in the Fourteenth Amendment necessarily encompassed the freedom of a bakery employee to agree without state interference to work for more than sixty hours a week or ten hours a day, he acted as if no other meaning of "liberty" were even possible. We now know better, of course, and even those who would agree with Justice Peckham's ultimate conclusion would be unlikely to believe, as Justice Peckham appeared to believe, that the outcome was commanded solely by the plain meaning of the word "liberty." When legal decision-makers like Justice Peckham, who are actually (and perhaps, as in this case, necessarily) making a policy or political choice act as if there were no choice to be made—when they treat a policy choice as simply an exercise in knowing the plain meaning of a word—their behavior is sometimes described as formalistic. They act as if it is the form that matters, but in fact it is substance that is doing the work. And it is hard to deny that this form of judicial deception—or self-deception—is worthy of criticism.

Justice Peckham's formalism was the formalism of disingenuousness and fully entitled to the stigma it has attracted. When we look at another conception of formalism, however, the formalism of Justice Thurgood Marshall in *United States v. Locke,* for example, it is not so clear that formalism deserves to be treated as a vice at all. It is, to be sure, formalistic to take the literal meaning of the words "prior to December 31" in *United States v. Locke* as dictating a result other than what seems to be the most sensible one, because it is to treat the *form* of a legal rule as more important than its deeper purpose, or more important than reaching the best all-things-considered judgment in the particular context of a particular case. But although *Locke* is from this perspective formalistic, it is also formalistic in just the same way to use the 55-mile-per-hour speed

32. See Brian Bix, *Jurisprudence: Theory and Context* 179–90 (4th ed. 2006); Robert S. Summers, *Form and Function in a Legal System: A General Study* (2006); Frederick Schauer, "Formalism," 91 *Yale L.J.* 571 (1987).

33. 198 U.S. 45 (1905).

limit to penalize the driver who is driving safely at 70, to penalize the short-swing trader who in fact has no inside information, to allow those with twenty-one-dollar claims to demand a jury trial, and to prohibit otherwise qualified thirty-four-year-olds from becoming president. In all of these cases, law operates formally in treating the meaning of the words of a rule as more important than achieving the law's deeper purpose and reaching the ideal result in this particular case. Formalist this may be, but formalism is, as these and countless other examples demonstrate, a central feature of what makes law distinctive.[34]

That formalism is a part of legalism seems plain enough, but that does not mean that formalism is always desirable. Nor does it mean that a formalist approach to interpreting rules is what we do or should expect from all legal decision-makers at all times. Still, if we can get over the fact that the word "formalism" is typically used to condemn, we can see that formalism—in the sense of preferring the outcome dictated by the words on the printed page rather than the outcome that is best, all things considered—often has much to be said for it. Consider, for example, the numerous cases involving search warrants that turn out to have contained an erroneous address for the premises to be searched. Although many such cases uphold a warrant containing this kind of minor error,[35] there are many that reach the opposite conclusion. So in *United States v. Kenney*,[36] for example, the United States District Court for the District of Columbia invalidated a search of the premises at 2124 8th Street in Washington because the warrant had specified 2144 8th Street, and in *United States v. Constantino*,[37] the contraband actually found in a search of 710 Jacksonia Street was similarly suppressed because the warrant had specified 807 Jacksonia Street. For the courts in those cases, the formal, technical, and literal approach to interpreting the warrant was justified because the real issue was not whether the police officers had searched the right building but whether police officers should be empow-

---

34. "Of all the criticisms leveled against textualism, the most mindless is that it is 'formalistic.' The answer to that is, *of course it is formalistic!* The rule of law is about form." Antonin Scalia, *A Matter of Interpretation: Federal Courts and the Law* 25 (1997).

35. E.g., United States v. Lora-Sorano, 330 F.3d 1288 (10th Cir. 2003).

36. 164 F. Supp. 891 (D.D.C. 1958).

37. 201 F. Supp. 160 (W.D. Pa. 1962). See also United States v. Ellis, 971 F.2d 701 (11th Cir. 1992).

ered to decide for themselves which premises were *really* to be searched, the exact language of the warrant notwithstanding.

If the formalism of treating search warrants literally is seen as, at the very least, plausible, then it turns out that formalism itself is not necessarily or always to be considered a vice. Rather, the virtues of formalism are part of a larger consideration of whether decision-makers of a certain type should be empowered to decide when the literal language of some rule (and to which the search warrant description, while not exactly a rule, is analogous) should give way to a less constrained determination of purpose, reasonableness, or common sense, for example. Those who defend the result in *United States v. Locke*,[38] for instance, do not maintain that denying Mr. Locke's claim because he filed *on* December 31 rather than *prior to* December 31 is the best or most reasonable outcome in *that* case. Rather, they argue that the real question is whether and when judges should be empowered to decide when the literal language of an act of Congress should be set aside in the service of what the judges believe Congress must have intended or what outcome Congress would have preferred. And when the question is reformulated in this way, it is no longer clear that a formal approach to legal rules is necessarily or always to be criticized, even if the results of that formalism will in particular cases often seem strange and at times even ridiculous.

None of this is to say that law is always formal in this way, or that it should be. As we have seen, courts often do ignore or go around the literal language of a rule when that language is inconsistent with obvious legislative purpose, and it is a mistake to argue that *United States v. Locke* is more representative of legal analysis than *Church of the Holy Trinity* or *United States v. Kirby*. Both the formal and the nonformal (or *purposive*) approaches are professional, respectable alternatives for a judge or advocate in the American legal system, and countless examples can be found in support of both of them. As a result, it is not uncommon to see cases in which one of the parties is arguing on the basis of the letter of the law and the other is relying on a law's spirit, purpose, or rationale. But even when spirit or purpose or rationale prevails, the law remains pervasively formal. It is common for literal language to give way to the purpose behind a *particular* legal rule, as in *Church of the Holy Trinity*, but it is considerably rarer for the purpose behind a rule also to give way when a judge determines that enforcing even that purpose would be in-

---

38. Including this author. *See* Frederick Schauer, "The Practice and Problems of Plain Meaning," 45 *Vand. L. Rev.* 715 (1992).

consistent with justice, or with larger conceptions of fairness or good policy. When a court denies relief to a litigant with an otherwise valid claim because he has failed to comply with a rule of procedure, for example, the court is recognizing that its job is not merely to decide which of the parties, all things considered, is more worthy.[39] So too when a party is allowed to escape from a contractual promise because of the absence of a requisite contractual formality,[40] or when, prior to the rise in the doctrine of comparative negligence, a plaintiff who was slightly at fault was denied relief against a substantially at-fault defendant.[41] In all of these cases, the pervasive formality of law—its tendency to take its rules and their words seriously even though in some cases they might work an injustice—is what distinguishes law from many other decision-making contexts.

At times law does act otherwise. A prominent example is *Riggs v. Palmer*,[42] in which Elmer Palmer, named as the beneficiary in his grandfather's will, had attempted to accelerate his inheritance by the expedient strategy of murdering the testator. The case did not involve Elmer's criminal conviction for killing his grandfather. To this, Elmer had little defense, and he was duly sentenced to a lengthy prison term. Nevertheless, Elmer claimed that even though he was convicted of and was paying the penalty for murder, he was still entitled to the inheritance. The relevant rule, the New York Statute of Wills, said nothing about murderous beneficiaries and provided only that, upon the death of the testator, the beneficiary under a valid will was entitled to inherit. That was the case here, Elmer argued, and so although he knew that he had to go to prison, he also believed that he was entitled to his grandfather's estate.

The Court of Appeals famously[43] rejected Elmer's claim, concluding that the literal language of the Statute of Wills must yield to the principle

39. See, e.g., General Mills, Inc. v. Kraft Foods Global, Inc., 495 F.3d 1378 (Fed. Ct. 2007); Speiser, Krause & Madole, P.C. v. Ortiz, 271 F.3d 884 (9th Cir. 2001).

40. See Robert S. Summers, "Why Law Is Formal and Why It Matters," 82 *Cornell L. Rev.* 1165 (1997).

41. See, e.g., Miller v. United States, 196 F. Supp. 613 (D. Mass. 1961); Co-Operative Sanitary Baking Co. v. Shields, 70 So. 934 (Fla. 1916).

42. 22 N.E. 188 (N.Y. 1889).

43. The case is analyzed extensively by the legal philosopher Ronald Dworkin in *Taking Rights Seriously* (1977) and *Law's Empire* (1986). Dworkin resoundingly applauds the result and takes it as highly typical of the American (and, to him, better) approach to legal decision-making.

that no person should profit from his own wrong. But there was a dissent even in that case, and it is by no means clear that setting aside the result indicated by a concrete rule in the service of larger and less concrete conceptions of justice is an accurate characterization of the typical nature of legal decision-making. In extreme cases, of which *Riggs v. Palmer* seems an obvious example, specific rules are often set aside, but in cases less extreme than this it is far more common for the rule to be applied even when it seems as if some injustice is done in the process. Indeed, there are many cases in which beneficiaries who were responsible for the death of the testator were allowed to inherit, including one in which the beneficiary was convicted of voluntary manslaughter of the person from whose death he would benefit,[44] another in which the beneficiary was found guilty of being an accessory after the fact in the murder of the testator,[45] still another in which a remainderman had killed the holder of a life estate in order that the killer could take the estate sooner,[46] and, finally, a case in which a "selfish, angry, resentful, indignant, bitter, self-centered, spiteful, vindictive, paranoid, and stingy" woman whose gross negligence served to "shorten the decedent's life" was nevertheless allowed to inherit sooner than would otherwise have been the case.[47]

Just as there are cases in which a rule is allowed to prevail even when an injustice is done in the process, so too are there even more cases in which courts have enforced what they see as bad rules because of the view that changes in bad rules, at least those bad rules that have come from a legislature, are for a legislature and not a court to make. In *Blanchflower v. Blanchflower,*[48] for example, the Supreme Court of New Hampshire was faced with the question whether same-sex adultery could count as adultery for purposes of the New Hampshire at-fault divorce statute, a statute whose language made it clear that adultery could be committed only with a person of the opposite sex. The court appeared to believe that the statute was both anachronistic and morally dubious on equality grounds but nevertheless concluded that any change was to be made by the legislature and not a court. For the Supreme Court of New Hampshire, like the dissenting judge in *Riggs,* like the courts that differ

44. Bird v. Plunkett, 95 A.2d 71 (Conn. 1953).
45. Reynolds v. American-Amicable Life Ins. Co., 591 F.2d 343 (5th Cir. 1979).
46. Blanks v. Jiggetts, 64 S.E.2d 809 (Va. 1951).
47. Cheatle v. Cheatle, 662 A.2d 1362 (D.C. 1995).
48. 834 A.2d 1010 (N.H. 2003).

from *Riggs* and allow people to profit from their known wrongs, and like the Supreme Court in *Locke,* what a legal rule actually says in the literal or plain language of its words made a substantial difference. The letter of a rule may not, as the majority opinion in *Riggs* and the decisions in *Church of the Holy Trinity* and *Kirby* show, always make a difference, and it may not always make all of the difference, but to ignore the ubiquitous importance of what a legal rule literally says is to ignore something very important about rules.

The importance of what a rule actually says is not just a point about rules. More pervasively, to ignore the even more ubiquitous importance of what rules do even when what they do appears unfair is to ignore something very important about law itself. It is not law's purpose, of course, to be unfair for the sake of being unfair. But there is an important group of values—predictability of result, uniformity of treatment (treating like cases alike), and fear of granting unfettered discretion to individual decision-makers even if they happen to be wearing black robes—that the legal system, especially, thinks it valuable to preserve. These values often go by the name of the Rule of Law, and many of the virtues of the Rule of Law are ones that are accomplished by taking rules seriously as rules. In doing so, law remains irreducibly formal and thus at times seemingly unfair in particular cases. But law is more than simply doing the right thing in each individual case. At times law's unwillingness to do just that will seem wrong, but what makes law what it is—usually for better but sometimes for worse—is that it takes larger institutional and systemic values as important, even if occasionally at the expense of justice or wise policy or efficiency in the individual case. There are many ways in which law does this, but the principal one is by taking rules seriously. Understanding when, why, and how rules—as rules—are important in law will take us a long way toward understanding law itself.

THE PRACTICE AND PROBLEMS
OF PRECEDENT

—different levels of courts etc. (handwritten)

3.1 Precedent in Two Directions

Law characteristically faces backward. Unlike most forms of policy-making, which are concerned with a proposed policy's future consequences, legal decision-making is preoccupied with looking over its shoulder. Frequently in law, but less so elsewhere, it is not enough that a decision produces desirable results in the future; the decision must also follow from or at least be consistent with previous decisions on similar questions. Indeed, legal reasoning's commitment to *precedent* is even stronger than that. By ordinarily requiring that legal decisions follow precedent, the law is committed to the view that it is often better for a decision to accord with precedent than to be right, and that it is frequently more important for a decision to be consistent with precedent than to have the best consequences.

The practice of precedent is more complex than sketched in the previous paragraph, and this chapter is devoted to exploring variations on the basic theme that courts are expected to follow or obey precedents—decisions from the *past*. But before getting too far into the complexities, it is important to distinguish two different ways in which the obligation to follow precedent arises in the legal system. One we can call *vertical* precedent. Lower courts are normally expected to obey the previous decisions of higher courts within their jurisdiction, and this relationship of lower to higher in the "chain of command" is usefully understood as vertical. Federal district courts are obliged to follow the precedents of the courts of appeals of their circuit, and the courts of appeals are obliged to follow the precedents of the Supreme Court. The same holds true in state systems, which typically have a similar structure and impose equivalent obligations. Indeed, we refer to courts as higher and lower precisely because higher courts exercise authority over lower ones, an authority manifested principally in the obligation of lower courts to treat the decisions of higher courts as binding upon them.

In addition to being obliged to follow the decisions of courts above them in the judicial hierarchy, courts are also, although less obviously and sometimes more controversially, expected to follow their *own* earlier decisions. Here the relationship is *horizontal,* because the obligation is between some court now and the *same* court in the past. Horizontal precedent is thus not a matter of higher or lower courts, but rather an artificial or imposed hierarchy from earlier to later. The earlier decision is superior not because it comes from a higher court; rather, the earlier decision becomes superior just because it is earlier. This obligation of a court to follow its own previous decisions is typically known as *stare decisis*—Latin for "stand by the thing decided"—and it is a distinct form of constraint by precedent. Under the doctrine of stare decisis, a court is expected to decide issues in the same way that *it* has decided them in the past, even if the membership of the court has changed, or even if the same members have changed their minds. Like vertical precedent, stare decisis—horizontal precedent—is about following the decisions of others. But although both vertical and horizontal precedents involve following the decisions of others, the distinction between a court's following the decision of a higher court and its following its own previous decisions is important enough in numerous contexts to be worth emphasizing even before we see just what the obligation to follow entails, and before we examine the complications that are involved when these obligations arise in actual practice.

3.2 Precedent—The Basic Concept

The core principle of decision-making according to precedent is that courts should follow previous decisions—that they should give the same answers to legal questions that higher or earlier courts have given in the past. What counts as the same question will occupy much of our attention, but first we need to examine just what the obligation to follow a precedent is. In doing so, it will help to introduce some additional clarifying terminology. So although in the case of vertical precedent the earlier decision comes from above, and in the case of horizontal precedent—stare decisis—it comes from the same court in the past, in both instances a court is expected to follow an earlier decision in another case. For the sake of clarity, we can label the court now making the decision the *instant court* and its current controversy the *instant case*. And we can call the previous court (including the same court in an earlier case) the *precedent court* and its decision the *precedent case*. Questions about the force and consequences of precedent will thus always involve the effect of some decision by the precedent court in the precedent case on the issue now before the instant court in the instant case.

So now we can turn to the nature of precedential obligation. Initially, understanding the idea of precedent requires appreciating the difference between *learning* from the past, on the one hand, and *following* the past just because of the fact of a past decision, on the other. With respect to the former, which is not really precedential reasoning at all, the instant court may *learn* from a previous case, or be *persuaded* by some decision in the past, but the decision to do what another court has done on an earlier occasion is not based on the previous case's status as a precedent. Instead the decision exemplifies the fundamental human capacity to learn from others and from the past. There are many instances in which the instant court will be persuaded by the reasoning of another court, but if the instant court is genuinely persuaded, then it is not relying on—*obeying*—precedent at all.[1] To see why this is so, consider a simple nonlegal example: Suppose I am boiling an egg. I boil it for six minutes, and am pleased to discover that it is cooked to precisely my preferred hardness. Consequently, the next time I boil an egg I do so, not surprisingly, for six minutes. I have learned from the previous "case," but when I boil the second egg for six minutes, I am not boiling it for six minutes *because* I boiled it for six minutes on the previous occasion. I am boiling it for six minutes because six minutes is the right time. I know this because I have learned from the previous action, but on subsequent occasions I make the decision because of what I then know.

This kind of learning from past experience pervades public decision-making. When Ronald Reagan ran for president in 1980, he focused his campaign, unlike earlier Republican candidates, on issues likely to attract Democratic union members and southern Democrats, and he took

---

1. The conception of *following* or *obeying* offered here is consistent with that in the jurisprudential literature, much of which is focused on the question of whether there is a moral obligation to obey the law. See Donald H. Regan, "Reasons, Authority, and the Meaning of 'Obey': Further Thoughts on Raz and Obedience to Law," 3 *Can. J.L. & Jurisp.* 3 (1990).

positions consistent with the preferences of those groups. The strategy was successful and subsequently adopted by other Republican political candidates. But these other candidates followed Reagan's strategy not because Reagan had used it, but because Reagan's success had convinced them that it was the right strategy.

The same phenomenon exists in law.[2] In *Henningsen v. Bloomfield Motors, Inc.,*[3] the Supreme Court of New Jersey concluded that there was such disparity of bargaining power between an automobile dealer and the typical purchaser of a car that the court would not enforce a buyer's waiver—even a written and signed one—of what would otherwise have been the normal warranties. So with *Henningsen* having been decided, suppose that an appellate judge from a different state reads the opinion in *Henningsen* and comes away persuaded that it represents the fairest approach to contractual waivers in the modern era of corporate dealerships and impersonal consumer transactions. She had never before considered the possibility of coercively unequal bargaining power, nor even imagined that the terms of a contract should not be enforced except in cases of fraud, duress, or incapacity. But reading *Henningsen* has persuaded her to modify her previous beliefs about the so-called sanctity of contract. She now believes that there are circumstances in which written and signed contractual provisions should be unenforceable even where there is neither explicit fraud nor any of the other traditional grounds for nonenforcement of a contract. Accordingly, when the opportunity arises, she reaches a decision consistent with *Henningsen* and writes an opinion that mostly tracks that case. In order to acknowledge the source of her learning, and also to give research guidance to others, she cites the New Jersey decision. But her current decision is not dictated by the existence of the New Jersey case—she is not *obeying* the decision in New Jersey. She has reached her decision because, having been persuaded by *Henningsen,* she now believes that unconscionable contractual provisions based on extreme disparities of bargaining power in consumer transactions should not be enforced. As with my learning how long to boil an egg from my previous action, and as with political candidates learning strategies from earlier successful ones, the judge in this hypo-

2. See Larry Alexander, "Constrained By Precedent," 63 *S. Cal. L. Rev.* 1 (1989); Lon L. Fuller, "Reason and Fiat in Case Law," 59 *Harv. L. Rev.* 376 (1946): Frederick Schauer, "Precedent," 39 *Stan. L. Rev.* 571 (1987).

3. 161 A.2d 69 (N.J. 1960).

thetical example has not made her decision in the instant case just because of what the New Jersey court did or because she was in any way obliged to follow a court in New Jersey. She made it because she learned something from another case that now genuinely reflects her current beliefs. It is not that much different from having learned about unconscionability from a book about economics or philosophy, or even from a conversation at the gym. The fact that the source of learning happened to be a court in another state is barely more than a coincidence.

These examples illustrate a common way in which judges use prior cases, but it is not, strictly speaking, reasoning from precedent—the prior case's status as a previous judicial decision has actually made no difference. In contrast, reasoning from precedent—and maybe it is a mistake to call it "reasoning" at all—is following a previous decision just because of its status as a decision of a higher court or of the same court on an earlier occasion, not because the follower in the instant case has been persuaded by the reasoning of the precedent case. Some lower court judge in New Jersey, for example, might still believe after *Henningsen* that all nonfraudulent contractual provisions should be strictly enforced according to their terms and that the *Henningsen* court's concern for the consumer was misplaced. Even after reading *Henningsen,* he remains unpersuaded. Yet however much he continues to believe in the strict enforceability of written provisions, and even though he believes *Henningsen* to have been wrongly decided, he is still obliged, as a lower court judge in the same jurisdiction, to follow *Henningsen* despite being convinced of its error. So too for stare decisis. If in 1970, ten years after *Henningsen,* the majority of the New Jersey Supreme Court consisted of justices not on the court at the time of *Henningsen,* and if those new justices believed *Henningsen* to have been erroneously decided, the obligations of stare decisis would still have obliged them to decide the same issue in the same way. They would have been constrained to follow a decision they thought mistaken just because of its existence as a previous decision of the same court. The British legal theorist P. S. Atiyah puts it directly: "The concept of a system of precedent is that it constrains judges in some cases to follow decisions they do not agree with."[4]

4. P. S. Atiyah, "Form and Substance in Legal Reasoning: the Case of Contract," *in The Legal Mind: Essays for Tony Honoré* 19, 27 (Neil MacCormick & Peter Birks eds., 1986). See also Lionel Smith, "The Rationality of Tradition," *in Properties of Law: Essays in Honour of James Harris* 297 (T. Endicott, J. Getzler, & E. Peel eds., 2006).

The basic idea should now be clear. When courts are constrained by precedent, they are obliged to follow a precedent not only when they think it correct, but even when they think it incorrect. It is the precedent's source or status that gives it force, not the soundness of its reasoning[5] nor the belief of the instant court that its outcome was correct. When it is argued, for example, that even those Supreme Court Justices who believe *Roe v. Wade*[6] to have been wrongly decided should nevertheless follow it in subsequent cases, the argument is not (or not only) that those Justices should change their minds about *Roe v. Wade*. Rather, the argument is that those Justices should follow *Roe* even if they continue to think that it was decided incorrectly.

3.3 A Strange Idea

Having seen that following precedent obliges judges to make decisions other than the ones they, in their best judgment, would have made absent the precedent, we can appreciate that constraint by precedent is in many respects counterintuitive, at least from the perspective of the constrained judges. From their perspective, the obligation to follow precedent—whether vertical or horizontal—often instructs them to reach what they think is the wrong decision.[7] So why would the law operate in this way, and why would the legal system require its judges to do something other than make decisions according to their own best legal judgment?

With respect to vertical precedent, the justifications for precedential constraint are fairly obvious. Just as children are expected to obey their parents even when they disagree, as privates are expected to follow even those orders from sergeants they believe wrong, as Catholics are expected to follow the dictates of the pope even if they think those dictates mistaken, and as employees are expected to follow the instructions of their supervisors, lower court judges are expected to follow the "instruc-

5. "If the precedent is truly binding on [the judge], and if he loyally accepts the principle of stare decisis, he will not even pause to consider what substantive reasons may be given for the opposite decision." Atiyah, *supra* note 4, at 20.

6. 410 U.S. 113 (1973).

7. Justice Scalia, who disapproves of stare decisis at the Supreme Court level, has said that "[t]he whole function of [stare decisis] is to make us say that what is false under proper analysis must nevertheless be held to be true." Antonin Scalia, *A Matter of Interpretation: Federal Courts and the Law* 139 (Amy Gutmann ed., 1997).

tions" of those courts above them in what the military calls the "chain of command." Whatever we might think about the obligation of currently disagreeing Justices to follow the Supreme Court's own earlier decision in *Roe v. Wade,* expecting lower courts to follow *Roe* as long as it is not overruled seems hardly surprising.[8] With respect to vertical precedent, constraint by precedent appears to be little more than the legal system's version of the kind of hierarchical authority that exists in most governmental and nongovernmental institutions.

When we turn to horizontal precedent, however, the arguments in its favor are less obvious. Stare decisis is a pervasive principle of the common law,[9] but it is far less so in nonlegal contexts. Scientists, for example, are not expected to reach the same conclusions as their predecessors just because their predecessors have reached them. It would be surprising if Congress were to make the same decisions as previous Congresses only because previous Congresses had made them. And no one believes that presidents should follow those decisions of their predecessors with which they disagree. Indeed, we often elect them not to. Thus it is no surprise that books about logic typically treat arguments from precedent as fallacies, because the fact that someone has reached a conclusion in the past says nothing about whether it is the correct conclusion now.[10] Even in law, the idea of precedent often seems strange, and Oliver Wendell Holmes once remarked that it was "revolting" that courts would be bound by precedents which "persist . . . for no better reasons than . . . that so it was laid down in the time of Henry IV."[11] And Jeremy Bentham, who was a very good hater, reserved special hatred for the system of precedent in general and stare decisis in particular, describing it as

8. It was in an abortion case, for example, that Judge Emilio Garza observed that "[f]or the second time in my judicial career, I am forced to follow a Supreme Court opinion I believe to be inimical to the Constitution." Causeway Medical Suite v. Ieyoub, 109 F.3d 1096, 1113 (5th Cir. 1997) (Garza, J., concurring).

9. It has not always been so. Although the obligations of vertical precedent go back to the beginnings of appellate courts in the eighteenth century or earlier, the constraints of stare decisis did not become accepted until the nineteenth century. See Thomas R. Lee, "Stare Decisis in Historical Perspective," 52 *Vand. L. Rev.* 647 (1999); Edward M. Wise, "The Doctrine of Stare Decisis," 21 *Wayne L. Rev.* 1043 (1975).

10. See, e.g., D. Q. Mcinerny, *Being Logical: A Guide to Good Thinking* 142 (2005); Christopher W. Tindale, *Fallacies and Argument Appraisal* 201 (2007).

11. Oliver W. Holmes, "The Path of the Law," 10 *Harv. L. Rev.* 457, 469 (1897).

"acting without reason, to the declared exclusion of reason, and thereby in opposition to reason."[12]

Yet as Holmes at other times recognized, even if Bentham did not, stare decisis does have something to be said for it. One argument in its favor was recognized by Justice Brandeis when he observed, famously, that "in most matters it is more important that [the question] be settled than that it be decided right."[13] In life, and especially in law, it is often valuable to have things settled so that others can rely on those decisions and guide their behavior accordingly. A company planning a commercial transaction needs to know which transactions are legally permissible and which not, and this confidence and reliance would be lost were the risks too great that the relevant legal rules would be continually subject to change. From the perspective of those who are subject to law's constraints, the gains from marginal improvements in the law are rarely sufficient to outweigh the losses that would come from being unable to rely even on imperfect legal rules and imperfect precedents.

From the perspective of the constrained court, stare decisis brings the advantages of cognitive and decisional efficiency. None of us has the ability to keep every issue open for consideration simultaneously, and we could scarcely function if all of our decisions were constantly up for grabs. Especially in a court, where narrowing the issues increases the ability to focus the arguments, treating some matters as simply settled makes life easier for the court, just as it does for those who are expected to plan their lives and their activities around the decisions that courts make. Justice Cardozo, while still a judge of the New York Court of Appeals, observed that "the labor of judges would be increased to the breaking point if every past decision could be reopened in every case,"[14] and in this pithy phrase he captured that human beings can only do only so much, and that doing some things well requires that we treat other things as best left for another time.

Stare decisis, in thus valuing settlement for settlement's sake and consistency for consistency's sake, serves a range of values all having something to do with *stability*. Stability is not all there is, of course, and even

12. Jeremy Bentham, "Constitutional Code," in 1 *Collected Works of Jeremy Bentham* 434 (F. Rosen & J. H. Burns eds., 1983).

13. Burnet v. Coronado Oil & Gas Co., 285 U.S. 393, 406 (1932) (Brandeis, J., dissenting).

14. Benjamin N. Cardozo, *The Nature of the Judicial Process* 149 (1921).

Brandeis recognized that just as it is sometimes more important that things be settled than that they be settled correctly, so too is it sometimes more important that things be settled correctly than that they be settled incorrectly or imperfectly just for the sake of settlement. Yet however important it is on occasion to be right, following the past without regard to its rightness is pivotal to how law operates. Stare decisis, far from being a silly appendage to a decision-making system whose principal aim is to make the right decision now, in fact reflects something deep and enduring about a decision-making system that often serves the values of stability, consistency, settlement, and respect for the past just as other branches of government and other decision-making systems remain more flexible, less stable, less predictable, and more focused on the future.

3.4 On Identifying a Precedent

It is easy to *say* that a court is expected to follow a past decision—whether its own in the case of stare decisis or that of a higher court in the case of vertical precedent—but it is rarely easy to determine what counts as a past decision. Occasionally the task will be straightforward. A Supreme Court case dealing with the permissibility of a state's total ban on abortion, for example, could hardly escape confronting *Roe v. Wade* as the relevant precedent. If someone argued in New Jersey that consumer purchasers of automobiles from corporate dealerships should be strictly held to their written waivers of warranties, *Henningsen* would dominate the arguments. And if the question were one of determining which of two conflicting statutes applied to a particular class of cases,[15] then a court's determination of that abstract issue of statutory interpretation would establish the law for future cases. More commonly, however, it is not nearly so clear which cases are to count as precedent cases, and, even more importantly, it is rarely obvious what those cases will be taken to stand for.

The task of identifying the relevant precedent and its holding is problematic largely because no two events are exactly alike. Therefore, no two cases will be exactly alike. In *Raffles v. Wichelhaus*,[16] for example, the English Court of the Exchequer concluded that there was no meeting of the minds and therefore no contract when a buyer of cotton thought

15. See Anastasoff v. United States, 223 F.3d 898 (8th Cir. 2000), *vacated as moot,* 235 F.3d 1054 (8th Cir. 2000).
16. 2 H. & C. 906, 159 Eng. Rep. 375 (Ex. 1864).

he was buying the shipment of cotton coming on one ship named *Peerless* and the seller thought he was selling the cotton shipment on a different ship that also happened to be named *Peerless*. Every case subsequent to *Raffles* will vary in some way, at the very least in terms of time. Still, it would be silly for someone to argue that *Raffles* was not a precedent for an otherwise similar case that arose in London rather than Liverpool, or in which both ships were named *Excelsior* instead of *Peerless,* or in which the cargo was tea and not cotton. When there is a precedent case that so resembles the instant case that any differences are trivial, lawyers and judges often say that the precedent is "on all fours," and in such cases the identification of the precedent rarely creates problems.

Typically, however, the differences between the instant case and some possible precedent case are more substantial than those between *Raffles* and a *Raffles*-like case with only different ships, different ports, and different cargos. When that happens, two interrelated problems arise. The first is the initial identification of the relevant precedent. Is some previous decision to be treated as a precedent case at all? The second problem is the determination of what that precedent case will now be taken to stand for. In a world in which there is no complete identity between any two cases or any two events, these tasks involve determining whether there is a *relevant* similarity between some possible precedent case and the instant case, for only when there is will the instant court be under an obligation to follow what the precedent court has held.

The problem of determining relevant similarity can be illustrated by examining two cases often used to explore the nature of precedent. First is Judge Cardozo's decision for the New York Court of Appeals in *MacPherson v. Buick Motor Company.*[17] At more or less maximum particularity, *MacPherson* held that the Buick Motor Company, a manufacturer of passenger automobiles, would be liable to a purchaser of a Buick for damages produced by Buick's incorporation into its automobile of a defective wheel manufactured by someone else, despite the lack of privity of contract between the purchaser and the Buick Motor Company. Yet even though *MacPherson* would pretty obviously be a precedent for a claim about a defective Oldsmobile or Toyota or for a case involving defective automobile parts other than wheels, most subsequent cases will not be so similar. If the injury in a subsequent case were caused by a foreign substance in a product normally less dangerous than a car, for

17. 111 N.E. 1050 (N.Y. 1916).

example, would *MacPherson* still be considered controlling precedent? Some time after *MacPherson* was decided, there arose in Great Britain an equally prominent case resembling it, *Donoghue v. Stevenson*.[18] In that case the consumer, Mrs. Donoghue, a patron at the Wellmeadow Café in Paisley, Scotland, was with a companion who ordered a glass of ginger beer for her. Mrs. Donoghue drank about half a glass of the ginger beer, and the proprietor then refilled her glass from the opaque bottle, at which time the remnants of a dead snail tumbled into Mrs. Donoghue's glass. The sight and smell of the decomposed snail caused Mrs. Donoghue gastric distress and mental shock, and she subsequently sued the manufacturer (which was also the bottler) of the ginger beer.

As in *MacPherson,* the defendant manufacturer claimed in *Donoghue* that the action was barred because of the lack of privity between consumer and manufacturer. Were the case to have arisen in New York after *MacPherson,* the plaintiff would undoubtedly have argued that the issue had already been decided, thus obliging the court to reach the same result that had been reached in *MacPherson.* But the defendant would have argued that the two cases were different and that *MacPherson* did not stand for the proposition that privity was unnecessary in a case not involving inherently dangerous machinery such as an automobile. And with these as the two opposing positions, how is the court in the instant case—the hypothetical post-*MacPherson* New York ginger beer case— to decide whether *MacPherson* is a precedent and just what it is a precedent for?

Precisely this question has been the subject of debate for generations. A common view is that the precedent case is a precedent not only for more or less identical cases arising in the future, but also for *similar* cases—cases involving similar facts. But what is it that makes one nonidentical factual situation similar to another? We are confident that cases involving defective Toyotas are similar to ones involving defective Buicks, but is an opaque beverage container with a nauseating foreign substance in it similar to or different from a car with a defective wheel? The two situations have in common that both were consumer transactions, the defects caused injury or illness, and the defect was not immediately apparent (which is why it was important in *Donoghue* that the bottle was opaque). They are different in that cars are different from ginger beer, cars are costly and ginger beer is not, and cars were sold by

18. [1932] A.C. 562 (H.L.).

manufacturer-specific dealerships but ginger beer was sold in cafés that stocked all sorts of different beverages. Like any two sets of facts, the facts of *MacPherson* and the facts of the ginger beer case are similar in some respects and different in others.[19] And if that is so, then how is the instant court to decide whether the two are similar enough for the first to be a (binding) precedent for the decision of the second?

One possibility is that some things just *are* similar to others, with the responsibility of law being to treat as similar those things that really are similar in some deep and prelegal sense. Under this view, what makes a variant on *MacPherson* involving Toyotas and not Buicks and another involving brakes and not wheels sufficiently similar to *MacPherson* is that Toyotas are similar to Buicks in that both are passenger cars, and brakes are similar to wheels in that both are parts of cars whose defective manufacture can cause serious injury. But this approach to similarity— one premised on the idea that there are natural similarities—will not work. *MacPherson,* as we know, was a case about tort liability and defective manufacture, but in some subsequent case about securities regulation or banking it might not be so clear that the Toyota Corporation, based in Japan, should be treated the same as the Buick Motor Company, based in Detroit. And if it turned out that wheels were ordinarily purchased from a wheel manufacturer but that brakes were manufactured by the automobile company itself, then in some kinds of products liability cases brakes might no longer be relevantly similar to wheels.

Philosophers often talk about natural kinds, by which they mean things that are fundamentally different from each other in nature and not as a matter of human categorization or sorting. Zebras are different from rocks not because humans have decided that they are, but because they are different in nature. What makes a zebra a zebra and a rock a rock is not decided by humans or their institutions, but by the natural design of the universe. But even with respect to natural kinds, law has its own goals and its own values, and so it might elect to treat things that are naturally different as similar, as when it applies the same products liability rules to sales of fruit trees and sales of bottled water, and the fact that there might be the same products liability rule for both is independent of

19. And because any two acts, events, or cases are alike in some respects and unalike in others, the value of a system of precedent cannot be grounded in the mandate to treat like cases alike. See David Lyons, "Formal Justice and Judicial Precedent," 38 *Vand. L. Rev.* 495 (1985).

the fact that fruit trees and water are different natural kinds. Conversely, the law might have different rules for things that are naturally similar. The diamond I purchase is (usually) mine in the eyes of the law, but the diamond I steal is (usually) not, and this is so even though the diamond I purchase and the diamond I steal are naturally and prelegally similar.

If even natural kinds are not naturally similar for the law, then nothing is naturally similar for the law. Two items might appear prelegally similar, but that is usually because their similarity is based on some common need or goal. Most people might take red handbags and blue handbags to be similar, for example, because they perform a similar function, but if the question were whether the handbags matched a certain pair of shoes, the two would no longer seem so similar. Nor would they be similar in an intellectual property case in which the different colors might make the products easily distinguishable. So too with why Toyotas may not be similar to Buicks for purposes of import tariff legislation, and why vodka is similar to water in the eyes of the airport inspectors of the Transportation Safety Administration but not in the eyes of those who enforce the laws prohibiting the sale of alcohol to minors. To suggest that there are certain natural similarities that answer the question of which cases are similar to others appears to send us down a quite false path.

This is not to say that the law never bases its determinations of similarity and difference on the similarities and differences that exist in the prelegal world. In *The Path of the Law,* Holmes offered the following probably apocryphal story:

> There is a story of a Vermont justice of the peace against whom a suit was brought by one farmer against another for breaking a churn. The justice took time to consider, and then said that he had looked through the statutes and could find nothing about churns, and gave judgment for the defendant.[20]

Holmes was obviously making fun of the Vermont justice of the peace, and Holmes's point was that no one but a non-legally-trained bumpkin could possibly imagine that "churn" could be a legally relevant category. This becomes clear when Holmes goes on the observe that

> [a]pplications of rudimentary rules of contract or tort are tucked away under the heads of Railroads or Telegraphs or . . . Shipping

20. 10 *Harv. L. Rev.* 457, 474–75 (1897).

. . . , or are gathered under an arbitrary title which is thought likely to appeal to the practical mind, such as Mercantile Law. If a man goes into law it pays to be a master of it, and to be a master of it means to look straight through all the dramatic incidents and to discern the true basis for prophecy.[21]

Holmes's little story has become famous, but Holmes may nonetheless have been wrong.[22] It is true that law often treats as similar those things that are prelegally or extralegally different, as when it uses legal categories like contract to encompass contracts for labor and contracts to sell lettuce, and when the category of "security" under the Securities Act of 1933 is understood to encompass not only stocks and bonds, but also some insurance policies, some bank accounts, and some fractional ownership interests in land, racehorses, oil paintings, fruit trees, and wine.[23] But just as often, and more so each day, law bases its determinations of legal similarity on the similarities that exist in the extralegal world. Under the lead of Karl Llewellyn, whose contributions to Legal Realism will be featured in Chapter 7, much of the Uniform Commercial Code is designed to reflect and track the practices of real merchants in their ordinary dealings.[24] That most aspects of contracts for the sale of securities are governed by securities-specific federal statutes and not by the state law of contracts shows that the genuine distinction between securities and other objects of contracting is reflected in the law as well. And the fact that long before he became a Supreme Court Justice, Louis Brandeis could be the coauthor of an article entitled "The Law of Ponds[25] exemplifies the way in which legal categories such as ponds are, more often than Holmes supposed, built on the categories of the prelegal world. Holmes might have been right that there was no such thing as churn law, but he was quite mistaken in suggesting that there *could be* no such thing as churn law.

21. 10 *Harv. L. Rev.* at 475.
22. See Frederick Schauer, "Prediction and Particularity," 78 *B.U. L. Rev.* 773 (1998).
23. See, e.g., Rutheford B. Campbell, Jr., "Racing Syndicates as Securities," 74 *Ky. L.J.* 691 (1985).
24. See, e.g., Zipporah Batshaw Wiseman, "The Limits of Vision: Karl Llewellyn and the Merchant Rules," 100 *Harv. L. Rev.* 465 (1987).
25. Samuel D. Warren & Louis D. Brandeis, "The Law of Ponds," 3 *Harv. L. Rev.* 1 (1889).

Thus, it is possible that determinations of similarity for the purpose of assessing what is to be a precedent will in some contexts reflect law's sense of similarity for law's purposes only, and will in other contexts reflect those judgments of similarity that come from the outside world. But as long as both of these possibilities exist, and as long as even prelegal determinations of similarity and difference are based on context and purpose, then it seems impossible to conclude that a legal determination of similarity is just a matter of seeing whether the facts in the instant case really *are* similar to the facts of the precedent case.

With the path of natural similarity being a false one, we must look for something else that will tell us whether and when an earlier case claimed to be a precedent is actually a precedent for the instant case. And this something else is often thought to be what is called, especially in common-law jurisdictions outside the United States, the *ratio decidendi* of the precedent case—the basis or rationale for the court's decision.[26] We need to know not only *what* the precedent court decided, but *why* it decided it. So a common view in England and elsewhere is that, like rules, precedent cases have justifications or rationales lying behind their outcomes, and a precedent case is a good precedent, and thus binding, for all subsequent cases falling within the ratio decidendi of the precedent case. So far so good, but now how do we know why the precedent court decided what it did? How do we know what the ratio decidendi was? One possibility is to look to the facts of the precedent case as described by the precedent court and to take those facts, in conjunction with the outcome of the case, as the ratio decidendi; indeed, this was what the legal theorist Arthur Goodhart influentially proposed.[27] But Goodhart's solution turns

26. See Geoffrey Marshall, "What is Binding in a Precedent?," *in Interpreting Precedents: A Comparative Study* 503 (D. Neil MacCormick & Robert S. Summers eds., 1997).

27. Goodhart, an American, was professor of jurisprudence at Oxford from 1931 to 1951. His claim that the ratio decidendi consisted of the material facts as found by the court combined with the result was set forth in Arthur L. Goodhart, "Determining the Ratio Decidendi of a Case," 40 *Yale L. Rev.* 161 (1930). Goodhart's claim spawned a vigorous debate some years later. See Arthur L. Goodhart, "The Ratio Decidendi of a Case," 22 *Mod. L. Rev.* 117 (1959); J. L. Montrose, "Ratio Decidendi and the House of Lords," 20 *Mod. L. Rev.* 124 (1957); J. L. Montrose, "The Ratio Decidendi of a Case," 20 *Mod. L. Rev.* 587 (1957); A. W. B. Simpson, "The Ratio Decidendi of a Case," 20 *Mod. L. Rev.* 413 (1957); Julius Stone, "The Ratio Decidendi of the Ratio Decidendi," 22 *Mod. L. Rev.* 597 (1959).

out not to help very much. If the facts are that Mr. MacPherson bought a Buick from a dealer who had bought it from the Buick Motor Company and the wheel of the Buick broke, causing an injury to Mr. MacPherson, and the outcome is that Mr. McPherson prevailed against the Buick Motor Company, we still do not know the *level of abstraction,* or *level of generality,* at which to understand these facts, and without more we cannot know *why* the court decided the way it did.[28] Was it something about Buicks, something about cars, something about wheels, something about consumer products, something about inherently dangerous products (as cars were thought to be in 1916), or something else? By themselves the facts and the result are not going to provide the reasons for the precedent court's decision, and without the reasons we have no way to tell whether *MacPherson* is a Buick case, a wheel case, a car case, a consumer product case, or something else entirely. Similarly, if a court decides that a person who unlawfully sells liquor to a minor is liable for alcohol-related injuries caused by that minor,[29] is that to be understood as supporting (or dictating) similar vicarious liability for one who lawfully sells liquor to an adult? Or one who unlawfully sells a gun that is subsequently used in an armed robbery? Or one who lawfully sells a gun that is used for the same purpose? And is the actual case of *Donoghue v. Stevenson* precedent for a case in which the bottle is transparent and thus capable of being inspected by the consumer? In none of these cases is it possible to say, Goodhart's view notwithstanding, that the court's statement of the facts combined with the result gives us anything close to an answer.

If in such cases the bare statement of the facts and the outcome cannot tell us what the precedent case fully "stands for," then it is tempting to say that the question of legal similarity is itself determined by the law. That is why discussions of precedent, including Goodhart's, commonly talk not about facts but about *material* facts. In concluding that the *holding* of the case—the term more common in the United States than ratio decidendi, although there are slight differences in meaning—is a combination of the material facts and the outcome, Goodhart and others solved the level of generality problem, but at the cost of undermining the core of their view. So to Goodhart it would have been an error to say that the car being a Buick was a material fact, because the car's "Buickness"

---

28. See John Bell, "The Acceptability of Legal Arguments," *in The Legal Mind: Essays for Tony Honoré* 45, 47 (Neil MacCormick & Peter Birks eds., 1986).
29. See, e.g., Congini v. Portersville Valve Co., 470 A.2d 515 (Pa. 1983).

was no more material than the fact that Mr. MacPherson's last name began with the letter "M." Under this view, a fact is material when a legal rule makes it legally important. It is a legal rule that tells us when two things are similar, and thus it is a legal rule that tells us the level of generality at which the facts should be understood and described by the deciding court. It is therefore a legal rule that would tell us that "automobile" is a legally material category while "Buick" is not. But although this is often so, relying on a legal rule to tell us which cases are materially similar and which are not avoids the very question we are trying to answer. If the standard for materiality comes from outside the precedent case—a statute, for example—then the statute is doing the work and we do not have an example of precedential constraint at all. That is, if a statute says that properties *p, q,* and *r* are material, and if the precedent case exhibits those properties, then the search for those properties in the instant case is a search for the properties that the statute and not the precedent case have made legally relevant. And much the same applies to determinations of materiality made by single or multiple cases other than the precedent case. If a preexisting legal rule makes some part of the precedent case material, then we need to look to the source of the understood rule and just apply that, rather than thinking that it is the precedent case that is exerting the constraint. If it is a legal rule that tells us why "Buickness" is not a legally material property, then a court in a post-*MacPherson* case ought to be following *that* legal rule and not anything that can be found in *MacPherson* itself.

It is thus difficult to understand how materiality can come from the statement of even material facts by themselves. If a rule external to those facts determines materiality, it is that rule and not the precedent case that is carrying the load. And if the determination of materiality does not come from a rule external to the case, then it looks as if the idea of precedential constraint might be illusory, because there is no barrier to the instant court calling on similarities if it wishes to reach a result consistent with that reached in an earlier case or calling on differences if it wants to reach the opposite result. And because any two events or factual situations resemble each other in some respects and differ in others, the response that the law determines relevant similarity is no response at all.

Before we throw up our hands in despair, however, and conclude that there really is no effective precedential constraint in most situations, we need to remember that in the overwhelming majority of cases the precedent court not only gives us facts and the outcome, or conclusion, but also tells us *why* it reached the conclusion it did. In other words, the question is not so much one of extracting the ratio decidendi from a case as of simply reading what the court said the ratio decidendi was.[30] If in *MacPherson* Judge Cardozo had said something like, "We reach this outcome because purchasers of consumer products have less of an ability to detect or correct manufacturing flaws and because manufacturers like Buick have a greater ability to insure against or bear the loss," then it would be far easier than without that statement to say that *MacPherson* is precedent for any case involving a consumer and a manufacturer, and that would be because that is just the way Judge Cardozo said it.

Sometimes a court will be even clearer and simply say what the rule is. If Judge Cardozo had said, "We hold that in all cases involving a non-business consumer and a manufacturer of goods, the consumer may recover against the manufacturer for defects in manufacture without regard to privity between manufacturer and consumer," the question of what the case stood for—what it was a precedent for—would virtually disappear, because now there would be a court-generated *rule* that could be applied in future cases.[31] But even when the holding is not signaled in quite so explicit a form, the court's words remain the lodestar for locating its holding. When asked to say *why* it reached the result it reached, a court will describe the facts of the case before it as an example of a type, but the type is necessarily more general than the particular example of

30. The extraction of the ratio decidendi is a much more important issue in Great Britain than in the United States, because under traditional British appellate practice, as well as that in some other British Commonwealth countries, there is no requirement that there be a single majority opinion or opinion of the court. The three or five or more judges who hear a case typically will each give his own individual opinion. The outcome reached by the majority of those judges is the outcome in the case, but determining what the case stands for is inevitably a process of determining which propositions of law and which rationales attracted the agreement of a majority of the judges. So if Judge A decides for the plaintiff for reasons *x, y,* and *z,* and Judge B decides for the plaintiff for reasons *p, q,* and *x,* and if Judge C decides for the defendant, then the ratio decidendi is *x,* the reason (and the only reason) shared by a majority of judges. Where this practice of individual opinions does not exist, as it does not in the United States (except to the extent to which an increasingly divided Supreme Court appears to be moving in that direction), the question of determining the ratio decidendi is less complex.

31. See Larry Alexander, "Constrained By Precedent," note 2 *supra.* See also Larry Alexander & Emily Sherwin, "Judges as Rule Makers," *in Common Law Theory* 27 (Douglas E. Edlin ed., 2007).

the type—philosophers call it a "token"—that happened to arise in the specific case. So when, for example, the Supreme Court decided *New York Times Co. v. Sullivan,*[32] which dramatically revamped American libel law on First Amendment grounds, it described the plaintiff, Commissioner Sullivan, not only as a police commissioner (which itself would have been an abstraction from Sullivan himself and from Sullivan's particular job), but also as a "public official." And it described the *New York Times* not just as the unique *New York Times,* and not even just as a newspaper, but as "the press." As a result, *New York Times v. Sullivan,* from the beginning, stood as a precedent for all libel cases involving public officials suing the press, and that is precisely because, and only because, the Supreme Court *said* just that. If the Court had described Sullivan as a police official, and if in a subsequent case it were to have been argued that *New York Times v. Sullivan* was precedent for a case in which the libeled plaintiff had been a public official having nothing to do with law enforcement, one side would have argued that it would be good to understand *Sullivan* as being about all public officials, and the other side would have argued for a narrower interpretation, but neither side would have been able to maintain that its preferred interpretation was *compelled* by the earlier case, as would have been possible under the language of the Supreme Court's actual opinion.[33]

3.5 Of Holdings and Dicta

The perceptive legal sophisticate will detect some tension between the foregoing account and the traditional distinction between the *holding* of a case and the *dicta* that may accompany it.[34] On the traditional account,[35] the holding—which is very close to but not identical with the ratio decidendi—is the legal rule that determines the outcome of the case. So when we say that the holding in *International Shoe Co. v. Washington*[36] is that states may exercise personal jurisdiction over out-of-state de-

32. 376 U.S. 254 (1964).
33. This is not to say that the hypothetical narrower *New York Times v. Sullivan* would not have been relevant to a subsequent case seeking to broaden it. The nature of such arguments will be the focus of Chapter 5.
34. We will return to the topic of holding and dicta in Chapter 9, which focuses even more closely than we do here on the nature of judicial opinions.
35. See, e.g., Glanville Williams, *Learning the Law* 62–88 (10th ed., 1978).
36. 326 U.S. 310 (1945).

fendants as long as there are sufficient minimum contacts with the state as not to offend traditional notions of due process, we have stated a legal rule. Sometimes the court is making up the rule anew, and sometimes it is simply echoing a statement of the rule that can be found in an earlier case or distilled from multiple previous cases. But there is nothing very mysterious about the idea of a holding—it is the legal rule that, as applied to the facts of the particular case, generates the outcome. So it is no error to say that the Court held in *International Shoe* that there must be minimum contacts with the forum state in order to support personal jurisdiction, but neither is it an error to include within the idea of a holding the stated reasons behind the rule and the application of that rule to the facts of the particular case. Thus, we might describe the *International Shoe* holding as the requirement of minimum contacts coupled with the Court's statement that it would be unfair to expect a defendant to defend a suit in a state to which it had virtually no connection, this general statement then being combined with the conclusion that because the International Shoe Company's salesmen had done business in Washington, there were sufficient minimum contacts to uphold the exercise of personal jurisdiction.

Nothing in this account of a holding is problematic by itself. The court states the rule of law on which it bases its decision, applies the rule of law to the facts before it, and announces a result. That is the holding. The problems come when a court does not explicitly say what its holding is and leaves it up to readers of the opinion to try to determine it. Under the traditional account, determining the holding can be accomplished by combining the court's statement of the material facts with the court's outcome, but we have seen that this approach is unsatisfactory. If the court does not say *why* the material facts are material, we are left with a statement of facts that can be interpreted at numerous levels of abstraction, and so we are left with no firm notion of what the court held and no way of reliably applying the precedent decision in the future. Only by stating its holding does the court allow subsequent courts actually to rely on (and obey) its holding, for without the statement, the holding could be almost anything at all. But with such a statement, and with our understanding of the central role that such a statement plays in marking the court's holding, the idea of a holding, just like the idea of a ratio decidendi, becomes much less mysterious.

Traditionally, everything other than the statements of the facts and the statement of the holding is an *obiter dictum*—literally, in Latin, something said in passing, or something said by the way. It is something extra, and something that is not strictly necessary to reach, justify, or explain the outcome of the case. Commonly shortened to "dicta," these unnecessary statements are often a court's observations about issues not actually before it, or conclusions about matters unnecessary to the outcome the court actually reached, or wide-ranging explanations of an entire body of law, or simply largely irrelevant asides. So in *Marbury v. Madison*,[37] Chief Justice John Marshall held that the Judiciary Act of 1789, upon which the subject-matter jurisdiction of the Court had been asserted, was unconstitutional. But he also went on to say that the Supreme Court possessed the power to exercise jurisdiction over the president of the United States, a conclusion that infuriated President Thomas Jefferson, not least because it was wholly unnecessary to the Court's conclusion and thus clearly dicta. If the Court had no subject matter jurisdiction after all, then there was no need for it to say anything at all about who would have been subject to that hypothetical jurisdiction. Somewhat less consequentially, when Justice Blackmun in *Flood v. Kuhn*,[38] the case that continued professional baseball's historical exemption from the antitrust laws, provided several pages on the history, poetry, literature, and great names of baseball throughout the ages, he included in his opinion material whose status as unnecessary to the outcome and thus as dicta would be difficult to deny.

Yet if providing reasons for their decisions is part of what we expect courts to do, and if providing reasons is a key to the actual workability of a system of precedent, then the traditional distinction between holding and dicta may be more problematic than commonly thought. Because a reason is necessarily broader than the outcome that it is a reason for,[39] giving a reason is saying something broader then necessary to decide the particular case. And that seems to be dicta. What is technically dicta—not totally necessary for the result—is precisely what it is that makes it possible for us to generalize from a very specific ruling and thus to use it

37. 5 U.S. (1 Cranch) 137 (1803).
38. 407 U.S. 258 (1972).
39. The basic idea is that what makes a reason a reason is that it is more general than what it is a reason for. When I say that I go to the gym regularly because it helps me lose weight, I am saying that something helping me to lose weight is a reason for any action (although not necessarily a conclusive one), and not just for my going to the gym on one particular occasion. For a full explanation, see Frederick Schauer, "Giving Reasons," 47 *Stan. L. Rev.* 633 (1995).

as a precedent in the future. So although at the extremes the distinction between holding and dicta is moderately clear—the statement of a new rule of law, as in *New York Times Co. v. Sullivan,* is a holding, and Justice Blackmun's ruminations about baseball lore are dicta—the realization that the system of precedent itself depends on what strictly speaking is dicta should give us pause before we make too much of the distinction, no matter how venerable a provenance it may have.

3.6 On the Force of Precedent—Overruling, Distinguishing, and Other Types of Avoidance

The chief purpose in distinguishing between vertical and horizontal precedent was to set the stage for explaining how the two differ in terms of constraining subsequent courts. Vertical precedent is commonly referred to as being *binding.* That is, a lower court is ordinarily understood to have no choice about whether to obey a precedent from a higher one. The lower courts in New York have no more of an option to disregard the holding in *MacPherson v. Buick* than to disregard a statute passed by the state legislature, and federal and state courts in the United States must treat Supreme Court rulings in cases like *Roe v. Wade* and *International Shoe v. Washington* as, in both the figurative and the literal sense, laying down the law.[40]

That the decisions of higher courts are binding does not mean that there is no play in the joints at the lower court level, even when there seems to be a binding precedent "on point." Sometimes it can be argued that the decision of the higher court is mere dicta and no part of the holding the lower court is expected to obey. In theory such an argument is possible, because even the doctrine of vertical precedent has traditionally been understood as being limited to what the higher court held and not including what the higher court happened to say along the way. In practice, however, the advocate in a lower court urging a result plainly inconsistent with the language in a higher court opinion has a steep uphill

---

40. In reality, of course, the law that is laid down would include the most recent decisions on the subject, including Planned Parenthood of Southeastern Pennsylvania v. Casey, 505 U.S. 833 (1992), in the case of abortion; and Burnham v. Superior Court, 495 U.S. 604 (1990), Bendix Autolite Corp. v. Midwesco Enterprises, Inc., 486 U.S. 888 (1988), and World-Wide Volkswagen v. Woodson, 444 U.S. 286 (1980), in the case of personal jurisdiction.

climb, and arguments that the obstructing language is mere dicta, or not part of the ratio decidendi, are usually unavailing.

Not so, however, when an advocate or a lower court judge can *distinguish* the instant case from the precedent case. Although it might be said that a binding precedent from a higher court simply obliges the lower court to follow it, it would be more accurate to say that a binding precedent obliges a lower court to follow it *or* to distinguish it from the instant case. In practice, a great deal of legal argument involves the attempt by one side to claim that some higher court case controls the result in the instant case, while the other side insists that there is a sufficient distinction between the two that the outcome in the precedent case need not be the outcome in the instant case.

Recall from Chapter 2, for example, the case of *Riggs v. Palmer*,[41] in which the New York Court of Appeals held that Elmer Palmer, having murdered his grandfather, could not claim an inheritance under his grandfather's will, the literal language of the New York Statute of Wills notwithstanding. Many years later, the effect of *Riggs* as a precedent was central to a case called *Youssoupoff v. Columbia Broadcasting System, Inc.*,[42] in which a man who had been a coconspirator in the 1916 murder of Rasputin (the adviser to the Russian royal family) sued for invasion of privacy as a result of a CBS television movie in which he was a featured character. The suit was brought in the New York state courts, and thus *Riggs* was controlling if applicable. CBS claimed that Youssoupoff's undeniable participation in the murder of Rasputin brought him within the "no man should profit by his own wrong" principle in *Riggs,* and Youssoupoff argued that the two cases could be distinguished because his wrong was not directly connected with the money he sought to recover. And in agreeing with Youssoupoff and refusing to dismiss the case, the trial court did not deny the binding force of *Riggs.* Instead, it said that the factual situation in the instant case was sufficiently distinguishable that there was no obligation on the part of the court to have reached the same outcome as in *Riggs.*

Another example, again from New York, comes from the cases of *Campo v. Scofield*[43] and *Bravo v. C. H. Tiebout & Sons, Inc.*[44] Both are

41. 115 N.Y. 506 (1889).
42. 265 N.Y.S. 754 (Sup. Ct. 1965).
43. 95 N.Y.S.2d 610 (App. Div. 1950).
44. 243 N.Y.S.2d 335 (Sup. Ct. 1963).

lower court cases involving "downstream" users of a negligently defective product that caused injury, just as in *MacPherson v. Buick.* And in both, the plaintiffs argued that *McPherson* was controlling. But in both of the cases the defendants argued that *MacPherson* was distinguishable, and the courts agreed. In *Campo,* which involved an injury caused by a machine designed to remove the tops of harvested onions, the court concluded that *MacPherson* applied only to defects not reasonably identifiable by the user. The existence of an "obvious and patent" defect could not support a claim against a remote manufacturer, even assuming the manufacturer was negligent. In *Bravo,* the plaintiff's failure to install a statutorily required safety device on a grinding wheel again rendered *MacPherson* distinguishable, even where there was manufacturer negligence and even where there would have been liability despite the statutory violation in the case of a claim brought by a direct purchaser.

In these and countless other cases, the lawyer for one party will argue that the instant case falls under a binding precedent and the lawyer for the other party will attempt to distinguish it. The arguments take the character they do precisely because the lower court is compelled to reach the same result in the instant case as in the precedent case when the facts are not distinguishable. With respect to stare decisis, however, things are different. Often the arguments resemble those of vertical precedent, with one party relying on the court's own past ruling and the other party seeking to distinguish it. But even where there are no plausible grounds to distinguish the cases, the obligation to obey a previous decision is rarely absolute in the way that the obligation to obey the decision of a higher court is. Unlike lower courts faced with higher court decisions, courts considering their own previous decisions have the capacity to *overrule* them on occasion.[45] They can recognize that the instant case presents the same issue decided in the precedent case but decide nevertheless to reject the earlier ruling.

Although courts may occasionally overrule their own previous decisions, doing so requires more than just the belief that the previous de-

---

45. Prior to the Practice Statement on Judicial Precedent of 1966, even the House of Lords in England was prohibited from overruling its own precedents, the view being that such a power was for Parliament alone. And the practice remains far less common in England than in the United States, indicating a stronger stare decisis norm there than here. See Rupert Cross & James Harris, *Precedent in English Law* (4th ed., 1991).

cision was in error. If that were all that were necessary, stare decisis would become meaningless, because it is precisely the point of stare decisis that a court should treat a previous decision as binding just because of its existence and not because it is perceived to be correct. If every time a court believed an earlier decision to be mistaken it could overrule that decision, then there would be no principle of stare decisis at all.

At times, however, a court will believe that one of its previous decisions is extremely wrong or that the consequences of a previously mistaken holding (in the eyes of the instant court) are so grave as to demand overruling. When the Supreme Court in *Brown v. Board of Education*[46] overruled *Plessy v. Ferguson*,[47] which held that separate but equal governmental facilities were constitutionally permissible, the *Brown* Court premised its action on the existence of what it then perceived to be a grave constitutional wrong. So too when the Supreme Court in *Mapp v. Ohio*[48] overruled *Wolf v. Colorado*[49] to hold that illegally obtained evidence would be inadmissible in a criminal trial in state as well as federal court. In these and other cases, the act of overruling is premised not on a current perception of mere error in the past, but rather on a current perception of error that is well beyond the range of normal mistakes, whether in the size of the mistake or in its consequences. The United States Supreme Court has described this heightened burden before overruling one of its own previous decisions in terms of the requirement of a "special justification,"[50] and the standard in England is that the previous decision be "manifestly wrong."[51] The modifiers—"special" and "manifestly"—are important, because it is the modifiers that make clear that the principle of stare decisis becomes meaningless if a court feels free to overrule all of those previous decisions it believes to be wrong. By requiring an elevated standard for the identification and consequences of perceived past error, the modifiers ensure that the obligation of a court to follow its own previous decisions is a genuinely constraining obligation, even if it is not an absolute one, one that cannot be overridden.

46. 347 U.S. 483 (1954).
47. 163 U.S. 537 (1896).
48. 367 U.S. 643 (1961).
49. 338 U.S. 25 (1949).
50. Dickerson v. United States, 530 U.S. 428, 443 (2000); Arizona v. Rumsey, 467 U.S. 203 (1984).
51. See William Twining & David Miers, *How to Do Things with Rules* 318 (4th ed., 1999).

4

AUTHORITY AND AUTHORITIES

4.1 The Idea of Authority

We have discussed rules and precedents in separate chapters because they differ in significant respects. Yet rule-governed and precedent-following decisions have much in common, including that both are *backward-looking*.[1] Rules made in the past control the events of the present, and following a rule made previously is different from making the decision that now appears to have the best consequences. So too with following a precedent, which involves adhering to an earlier decision as opposed to deciding what will be best for the future.

The backward-looking aspect of these modes of legal thinking is closely related to the concept of *authority,* for rules and precedents not only pull us backward, but also force us away from our own best judgment in favor of someone else's. When a court *follows* a rule, it does not decide for itself whether the rule is a good or a bad one. Nor does the court decide whether in this case to obey the rule. Instead, rules function as rules by excluding or preempting what would otherwise be good reasons for doing one thing or another.[2] Judges following a rule look to the rule *instead of* the intrinsic merits of the case. A police officer enforcing a

---

1. On the backward-looking aspect of legal reasoning, see Richard A. Wasserstrom, *The Judicial Decision: Toward a Theory of Legal Justification* (1961).

2. On the intrinsically *exclusionary* or *preemptive* aspect of rules, see especially Joseph Raz, *The Authority of Law: Essays on Law and Morality* (1979); Joseph Raz, *Practical Reason and Norms* (1975). See also Patrick Atiyah, "Form and Substance in Legal Reasoning: The Case of Contract," *in The Legal Mind: Essays for Tony Honoré* 19 (Neil MacCormick & Peter Birks eds., 1986); Robert S. Summers, "Two Types of Substantive Reasons: The Core of a Theory of Common Law Justification," 63 *Cornell L. Rev.* 707 (1978).

speed-limit rule is expected to focus on whether a driver was exceeding the speed limit and not on whether she was operating the vehicle un-safely. The Bureau of Land Management official who first rejected Mr. Locke's filing because it was a day late did not evaluate whether it would be good, all things considered, to accept this petition from this claimant at this time. He simply found that Locke had not filed prior to December 31.[3]

Just as rules exclude at least some of what would otherwise be considered in making a decision, so do precedents. A lower court bound by *MacPherson v. Buick Motor Company*[4] is not expected to determine whether it is wise to impose liability on a manufacturer when there is no privity between manufacturer and consumer. And the judge who understands that *Roe v. Wade*[5] is binding precedent knows that he is not to decide whether a complete ban on abortion is morally permissible, morally mandatory, or even constitutional. In these situations, it is sufficient that the precedent exists, for the very existence of a (binding) precedent precludes reevaluation of its wisdom and forecloses deciding whether following the precedent will produce the best result in the instant case.

With respect to both rules and precedents, the key idea is that they are *authoritative*. Their force derives not from their soundness but from their status, and philosophers of law refer to this feature of authority as *content-independence*.[6] When a rule (or a command, an order, or an instruction) is authoritative, its subjects are expected to obey regardless of their own opinions of its wisdom. In other words, what the rule says does not matter; where it comes from makes all the difference. When an exasperated parent yells, "Because I said so!" to a child, the parent may well

3. United States v. Locke, 471 U.S. 84 (1985), discussed in Chapter 1. Recall that the statute required that filing be "prior to December 31" of the relevant year, even though it is almost certain that Congress meant to say "*on or* prior to December 31."

4. 110 N.E. 1050 (N.Y. 1916) (Cardozo, J.), discussed at length in Chapter 3.

5. 410 U.S. 13 (1973).

6. The classic discussion of authority as content-independent is in H. L. A. Hart, "Commands and Authoritative Legal Reasons," in *Essays on Bentham: Jurisprudence and Political Theory* 243, 261–66 (1982). See also R. A. Duff, "Inclusion and Exclusion," 51 *Current Legal Probs.* 247 (1998); Kenneth Eimar Himma, "H. L. A. Hart and the Practical Difference Thesis," 6 *Legal Theory* 1, 26–27 (2000); Frederick Schauer, "The Questions of Authority," 81 *Geo. L.J.* 95 (1992). For a skeptical view of the idea of content-independence, see P. Markwick, "Independent of Content," 9 *Legal Theory* 43 (2003).

have first tried to explain to the child *why* she should do her homework or clean up her room. Only after such attempts at content-based persuasion have been unavailing does the parent resort to the because-I-said-so argument. And he does so precisely to make clear that the child should do as told whether the child agrees with the reasons for doing it or not. And so too in law, where the legal system demands that its judges—and the rest of us as well—follow even those rules and precedents that they think mistaken. Law's subjects are expected to obey the rules and precedents because of their source and status, regardless of whether they are persuaded by the content of their reasoning, and even if they are *not* persuaded by the content of their reasoning.

It is worth pausing over the unusual nature of content-independent authority. In most aspects of our lives, we base our decisions on the substance of the reasons we have and not on where those reasons come from. I eat spinach because it is good for me. Judge Cardozo decided the way he did in *MacPherson v. Buick* because he thought that outcome fairer and more efficient than what had previously been the law. These reasons—that spinach is good for me, that not requiring privity as a condition of liability for certain consumer transactions is fair—are *substantive reasons*. Sometimes these are called "first-order reasons."[7] They go directly to the content of the reason. If *I* did not think spinach was good for me (and assuming I did not like its taste), I would not eat it. And Judge Cardozo would not have reached the result in *MacPherson* if he had thought it unfair or bad policy. Normally, someone considering what to do or to decide will take a reason as a good substantive reason only if she believes in what the reason actually *says*. *Content-independent reasons,* however, are different, precisely because what the reason says does not matter.[8] It is the reason's source—"because I said so"—that gives it its power.

Like parents, those in authority often rely on their official or formal role to provide the content-independent reasons for subjects to follow their commands or instructions. Sergeants and teachers, for example, may initially try to induce their subordinates or students to understand

---

7. See Raz, *Practical Reason and Norms, supra* note 2.

8. In contrast to first-order reasons, content-independent reasons also have the character of *second-order reasons*. They are reasons about reasons, and one example is a reason that tells a decision-maker to ignore what would otherwise be good first-order reasons.

and internalize—to take on as their own—the substantive reasons for doing something. The essence of authority, however, exists not because of such internalization but apart from it. Perhaps the sergeant would like me to understand *why* I should have a sharp crease in my uniform pants, and surely the teacher would like me to see *why* I must memorize a Shakespeare sonnet; but in these and myriad other cases, the authorities wish it to be understood that I am to do as I am told just because of who told me to do it, even if I neither accept nor agree with the underlying substantive reasons for doing so.

It is controversial whether exercising or following authority is a good idea, and if so, in what contexts. Over the years many have argued that it is irrational for someone to do something she would not otherwise have done just because a so-called authority dictates it.[9] If Barbara has decided after careful thought to spend her life as a lawyer rather than as a physician, why should she act differently just because her father tells her she should? When Sam has concluded that he would like to smoke marijuana because he believes it makes him feel good and has few side effects, is it rational for him to put aside his own best judgment in favor of that of police officers and politicians? If an electronic signal says "Don't Walk" and there is no car in sight, does it make sense for me to stand obediently at the curb? And when a judge has determined what she believes would be the best result in the case before her, can it be rational for her to make a contrary ruling solely because a bare majority of judges of a higher court came to a different conclusion in a similar case? Authority may be ubiquitous in our lives, but for generations its basic soundness has been an object of persistent challenge.

Yet although authority has long been criticized, it has for just as long been defended. Socrates refused to escape from Athens on the eve of being put to death precisely because he accepted the authority of a state that had unjustly, even in his own mind, condemned him. President Eisenhower sent federal troops to Little Rock, Arkansas, in 1958[10] to enforce a Supreme Court decision—*Brown v. Board of Education*[11]—with

---

9. See, e.g., Heidi M. Hurd, *Moral Combat* (1999); A. John Simmons, *Moral Principles and Political Obligations* (1979); Robert Paul Wolff, *In Defense of Anarchism* (1970); Heidi M. Hurd, "Challenging Authority," 100 *Yale L.J.* 1611 (1991). See generally Scott J. Shapiro, "Authority," in *The Oxford Handbook on Jurisprudence and Philosophy of Law* 382 (Jules Coleman & Scott Shapiro eds., 2002).

10. See Cooper v. Aaron, 358 U.S. 1 (1958).

11. 347 U.S. 483 (1954).

whose outcome he disagreed,[12] and he did so because he accepted the authority of the Supreme Court, just as he expected the state of Arkansas to accept the authority of the federal government. Questioning the idea of authority may have a long history, but there is an equally long history of people accepting and defending it.[13]

The ultimate rationality of authority is not our principal concern here, nor is the question of the legitimacy of state authority in general. Knowing that authority is controversial, however, is important precisely because so many legal debates, both in court and out, are about the extent of law's authoritativeness. The debates about whether *United States v. Locke* was correctly decided,[14] and indeed the debates among the Justices in the case itself, are about the extent to which, if at all, a sloppily drafted act of Congress should be taken as authoritative, mistakes and all, just because Congress enacted it. Likewise, the question of when a court should overrule itself is about the authority of past decisions. And the debates over judicial responsibility for enforcing the Fugitive Slave Laws,[15] the laws of Nazi Germany,[16] and the racial laws of apartheid South Africa[17] are debates about the authority, if any, of immoral law.[18]

12. See Richard Kluger, *Simple Justice* 753–54 (1976); Kenneth O'Reilly, *Nixon's Piano: Presidents and Racial Politics from Washington to Clinton* 170–75 (1995).

13. See, e.g., Joseph Raz, *The Morality of Freedom* (1986); Raz, *The Authority of Law, supra* note 2; Robert P. George, "Natural Law and Positive Law," *in The Autonomy of Law: Essays on Legal Positivism* 321, 327–28 (Robert P. George ed., 1996); Scott J. Shapiro, "The Difference That Rules Make," *in Analyzing Law: New Essays in Legal Theory* (Brian Bix ed., 1998). A more qualified defense of official authority is Leslie Green, *The Authority of the State* (1988).

14. Compare Richard A. Posner, "Legal Formalism, Legal Realism, and the Interpretation of Statutes and the Constitution," 37 *Case West. Res. L. Rev.* 179 (1986), and Nicholas S. Zeppos, "Legislative History and the Interpretation of Statutes: Toward a Fact-Finding Model of Statutory Interpretation," 76 *Va. L. Rev.* 1295, 1314–16 (1990), with Frederick Schauer, "The Practice and Problems of Plain Meaning," 45 *Vand. L. Rev.* 715 (1992).

15. See Robert M. Cover, *Justice Accused: Antislavery and the Judicial Process* (1975).

16. See Lon L. Fuller, "Positivism and Fidelity to Law: A Reply to Professor Hart," 71 *Harv. L. Rev.* 630 (1958); Stanley L. Paulson, "Lon L. Fuller, Gustav Radbruch, and the "Positivist" Theses," 13 *L. & Phil.* 313 (1994).

17. See David Dyzenhaus, *Hard Cases in Wicked Legal Systems: South African Law in the Perspective of Legal Philosophy* (1991).

18. An important analysis of the issues is Kent Greenawalt, *Conflicts of Law and Morality* (1987).

So although explicitly philosophical treatments of authority rarely surface in legal argument, the fact that authority itself is deeply contested is a looming presence in the operation of the law, because content-independent authority lies at the heart of legal reasoning and argument. Lawyers do try to convince judges that their client is substantively right, but the language they use is the language of authority. The good lawyer will encourage the judge to see the substantive justice of his client's position, but he relies on the authority of rules and precedents as a way of saying to the judge that she should rule in his client's favor even if she disagrees that it is the right substantive outcome.

In law, the concept of authority is typically associated with legal *sources*. Indeed, legal sources—constitutions, statutes, regulations, and reported cases, most commonly—are often referred to as *authorities*, whether they are used in an authoritative way or not. For example, what American lawyers call a "brief," a written argument on a matter of law, is sometimes referred to as a "memorandum of points and authorities." In this broader sense, a legal authority—not only a constitution, statute, regulation, or reported judicial opinion, but also at times a learned treatise or an article in a law review—may sometimes be used not because it is authoritative, but because it is a repository of genuine wisdom, experience, or information. A citation in a judicial opinion to a pithy phrase from Holmes or Cardozo, for example, may differ little from a speech in which a member of Congress quotes Abraham Lincoln or Winston Churchill. Thus, we should not be seduced by labels into thinking that everything called an "authority" in legal argument is being offered or used for reasons of its authority. Just as there is an important difference between learning how to do something from a book and taking something in that same book as correct just because it is in the book, so too is there an important difference between authority-based reasoning and the various other uses to which legal decision-makers may put a host of published materials.

But although legal arguments and judicial opinions often use sources in this nonauthoritative way, law remains pervaded—indeed, characterized—by the use of genuinely authoritative sources. Such sources, unlike quotations from famous judges or references to the law of other jurisdictions, provide reasons for making a decision in a certain way by virtue of their very existence and not of their content. And so although these source-based and content-independent reasons will often be consistent with what a judge would have done even without them, sometimes they will not. Relying on genuinely authoritative sources may thus dictate that a judge make a decision other than the one she would have made herself, even after taking into account all the wisdom and information that she can obtain from her own knowledge and that of others. And in this way legal reasoning differs, in degree even if not in kind, from the reasoning in other decision-making environments. In other decision-making environments, authority may play some role, but first-order substantive considerations typically dominate. In law, however, authority is dominant, and only rarely do judges engage in the kind of all-things-considered decision-making that is so pervasive outside of the legal system.[19] Far more commonly, legal argument relies on sources, not only because the law treats so many of them as authoritative, but also because the way in which legally authoritative sources replace first-order substantive considerations remains the touchstone of legal reasoning.

4.2 On Binding and So-Called Persuasive Authority

Once we understand that genuine authority is content-independent, we can see that persuasion, on the one hand, and the acceptance of authority (whether voluntarily or not),[20] on the other, are fundamentally opposed notions. To be *persuaded* that global warming is a problem, or that freedom of speech encompasses the right to encourage racial hatred, is to accept as sound the substantive reasons for those conclusions. And when we are genuinely persuaded by substantive reasons, we have no need for authoritative pronouncements. A scientist who concludes that global warming is a problem does so not because seven Nobel Prize winners have said so but because her own investigation justifies the conclusion.

19. At times the word "pragmatic" is used to describe or promote just this kind of all-things-considered decision-making even in the legal system, but the more sophisticated versions of so-called legal pragmatism—e.g., Richard A. Posner, *How Judges Think* (2008)—accept the largely authority-based nature of legal reasoning.

20. One reason for my accepting the authority of some source or of someone *in* authority is my own belief that it is, for one reason or another, the right thing to do. But another reason is that something bad will happen to me if I do not. Authority and *legitimate* authority are two different things, and the concentration camp prisoner who does what the Nazi guard tells him to do solely for fear of being sent to the gas chamber is still treating the guard's orders as authoritative—it is the source of the order and not its content that leads the prisoner to comply.

But when *I* conclude that global warming is a problem, it is not because I genuinely know it to be correct, for I have no authority-independent way of knowing. Rather, I reach that conclusion because it is what many authorities whose authority I accept have said. It is not that I am persuaded that global warming is a problem. It is that I am persuaded that people whose judgment I trust are persuaded that global warming is a problem.

The same distinction permeates the law.[21] It is one thing for a public official or lower court judge to believe that the best understanding of the principle of freedom of speech permits the advocacy of racial hatred. It is quite another to conclude that advocacy of racial hatred is to be permitted in the United States because the Supreme Court said so in *Brandenburg v. Ohio*.[22] In the former the substantive reasons are doing the work, while in the latter it is authority pure and simple. A lower court judge must follow *Brandenburg* even if he thinks it mistaken and even if his own legal analysis leads him to conclude that advocacy of racial hatred is not constitutionally protected. The precedent is cloaked with authority, and so the judge is obliged to obey it regardless of what he thinks of its soundness.[23]

Precedents like *Brandenburg* are typically referred to as *binding*. A lower court judge is bound, or compelled, to follow them. Or, to be more precise, binding authorities are those that a lower court must follow or distinguish, just as a lower state court in New York must follow *MacPherson v. Buick* or explain why the current case is different. The court is not permitted to concede *MacPherson*'s applicability but refuse to apply it. Nor may it overrule *MacPherson*. It must follow *MacPherson,* just as it must follow the Constitution of the United States, the Con-

21. "[A]uthority and hierarchy play a role in law that would be inimical to scientific inquiry." Richard A. Posner, *The Problems of Jurisprudence* 62 (1990). Judge Posner exaggerates, because genuine authority does exist in science. See C. A. J. Coady, "Mathematical Knowledge and Reliable Authority," 90 *Mind* 542 (1981); John Hardwig, "The Role of Trust in Knowledge," 88 *J. Phil.* 693 (1991). But Posner's basic point that authority is far more important in law than in science is nevertheless sound.

22. 395 U.S. 444 (1969) (per curiam).

23. See Larry Alexander, "Constrained By Precedent," 63 *S. Cal. L. Rev.* 1 (1989); Evan Caminker, "Why Must Inferior Courts Obey Superior Court Precedents?," 46 *Stan. L. Rev.* 817 (1994); Michael Gerhardt, "The Role of Precedent in Constitutional Decisionmaking and Theory," 60 *Geo. Wash. L. Rev.* 68 (1991); Frederick Schauer, "Precedent," 39 *Stan. L. Rev.* 571 (1987).

stitution of the State of New York, and any applicable federal or New York statute. And because the court has no choice about whether to follow such authorities, they are sometimes referred to not as "binding" but as *mandatory*. They are mandatory in the sense that they must be used and in the sense that they must be followed.

The briefest glance at almost any judicial opinion, however, will show that courts often support their arguments by references to various decisions and other sources that they are bound neither to use nor to follow. A New York state court may cite to a case decided in Vermont, just as the United States Court of Appeals for the Third Circuit may refer to cases from other circuits or from the district courts of its own circuit. The courts are not even required to cite to these "authorities," let alone follow them. Not only is the Third Circuit not required to follow a similar case in the United States District Court for the Western District of Virginia, it is not even required to acknowledge its existence. Yet such citation to nonbinding sources is ubiquitous, and so too is citation to legal treatises and articles in law journals. Such *secondary* sources, like the decisions from other jurisdictions, are commonly found in judicial opinions, but no judge is required to use or even to refer to them, and the judge who supports a conclusion with reference to a learned treatise or law review article is referring to a source whose use is entirely at the discretion of the opinion-writing judge.

Sometimes cases from other jurisdictions and from lower courts, learned treatises, law review articles, and nonlegal sources (like dictionaries, newspaper articles, and journals from nonlegal disciplines) are referred to as *persuasive* authorities, the idea being that a court will use them only if it is persuaded by the reasoning of the cited source.[24] But if the court citing such material is genuinely persuaded, then it is misleading to think of the sources as authoritative at all, for persuasion and authority are fundamentally opposed notions. It is far better to describe these nonbinding sources as nonmandatory or, more felicitously, *optional*.

As we will see in the next section, referring to mandatory authorities as "binding" is somewhat misleading as well. A better and more accurate distinction than the one between binding and persuasive authority, there-

24. See, e.g., Morris L. Cohen, Robert C. Berring, & Kent C. Olson, *How to Find the Law* 3 (9th ed., 1989); Robin Wellford Slocum, *Legal Reasoning, Writing, and Persuasive Argument* 13–24 (2d ed., 2006).

fore, is one between optional and mandatory authorities, for the real difference is whether the decision-maker has a choice whether to use the authority. In a products liability case in the Minnesota state courts, a law review article about Minnesota products liability law is obviously pertinent, but its use is optional in the same way that an Arizona products liability case dealing with very similar facts would be optional in the Minnesota courts. By contrast, a Minnesota products liability *statute* is also pertinent, but a Minnesota court has no choice but to use it.

The distinction between mandatory and optional authorities explains why a judge in the United States District Court for the Southern District of New York is *required* to follow Second Circuit Court of Appeals and Supreme Court decisions but *not required* to follow the conclusions of the Eastern District of New York, the New York Court of Appeals, the Third Circuit, *Wigmore on Evidence,* the *Harvard Law Review,* the High Court of Australia, or the European Court of Human Rights. Although the sources in this latter set are permissible, even if not mandatory, their permissibility distinguishes them from a host of *im*permissible sources. The Southern District judge may not be required to cite or rely on *Wigmore on Evidence,* but it is noteworthy that reliance on Wigmore is permissible in a way that reliance on or citation to astrology, private conversations with the judge's brother, and articles in the *National Enquirer* is not. It is thus not sufficient to distinguish mandatory from optional authorities, for distinguishing optional yet permissible from impermissible sources is also essential, as we shall see in section 4.4, for understanding the nature of legal argument.

But first there is more that needs to be said about optional authorities. It is true that optional authorities are ones that a court is not required to use, but if a court is not required to use an optional authority, then how does it select an optional source, and is there really no difference between an optional citation to an opinion from a court of appeals in another circuit and an optional citation to a quotation from Abraham Lincoln or Woody Allen?

With respect to some uses of optional sources, the judge might use and cite to a source because she is persuaded by the reasons the source offers in support of the source's conclusion. But then the source—the authority—is not being used *as* an authority, and little differentiates the persuasive opinion of a court in a different jurisdiction from the persuasive opinion of the judge's father-in-law. Good manners and the desire to give research direction to others will often counsel the judge to acknowledge the source of what she has now taken on as *her* ideas and conclusions, but the citation of the decision of another jurisdiction seems not to be a reliance on authority as we now understand the idea of authority. It will instead be the judicial equivalent of an academic paper that gives credit to the origins of the author's thinking.

If an optional source of guidance is used because of the user's belief in the substantive soundness of the source's reasoning, therefore, the source, even if by tradition and convention it is labeled an "authority," is not being used *as* an authority. But although this conclusion appears to make the idea of an optional authority as self-contradictory as that of a persuasive authority, there remains another interpretation. Although optional authorities are sometimes selected because they are persuasive, more often they are selected *as authorities* because the selector trusts the authority as an authority even if he does not agree with the conclusion or, more likely, believes himself unreliable in reaching a conclusion on which the authority, whether commentator or other court, is thought more reliable. So although a Tenth Circuit judge is under no obligation to rely in securities cases on conclusions reached by the Second Circuit or found in Loss and Seligman's treatise on securities regulation,[25] the judge might think that her own judgments about securities matters are unreliable enough that she would prefer to rely on a court or commentator she believes to be more expert in such matters. The Tenth Circuit judge who looks to the Second Circuit for guidance in securities cases is like a trial court relying on expert testimony or an amateur at car repair relying on the advice of an expert mechanic. The judge is persuaded not so much by the expert's reasons as by the (judge's inexpert evaluation of the)[26] expert's expertise,

25. Louis Loss & Joel Seligman, *Securities Regulation* (3d ed., 2004).

26. Nonexpert evaluation of expertise is a serious problem, albeit one typically discussed more in the context of the law of evidence than with respect to sources of law. But whether it is members of a jury (or a judge acting as trier of fact) trying to determine which of two opposing expert witnesses is correct (where all too often the decision is made on the basis of considerations such as whether the expert looks like a college professor) or a judge on an appellate court deciding between the opposing interpretations of two different scholars of a statute dealing with a topic about which the judge himself knows little, inexpert evaluation of expertise is a recurring dilemma. See Scott Brewer, "Scientfic Expert Testimony and Intellectual Due Process," 107 *Yale L.J.* 1535 (1998). Sometimes the answer lies in the ability

and thus the source is being used in a genuinely authoritative way, even though the authority is selected by its subject—the judge—rather than being imposed by the system on the subject.

We can now see that a common use of an optional authority is not one in which the judge is persuaded by the substance of what an optional source says, but instead is one in which she is persuaded that the source is more likely right than she would be if she made her own decision. So although a judge of the Southern District of New York is required to follow Second Circuit rulings even if he thinks that all of the judges of the Second Circuit are idiots, the same judge may rely on an optional authority because he is persuaded that the authority knows what he is talking about, even if the judge does not know enough about the subject to know if the authority is actually right. Relying on such an authority is optional and not mandatory, but because it is based on the source and not on the content, it nevertheless counts as a genuine reliance on authority. There is a difference between relying on an authority because the system demands it, as when a lower court obeys a higher one, and relying on an authority because the authority is perceived to be more expert, but both are examples of genuine authority.

Even more frequently, optional authorities are employed in a way that hovers precariously on the edge of genuine authority. Thus, when a lawyer in a brief, a judge in an opinion, or a scholar in a law review article makes reference to an authority, it is often to provide so-called support for some proposition. Judges will ask lawyers what support they have for an argument, and student law review editors incessantly ask authors to provide support for what they say. But the idea of "support" here is odd. The authority alleged to provide support is often not one that supports a proposition more than another authority negates it.[27] This kind of "sup-

---

of some people on some occasions to evaluate credentials expertly even if they do not have the ability to evaluate the conclusions reached by the people who have those credentials. A judge of the Sixth Circuit, for example, might be expert at knowing that the place to look for guidance is the Second Circuit on securities matters and the Tenth Circuit on questions of federal Indian law, even if he knows little about either securities or Indian law. Whether there can be expert evaluation of expertise without an evaluation of the substance of the expertise is itself a problem, but when such an evaluation is unavailable, the quandary is even larger.

27. There is a an ethical obligation for lawyers to cite to directly contrary controlling authority—see Model Rules of Professional Responsibility, Rule 3.3—but even apart from the significant qualifications provided by "directly" and "control-

port" is a peculiar sense of authority, because the balance of all the authorities might not point in one direction or another, or might even point against the very proposition allegedly being supported. Nevertheless, the conventions of legal citation require only that a proposition be supported by a reference to some court (or other source) that has previously reached that conclusion, even when other courts or sources have reached different conclusions, and even when there are more of the latter than the former. Often, therefore, to support a legal proposition with a source is to say no more than that at least one person or court has said the same thing on at least one previous occasion.

This kind of support may seem close to pointless, and it often is, but it does serve a purpose. Especially in a brief or judicial opinion, providing this kind of minimal support reflects not only law's intrinsically authoritative nature, but also law's related inherent conservatism, in the nonpolitical sense of that word. Perhaps surprisingly to many people, a legal argument is a better legal argument just because someone has made it before, and a legal conclusion is a better legal conclusion just because another court has reached the same conclusion on an earlier occasion. The use of an authority that is not necessarily more persuasive or more authoritative than one that could be marshaled for the opposite proposition provides at least the minimal assurance that the user of the authority is not simply making up the argument out of whole cloth.

So what conclusions can the reader of an opinion or brief or article draw from the fact that the author has provided assurance of minimal unoriginality? One conclusion would rest on the premise that that there are not, proportionally, that many legal propositions whose affirmation and denial are both supportable by respectable published sources. That is often so outside of law, and in science many of the basic principles would be so unanimously supported that respectable published conclusions to the contrary would be nonexistent. Were this so with law, then the fact that some conclusion of law had been reached previously by a court or credentialed commentator would be some indication of its soundness.

Thus, American judges often use the phrase "It won't write"[28] to refer

---

ling," the obligation is one that is (unfortunately) hardly universally followed. See Roger J. Miner, "Professional Responsibility in Appellate Practice: A View from the Bench," 19 *Pace L. Rev.* 323 (1999).

28. See Patricia M. Wald, "The Rhetoric of Result and the Results of Rhetoric: Judicial Writings," 62 *U. Chi. L. Rev.* 1371 (1995). See also Paul A. Freund, "An

to a conclusion they would prefer to reach but for which they cannot find sufficient support in the available authorities to justify the outcome. In effect they are saying that some legal propositions, even some legal propositions that would generate a desirable result in the particular case, are simply not legally supportable. The question, however, which we will take up in the discussion of Legal Realism in Chapter 7, is the frequency with which this is so, that is, the frequency with which one or another possible outcome in a case "will not write." If some citation to a case, rule, or principle is almost always available to support virtually any legal conclusion, as Legal Realists such as Karl Llewellyn sometimes insisted, then the requirement of support will not be much of a constraint. But if, in contrast, the existing stock of authorities, even optional and not mandatory authorities, is often entirely on one side of a legal question, then a requirement that legal conclusions be supported by legal authorities will genuinely constrain a judge's decisional freedom. The extent to which this is so, however, is an irreducibly empirical conclusion, and with respect to *this* conclusion, as we will see in Chapter 7, opinion is deeply divided.

If Llewellyn was even a little bit correct, the requirement for some support may often not be very constraining on a judge, but it is worth noting that requiring minimal support is still a form, albeit a weak one, of genuine authority. The author of a brief or opinion who provides some support in order to deny genuine novelty is asking the reader to take the supported proposition as being at least slightly more plausible because it has been said before than if it had not been. And this is being done, typically, on the basis of the very existence of the source itself rather than of the substantive reasoning contained in it. One could well ask why the legal system is so concerned about the existence of one supporting "authority" even when the weight of authority might go in the other direction. But although the practice is questionable, the point is only that even this weaker and arguably more common form of citation to authority is a variant on genuine authority and is consistent with the authoritative character of the law itself. The lawyer who points to an authority for support is in effect claiming an endorsement for her argument, and

Analysis of Judicial Reasoning," in *Law and Philosophy* 282, 284 (Sidney Hook ed., 1984); Patrick J. Schiltz, "The Citation of Unpublished Opinions in the Federal Courts of Appeals," 74 *Fordham L. Rev.* 23, 50 (2005).

in law, as in life, having one endorser is at least better than having none at all.

4.3 Why Real Authority Need Not Be "Binding"

But what of mandatory authorities? Are they as "binding" as the traditional terminology suggests? The answer depends on what is meant by "binding," and it turns out that speaking of "binding" authority can be just as misleading as speaking of "persuasive" authority.

Typically, when we imagine a rule or constraint as binding, we think of it as unavoidable, as leaving no choice. Binding constraints are those we suppose to be absolute and incapable of being overridden by other considerations. The image of a binding authority is most commonly an image of an authoritative constraint from which the decision-maker cannot escape. If a precedent is binding, then a court bound by it simply must follow it. Period.

There is no reason, however, why even a binding authority should be understood in this way. Although a binding authority creates an obligation on the part of the bound court to use that authority, such an obligation, like any other obligation, need not be absolute in order to oblige. In life as much as in law, genuine obligations can be overridden by even stronger ones without losing their force as obligations. I am obliged to keep my promises, so it is said and so I believe, and thus I must keep my lunch date with you even if I no longer find you interesting or have subsequently received a better offer. But if a close relative has fallen ill, it is understood that my obligation to keep my lunch date is overridden by the even stronger one to attend to ailing relatives. And when the police officer refrains from giving a speeding ticket to the man who is rushing his pregnant wife to the hospital, the officer properly understands that the obligation to obey (and to enforce) the speed limit can be outweighed by a still more pressing obligation. Indeed, rights operate in the same way. It is not that the government may never, under the equal protection clause of the Fourteenth Amendment, draw a distinction based on race. Rather, the government may draw such a distinction only if it has a *compelling interest* in doing so,[29] and the fact that the interest must be compelling

29. Adarand Constructors, Inc. v. Pena, 515 U.S. 200 (1995); Loving v. Virginia, 388 U.S. 1 (1967).

(rather than simply substantial, legitimate, or rational) shows exactly how a right, like a rule and like an obligation, can make a genuine difference without being absolute. What there is a reason to do is different from what should be done, all things considered, just as what there is a right to do is different from what the right-holder actually gets to do, all things considered.

Just as obligations can be obligatory without being absolutely so, so too can authorities be authoritative without being absolutely authoritative. The existence of an authoritative reason is not inconsistent with there being other outweighing authoritative reasons or outweighing reasons of other kinds. Most authorities are therefore not binding or controlling in the absolute sense, and treating a source as authoritative or even mandatory does not entail following it come what may. A judge of the United States District Court for the District of Maryland is bound by the decisions of the Court of Appeals for the Fourth Circuit, but he is also bound by the decisions of the Supreme Court, and if in some case the relevant Fourth Circuit precedent turns out to dictate one outcome while the relevant Supreme Court case indicates another, the obligation to follow the Supreme Court will override the obligation to follow the Fourth Circuit. Similarly, the best understanding of stare decisis is that a subsequent court is bound to follow the earlier decisions of the same court, but this too is not an absolute obligation. When the Supreme Court says that it will only overturn its own precedents when there is a "special justification" for doing so,[30] it is emphasizing that it is not sufficient for overruling that the Court now believes that the previous Court was mistaken. Something more is required, something "special," but there is no indication that this higher burden of justification cannot on occasion be satisfied. In this respect, the Supreme Court's approach is consistent with that of appellate courts generally, which typically retain the power to overrule their own earlier decisions, but which emphasize that overruling is exceptional and that it will occur only when the reasons for doing so are especially weighty. The earlier case is a binding precedent, but here, unlike in the situation involving vertical precedent, where we understand binding to mean nonoverridable by any other consideration, the binding force of stare decisis is real but decidedly nonabsolute.

30. Arizona v. Rumsey, 467 U.S. 203 (1984).

4.4 Can There Be Prohibited Authorities?

We have distinguished mandatory from optional authorities, but we need to return to the idea of a *prohibited* authority. Are there sources that simply may not be used at all? It turns out that the answer to this question is yes, although the issues are complex. Consider, for example, the practice of some American courts, especially federal courts of appeals, of issuing "no citation" or "no precedential effect" rules encompassing many of the cases the court decides.[31] Under these rules, the court typically issues with its judgment a brief opinion for the benefit of the parties, but by the court's rules that opinion, even if publicly available, can be neither cited nor relied upon as authority in subsequent cases. The practice has generated controversy,[32] and in the federal courts Rule 32.1 of the Federal Rules of Appellate Procedure now prohibits the individual circuits from issuing no-citation rules, even though Rule 32.1 says nothing about the ability of a court to declare that one of its decisions will have no precedential effect, just as the Supreme Court's denials of certiorari have no precedential effect.[33] But although no-citation rules have been eliminated in the federal courts, some of them still exist in the state courts,[34] and they have the effect of creating a class of prohibited citations, prohibited sources, and prohibited precedents. Moreover, the still-permitted practice of designating some opinions as having no precedential effect verges on treating such opinions as prohibited authorities. Even with the recent change in the rules, therefore, the question persists. Does a court get to

---

31. See Jessie Allen, "Just Words? The Effects of No-Citation Rules in the Federal Courts of Appeals," 29 *Vt. L. Rev.* 555 (2005); William L. Reynolds & William M. Richman, "The Non-Precedential Precedent—Limited Publication and No-Citation Rules in the United States Courts of Appeals," 78 *Colum. L. Rev.* 1167 (1978); Lauren Robel, "The Practice of Precedent: Anastasoff, Noncitation Rules, and the Meaning of Precedent in an Interpretive Community," 35 *Ind. L. Rev.* 399 (2002); Amy E. Sloan, "A Government of Laws and Not Men: Prohibiting Non-Precedential Opinions by Statute or Procedural Rule," 79 *Ind. L.J.* 711 (2004).

32. *Compare* Hart v. Massanari, 266 F.3d 1155, 1170–74 (9th Cir. 2001) (Kozinski, J.), *with* Anastasoff v. United States, 223 F.3d 898, 899–905 (8th Cir. 2000), *vacated as moot*, 235 F.3d 1054 (2000) (en banc).

33. See Teague v. Lane, 489 U.S. 288, 296 (1989).

34. E.g., Texas Rule of Appellate Procedure 90(i). Tex. R. App. Proc. 90(i).

control what will count as precedent before it, and can it say that some of what it decides cannot subsequently be used?

If we view precedents simply as predictions, it seems odd to prohibit their use. But it seems even odder, as we will see in Chapter 7, for someone arguing before a court to be predicting what that court will do, as opposed to urging the court to do what it *should* do. If we persist in the strange belief that courts do not make law, then perhaps a judicial decision can be understood as evidence of the preexisting law, and under this premise it would be questionable to prohibit a lawyer from providing to a court any available evidence of what the law is. But a judicial decision is not evidence of what the law is. It is the law. And if it is the law, then there is no reason why a court, any less than a legislature, should not have the ability to decide when it will make law and when it will not. In treating some sources as in effect not authoritative at all, courts adopting no-citation or no-precedential-effect rules appear to be worried that what the court may have said entirely for the benefit of the parties, and with little consideration of the implications for other cases, will be used as reason in subsequent cases.[35] These rules are ones by which a court denies the authority, and not only the absolute authority, of its casual, rushed, or largely party-focused statements. And there seems little reason that we should deprive courts of the power to do just that.[36]

There is a parallel here to the 2006 decision by the Middlebury Col-

---

35. A court giving reasons for its decision in one case is announcing reasons that will apply in subsequent cases. Because reasons are always more general than the outcomes that they are reasons for, courts will often try to assess whether the reasons they give for a good result in the first case will have the effect of producing less-than-good results in subsequent cases. And courts will sometimes consider reaching the wrong outcome in the case before it in order to avoid laying down a rule that will produce poor outcomes in future cases. See M. P. Golding, "Principled Decision-Making and the Supreme Court," 63 *Colum. L. Rev.* 35 (1963); Kent Greenawalt, "The Enduring Significance of Neutral Principles," 78 *Colum. L. Rev.* 982 (1978). If a court wishes to avoid both a poor outcome in the case before it and poor outcomes in future cases because of what it said in the first case, it can reach the right outcome in the case before it while restricting its use in future cases. See Frederick Schauer, "Do Cases Make Bad Law?," 73 *U. Chi. L. Rev.* 883 (2006); Frederick Schauer, "Giving Reasons," 47 *Stan. L. Rev.* 633 (1995).

36. The Supreme Court did pretty much the same thing when it made clear in Bush v. Gore, 531 U.S. 98 (2000), that its decision was to be understood as restricted to the unique circumstances of the 2000 presidential election. It is also noteworthy that the Court itself has never subsequently cited that case.

lege Department of History to prohibit students from citing *Wikipedia* in their class papers. The department's worry was not primarily that Middlebury students would take whatever is on *Wikipedia* as unchallengeable gospel, but rather that the students would take *Wikipedia* entries as serious sources of information and authoritative guidance. Indeed, Middlebury's prohibition on *Wikipedia* is similar to the strong warnings against citation to *Corpus Juris Secundum* or *American Jurisprudence* routinely included in legal writing instruction for law students.[37] And perhaps the prohibition on *Wikipedia* is also analogous to the Supreme Court's boilerplate statement in every one of its decisions on the merits that the syllabus of the decision is prepared by the Reporter of Decisions, not the Court itself, and accordingly is not to be treated as authoritative.[38]

Some of the considerations that influenced the Middlebury History Department also apply to the hotly debated question of whether American courts should cite to or rely on foreign law, a debate that surfaced in Supreme Court opinions on capital punishment[39] and homosexual sodomy[40] and has been widely discussed in the law reviews.[41] For Justice Scalia and other opponents of citation of foreign law, the concern is not that foreign law would be considered absolutely binding, because no one has urged such a position. Rather, the opponents worry that the typical reference to foreign or international law, even if optional, treats foreign law as a legitimate source, albeit not a binding one, and thus as genuinely

37. See William H. Manz, "The Citation Practices of the New York Court of Appeals," 49 *Buff. L. Rev.* 1273, 1287 (2001).

38. United States v. Detroit Timber & Lumber Co., 200 U.S. 321, 337 (1906).

39. See Roper v. Simmons, 543 U.S. 551 (2005); Atkins v. Virginia, 536 U.S. 304 (2002).

40. Lawrence v. Texas, 539 U.S. 558 (2003).

41. See, e.g., Roger P. Alford, "In Search of a Theory for Constitutional Comparitivism," 52 *UCLA L. Rev.* 639 (2005); Vicki C. Jackson, "Constitutional Comparisons: Convergence, Resistance, Engagement," 119 *Harv. L. Rev.* 109 (2005); David S. Law, "Generic Constitutional Law," 89 *Minn. L. Rev.* 652 (2005); Nelson Lund & John O. McGinnis, "*Lawrence v. Texas* and Judicial Hubris," 102 *Mich. L. Rev.* 1555 (2004); Michael D. Ramsey, "International Materials and Domestic Rights: Reflections on *Atkins* and *Lawrence*," 98 *Am. J. Int'l L.* 69 (2004); Mark Tushnet, "Transnational/Domestic Constitutional Law," 35 *Loy. L.A.L. Rev.* 239 (2003); Jeremy Waldron, "Foreign Law and the Modern *Ius Gentium*," 119 *Harv. L. Rev.* 129 (2005); Ernest A. Young, "Foreign Law and the Denominator Problem," 119 *Harv. L. Rev.* 148 (2005).

authoritative. For Justice Kennedy in *Lawrence v. Texas,* for example, the practices of the countries whose decriminalization of homosexual sodomy he cites are reasons for the United States to come to the same conclusion, even if those reasons are far from conclusive. Like other optional references to authoritative sources—the Tenth Circuit's reliance on the Second Circuit and the Second Circuit's reliance on *Loss and Seligman,* for example—neither the optionality nor the nonabsoluteness of the use of an authority is inconsistent with that authority's authoritativeness. To cite something is typically to imply that it is to be taken seriously, and those who would treat the citation of foreign law as questionable or impermissible, just like the appellate courts that prohibit citation to some of their less carefully considered opinions, wish to establish that some sources simply should not be taken seriously. Debates on this issue are likely to continue for some time, and they raise issues about democracy and lawmaking that are not germane here, but it is worth bearing in mind that these debates are about which sources should be taken as genuinely authoritative, even if not absolutely so. This is a debate that goes to the heart of the authoritative character of law itself, as the ensuing section will clarify.

4.5 How Do Authorities Become Authoritative?

Although we can distinguish between mandatory and optional authorities, the difference turns out to be one of degree rather than one of kind. In theory it would be possible for sources to become authoritative by virtue of a single discrete act, as with the provision in the West Virginia Constitution recognizing certain legislative decisions of Virginia (of which West Virginia had formerly been a part) courts as authority in West Virginia.[42] Far more commonly, however, the status of an authority *as* an authority is the product of an informal and evolving process by which some sources become progressively more authoritative as they are increasingly used and accepted. It was formerly the practice in English courts, for example, to treat as impermissible in a lawyer's argument or a judge's opinion a reference to a secondary source written by a still-living author. If the author of a treatise or (rarely) an article was dead, then citation was permissible, but not otherwise. The reasons for this practice remain somewhat obscure, although apparently it developed out of a concern

---

42. West Virginia Constitution, §2–1–1.

that it was far easier for those who are still living than those who are dead to change their minds. What is important, however, is that the prohibition gradually withered, a withering that commenced more or less with the citation by the House of Lords in 1945 to a work by the then still-living Arthur Goodhart.[43] Once the first citation to a living secondary author appeared, subsequent courts became slightly less hesitant to do the same thing, and then less hesitant yet, and over time the practice became more widely acceptable.[44]

There is nothing unique about the example of still-living authors of secondary sources. Rarely are there formal rules determining what is to be recognized as law. What the British legal philosopher H. L. A. Hart influentially called the "rule of recognition"[45] is far less a rule as such than it is a series of continuing changing practices or conventions, much like the fluid practices or conventions that constitute a language.[46] And so too are there rarely crisp rules that determine which authorities may legitimately be cited in a legal brief or argument or opinion. Rather, what counts as legal authority, and thus what counts as a legitimate source of law, is the product of an evolving practice in which lawyers, judges, commentators, and other legal actors gradually and in diffuse and nonlinear fashion determine what will count as a legitimate source and what will not, and thus will, in the same fashion, determine what will count as law and what will not. Justice Scalia, the Middlebury History Department, and the guardians of the no-citation rules thus have some genuine basis for worrying that legitimizing the use of this or that source will set in motion a considerably more expansive process. Indeed, a legal citation has an important double aspect. A citation to a particular source is not only a statement by the one citing it that this is a good source, but is also a statement by the citer (especially if a court) that sources *of this type* are legitimate.

43. See Neil Duxbury, *Jurists and Judges: An Essay on Influence* (2001); Frederick Schauer & Virginia J. Wise, "Legal Positivism as Legal Information," 82 *Cornell L. Rev.* 1080 (1997).

44. It is still less acceptable in Great Britain than it is in the United States, but the same can be said about the citation to secondary sources generally, whether their authors are dead or alive.

45. H. L. A. Hart, *The Concept of Law* (Penelope A. Bulloch & Joseph Raz eds., 2d ed., 1994).

46. See A. W. B. Simpson, "The Common Law and Legal Theory," *in Oxford Essays in Jurisprudence* 73 (A. W. B. Simpson ed., 1973).

Thus, we frequently see a progression in authoritativeness from prohibited to optional to mandatory, a common process by which sources become transformed from decidedly nonlegal "stuff" into mandatory authorities. Although the Tenth Circuit would be doing nothing wrong in the technical sense in failing to cite to the Second Circuit in a securities case, the failure to cite to the most prominent court on securities matters would be apt to raise some eyebrows. And the higher the eyebrows are raised, the more what seems superficially optional is in reality virtually mandatory.[47] The more there is an expectation of reliance on a certain kind of technically optional authority—it is virtually impossible to argue or decide an evidence case in the Massachusetts Supreme Judicial Court, for example, without referring to Liacos's *Handbook of Massachusetts Evidence*[48]—the more an authority passes from optional to mandatory.

Thus, for Justice Scalia (and others) with reference to foreign and international law, for legal writing instructors counseling first-year law students about which authorities are permissible citations and which are not, and for appellate courts wrestling with no-citation rules, what may appear to be minor questions about form are in fact fundamental questions about what is to count as law. When Justice Breyer, in *Parents Involved in Community Schools v. Seattle School District No. 1*,[49] provided three pages of sources, mostly historical and administrative sources not in the briefs or the record below, his citation practice not only speaks to what for him counts as law and what it is to *do* law, but also serves an authoritative function (although it would have been more authoritative had the opinion not been a dissent) in telling lawyers and judges what they can *use* to make a legal argument, and thus in telling lawyers and judges what law is.[50]

47. See J. M. Balkin & Sanford Levinson, "Legal Canons: An Introduction," in *Legal Canons* 3 (J. M. Balkin & Sanford Levinson eds., 2000).

48. Paul J. Liacos, *Handbook of Massachusetts Evidence* (6th ed., 1994). Given that the book, in all of its editions, has been cited 894 times by the Massachusetts Supreme Judicial Court and the Massachusetts Appeals Court, it would be a brave (or foolhardy) lawyer who attempted to argue a point of evidence before one of those courts without dealing with what Liacos has to say on the issue. To say that the source is not a mandatory authority thus appears to be a considerable oversimplification.

49. 127 S. Ct. 2738, 2800 (2007) (Breyer, J., dissenting).

50. And thus the debate at Middlebury College and elsewhere about *Wikipedia* is analogously not about citation or footnoting but about what it is to *do* history and thus about what history (as a practice) simply is.

Because law is an authoritative practice, a great deal turns on what the authorities are. Why the Supreme Court and the Congress of the United States but not the editorial board of the *New York Times?* Why the Federal Trade Commission but not the board of directors of Wal-Mart? Why *Loss & Seligman* but not Marx and Engels? Why the *Harvard Law Review* but not the *Village Voice?* Why the writings of Thomas Jefferson but not those of Jefferson Davis?

None of these seemingly rhetorical questions is strictly rhetorical. At least in American courts, citation practice is undergoing rapid change, and there has been a great increase not only in citations to non-American sources, but also to sources that not so many years ago would have been sneeringly dismissed as "nonlegal." In *Kumho Tire Co. v. Carmichael,*[51] for example, a case dealing with the qualifications of expert witnesses, Justice Breyer's majority opinion referred to a book, not cited below, entitled *How to Buy and Care for Tires.* Justice Breyer's willingness to depart from traditionally legal sources, however, is hardly unique to him. In *PGA Tour, Inc. v. Martin,*[52] the Supreme Court, with Justice Stevens writing for the majority, relied on and cited to a number of nonlegal sources—again, sources not in the record but located by the Justices (or, more likely, their clerks)—about the nature of golf in order to decide whether allowing a professional golfer with a circulatory ailment to ride in a golf cart in violation of the rules of high-level professional golf was required by the Americans with Disabilities Act. And in *Bush v. Gore,*[53] the majority thought it important to frame its entire decision with the proposition that 2 percent of all ballots cast in a presidential election do not register a valid choice for president. The Court plainly thought this important—the proposition gets its own subsection in the opinion—but to reach this conclusion, it relied on several newspaper articles that it located for itself (one from the *Omaha World-Herald,* for example), which document this historical phenomenon.

These examples are hardly exceptional. With increasing frequency, certainly in the United States and to some extent in other common-law jurisdictions, lawyers and judges have been citing to and sometimes relying on material contained in nonlegal journals from economics, sociology, psychology, and political science, in books about subjects other than

51. 526 U.S. 137 (1999).
52. 532 U.S. 661 (2001).
53. 531 U.S. 98 (2000) (per curiam).

law, and in articles in newspapers and popular magazines. If seen as just a change in citation practice, this might be at best an interesting shift in the form of judicial opinions. But these changes do not merely reflect a transformation in citation practice. They embody a change in what counts as a legal source, and thus in what counts as a *legal* argument; and what counts as a legal argument—as opposed to a moral, religious, economic, or political one—is the principal component in determining just what law is. The boundaries of law are set by the boundaries of legal authority, and law speaks as law through its sources. When previously prohibited authorities become optional, and when previously optional authorities become mandatory, the nature of legal sources has changed, and with that change comes a transformation in the nature of law itself.

THE USE AND ABUSE OF ANALOGIES

5.1 On Distinguishing Precedent from Analogy

It will strike some readers as odd that in an entire chapter on precedent, and then in another on legal authority, there has yet to be a single mention of the word "analogy." Analogies, after all, are a ubiquitous feature of legal argument and judicial opinions. In law, as elsewhere, people argue that because some current situation is like another from the past, then the current one should be dealt with in the same way as the previous one. And because most analogies drawn by lawyers and judges are analogies to previous cases, it is tempting, as it has been for many commentators, to assume that the legal concept of decision according to precedent, which we examined at length in Chapter 3, is actually a form of argument by analogy, or even that the two are the same.[1]

The temptation, however, should be resisted. Although the use of analogies is pervasive in legal argument, analogical reasoning is not the same as constraint by precedent.[2] The fact that lawyers routinely and

1. E.g., Edward H. Levi, *An Introduction to Legal Reasoning* (1949); Lloyd Weinreb, *Legal Reason: The Use of Analogy in Legal Argument* (2005); Barbara A. Spellman, "Reflections of a Recovering Lawyer: How Becoming a Cognitive Psychologist—and (in Particular) Studying Analogical and Causal Reasoning—Changed My Views about the Field of Law and Psychology," 79 *Chi.-Kent L. Rev.* 1187 (2004).

2. And thus it is correct to treat them as distinct but related topics, as in, for example, Grant Lamond, "Precedent and Analogy in Legal Reasoning," *in Stanford Encyclopedia of Philosophy* (N. Zalta ed., 2006), http://plato.stanford.edu/archives/sum2006/entries/legal-reas-prec. See also Frederick Schauer, "Why Precedent in Law (and Elsewhere) Is Not Totally (or Even Substantially) about Analogy," 3 *Perspectives on Psychological Science* 454 (2008).

loosely refer to any previous reported decision as a "precedent" helps foster the confusion, but a genuinely constraining precedent is different from a previous case that may be used analogically. In drawing analogies, we say that some aspect of a current problem is similar to some aspect of a past problem, and thus that we should learn—sometimes to follow and sometimes to avoid—from the previous event. When, for example, it was argued at the time of the first Iraq war, in 1991, that Saddam Hussein was "like" Adolf Hitler, the point was to show that because Hitler was a dangerous dictator who invaded other countries and needed to be stopped, it followed that Saddam Hussein, also a dangerous dictator who invaded other countries, needed to be stopped as well. Because few people would have disagreed with the proposition that it was important to stop Hitler, those who drew the analogy—especially President George H. W. Bush—hoped that others would agree that it was also important to stop Saddam.[3]

The analogical argumentative structure was the same for those who argued *against* the second Iraq war, in 2002, by using an analogy between that war and the war in Vietnam. Then the crux of their argument was that Iraq and Vietnam were both situations in which conventional warfare was impossible and in which American military knowledge of the culture, terrain, and language was minimal. Because Vietnam turned into a long, costly, and ultimately unsuccessful military venture, so the argument went, the similar situation in Iraq presented similar dangers and should therefore be avoided.

This type of analogical argument pervades legal discourse. Consider, for example, the argument that prohibiting same-sex marriage violates the equal protection clause of the Fourteenth Amendment because such prohibitions resemble the prohibitions on interracial marriage that the Supreme Court held unconstitutional in *Loving v. Virginia*.[4] Here the formal structure of the argument tracks that of the Iraq examples above: A prohibition on same-sex marriage is similar to a prohibition on interracial marriage because both prevent people who want to be married from marrying solely because of their immutable personal characteristics. The prohibition on interracial marriage was properly struck down. There-

3. See Barbara A. Spellman & Keith J. Holyoak, "If Saddam Is Hitler, then Who Is George Bush?: Analogical Mapping between Systems of Social Roles," 62 *J. Personality & Social Psych.* 913 (1992).

4. 388 U.S. 1 (1967).

fore, following this logic, the prohibition on same-sex marriage should be struck down as well.[5]

Following the terminology of cognitive psychologists who study analogy, we can refer to the earlier case as the *source*, or source analog, and the current case as the *target*.[6] When a lawyer uses an analogy in an argument (or a judge uses one in an opinion), the lawyer is claiming that some feature of the source case—treating people differently because of their immutable personal characteristics, for example—is present in the target case, and accordingly the target case should be decided in the same way as the source case.

Implicit in this standard picture of analogy is that the person drawing the analogy has a choice of source analogs and selects one from among multiple possibilities on the basis of its being the most useful in making a decision or the most valuable for persuading someone else of the wisdom of a decision already made. Lawyers use analogies, therefore, because they are helpful. They assist in making decisions, they help persuade others of the correctness of decisions already made, and they illuminate aspects of a current situation that may otherwise have been obscured. So when the first President Bush analogized Saddam Hussein to Adolf Hitler in order to encourage support for the first Iraq war, and when opponents of the second Iraq war analogized that war to the American misadventure in Vietnam, they both selected their source analogs—Hitler and Vietnam, respectively—from among multiple potential candidates because of the capacity of the ensuing analogy to persuade those who might otherwise have disagreed with their position.

Although sometimes analogies are used to argue against rather than

5. The characterization in the text is simplified in order to illustrate the argumentative structure, but full arguments in this vein can be found in, for example, William N. Eskridge, Jr., "Equality Practice: Liberal Reflections on the Jurisprudence of the Civil Union," 64 *Alb. L. Rev.* 853 (2001); Andrew Koppelman, "Why Discrimination against Lesbians and Gay Men Is Sex Discrimination," 69 *N.Y.U. L. Rev.* 197 (1994).

6. See generally *The Analogical Mind: Perspectives from Cognitive Science* (Dedre Gentner, Keith J. Holyoak, & Boris N. Kokinov eds., 2001); Keith J. Holyoak & Paul Thagard, *Mental Leaps: Analogy in Creative Thought* (1995); *Similarity and Analogical Reasoning* (Stella Vosniadou & Andrew Ortony eds., 1989); Keith J. Holyoak, "Analogy," *in The Cambridge Handbook of Thinking and Reasoning* 117 (Keith J. Holyoak & Robert G. Morrison eds., 2005); Isabel Blanchette & Keith Dunbar, "How Analogies Are Generated: The Roles of Structural and Superficial Similarity," 28 *Memory & Cognition* 108 (2001).

for some course of action—that cigarettes should not be banned because of the lessons of Prohibition, for example, or that the Supreme Court should not impose substantive (as opposed to procedural) constraints on legislation in the name of the due process clause of the Fourteenth Amendment because of the unfortunate consequences of *Lochner v. New York*[7]—even here the analogies are chosen because of the guidance they are believed to offer, the illumination they are believed to provide, the lessons they are thought to teach, or the persuasion they are thought to facilitate. Those who use analogies do not select analogies that would prevent the selector (or the object of the selector's attempt to persuade) from doing what would otherwise be (to the selector) a good idea, and decision-makers do not select or even see analogies that would impede a course of action that, but for the analogy, would be chosen. In other words, lawyers do not select analogies that they believe will not lead someone—judge or jury—to the conclusion that they are advocating, and judges do not select analogies that they believe will not help the reader of an opinion see the wisdom in their conclusion.

As we have seen, however, the legal concept of precedent is very different. A mandatory precedent will sometimes, by virtue of its authoritative status, block an otherwise preferred current decision. The very fact that we refer to mandatory precedents as "binding" underscores their constraining nature, a constraint that operates precisely because the judge is perceived to have little choice in the matter. Law's use of precedent thus differs substantially from law's use of analogy, for in the latter a previous decision is selected in order to support an argument now, while in the former a previous decision imposes itself to preclude an otherwise preferred outcome.

Consider Justice Potter Stewart's 1973 concurring opinion in *Roe v. Wade*.[8] The most significant precedent was the 1965 case of *Griswold v. Connecticut*,[9] invalidating a Connecticut law prohibiting the sale of contraceptives. For those Justices who agreed with the outcome in *Griswold*,

7. 198 U.S. 45 (1905). *Lochner* was the famous (or notorious) case in which the Supreme Court used the due process clause of the Fourteenth Amendment to strike down a New York statute regulating the working hours in bakeries. The decision prompted a dissenting Justice Holmes to denounce the majority for using the Constitution to choose among competing political and economic philosophies, a task he thought should be the legislature's and not the courts'.

8. 410 U.S. 113, 193 (1973) (Stewart, J., concurring).

9. 381 U.S. 479 (1965).

the result in *Roe* was largely unexceptional. From their perspective, *Roe* merely extended broad principles of privacy and substantive liberty set forth earlier in *Griswold*. Yet although Justice Stewart had been one of the dissenters in *Griswold,* he did not dissent in *Roe*. He continued to believe that the Constitution contained no right to privacy, but he concluded that *Griswold* and other cases had, to his dismay, resurrected the doctrine of substantive due process, and he concluded in *Roe* that the obligation to follow even those precedents he thought mistaken mandated that he follow them in *Roe,* making clear that he then "accept[ed]" the precedential authority of cases with which he disagreed.

Examples of such crisp respect for stare decisis may be rare in the Supreme Court, but they are not unknown. In the 1950s and 1960s, for example, Justice John Marshall Harlan often joined the majority in criminal procedure decisions from whose basic principles he had dissented in previous cases,[10] just as Justice Byron White in *Edwards v. Arizona*[11] in 1981 felt obliged to follow the Supreme Court's 1966 decision in *Miranda v. Arizona,*[12] a case in which he had been among the dissenters, and just as Justice Anthony Kennedy in *Ring v. Arizona*[13] stated explicitly that "[t]hough it is still my view that [the earlier case of] *Apprendi* was wrongly decided, *Apprendi* is now the law, and its holding must be implemented in a principled way."

These examples come from the Supreme Court, but that is where we are *least* likely to find genuine precedential constraint. Because the Supreme Court hears and decides barely more than seventy cases a year out of the more than nine thousand petitions for review presented to it, and because even the nine thousand represent cases far along in the judicial system, the Supreme Court would be the last place to look for cases whose outcomes are genuinely constrained by a previous decision. As we saw when we examined the selection effect in Chapter 2, legal outcomes genuinely dictated by a rule or precedent are disproportionately unlikely to be litigated or, if litigated, appealed, and thus the population of appellate cases, especially at the Supreme Court level, is heavily weighted toward disputes whose outcomes are not determined or even very much

10. See Henry J. Bourguignon, "The Second Mr. Justice Harlan: His Principles of Judicial Decision Making," 1979 *Sup. Ct. Rev.* 251.

11. 451 U.S. 477 (1981).

12. 384 U.S. 436 (1966).

13. 536 U.S. 584 (2002).

guided by existing precedents. When we examine the United States courts of appeals, however, things are different. Where appellate jurisdiction is a matter of right and not discretionary with the court and where more than 80 percent of the decisions are not only unanimous but also not thought deserving of even an officially published opinion, we find far more cases in which an existing mandatory authority appears to dictate a particular outcome regardless of what the judges believe might be the just or wise outcome but for the existence of binding precedents. And thus, when we take into account the full universe of courts, the point becomes clear: The legal system's use of precedent is not about a lawyer or judge retrieving one from among numerous candidates for the source analog, nor is it about using analogy to help a lawyer make an argument now or helping a judge reach a better decision now. Rather, it is about a judge's obligation to follow a mistaken (to her) earlier decision solely because of its existence. It is, to put it bluntly, about a judge's obligation to make what she believes is the wrong decision. "Stare decisis has no bite when it means merely that court adheres to a precedent it considers correct. It is significant only when a court feels constrained to stick to a former ruling although the court has come to regard it as unwise or unjust."[14]

Perhaps the most striking difference between precedential constraint and the classic case of reasoning by analogy is the typical lack of freedom that a follower of precedent perceives in the selection of the precedent. Whereas analogical reasoners are widely understood to have a choice among various candidate source analogs, such freedom is typically absent with respect to the genuine constraints of precedent. Justice Stewart would have thought bizarre the suggestion that finding another earlier case could allow him to avoid the constraints of *Griswold*, just as Justice White would surely have laughed at the idea that feeling constrained by *Miranda* in subsequent interrogation cases was simply a function of not having been creative enough to select the best source case. Although it is true that on occasion creative and effective advocates can persuade a court to see a case or an issue in an entirely new light, far more often a previous decision about issue X looms so large that it is implausible for a judge to avoid that decision by maintaining that the current case is really about Y and not about X. In a very attenuated sense, no 2004 forest green Toyota Corolla is the same car as any other 2004 forest green Toy-

14. United States *ex rel.* Fong Foo v. Shaughnessy, 234 F.2d 715, 719 (2d Cir. 1955).

ota Corolla, but there is nothing unusual when one owner of such a car says to another that "I have the same car." So too here. Any two previous cases, instances, acts, issues, or events are in some respects different, but in reality their equivalence is often inescapable, and in law (and sometimes elsewhere) it is frequently both obvious and unchallengeable that the current decision to be made is about the *same* question that has been asked and answered on a previous occasion.

Thus, it is characteristic of the ordinary instance of precedential constraint that the current issue is so widely perceived to be the same as one resolved in a prior decision that it is not open—politically or professionally—for the current decision-maker to maintain that there is a relevant difference. A foreign policy decision-maker in 1991 might have been able with roughly equivalent plausibility to analogize Saddam to Idi Amin (a brutal dictator with whose country—Uganda—the United States did not go to war) as to Hitler, but a Supreme Court Justice asked in 2008 to rule on the constitutionality of a state law totally prohibiting abortion would find it virtually impossible—logically, linguistically, psychologically, professionally, and politically—to distinguish that case from *Roe v. Wade*.

Once we understand that in the case of precedent the choice of source decisions is often not *perceived* as a choice at all—and is often simply *not* a choice at all—we can grasp the difference between analogy and precedent. Whereas in the case of analogy the lawyer or judge is looking for assistance in reaching the best decision (or in persuading someone else of the best decision), in the case of precedent the effect is just the opposite. When there is an unavoidable similarity between the source and the target, and when the judge because of the constraints of vertical precedent or stare decisis is required to decide the instant case (the target case) in the same way that the precedent case (the source case) was decided, a judge will be constrained to reach what she will sometimes believe to be a poor outcome. Whereas in the case of analogy a lawyer or judge is looking for a source case in order to help her make the best argument or the best decision now, with respect to genuine precedent the judge will be compelled to make what she may believe to be the wrong decision. Analogy is hugely important in law, and good lawyers and good judges know how to use analogies effectively. But they also understand that precedent may on occasion constrain, and they understand as well that using an effective analogy and recognizing the constraints of precedent are hardly the same.

5.2 On the Determination of Similarity

That arguments by analogy are different from the constraints of precedent does not imply that analogical reasoning is unimportant in law. To the contrary, analogical reasoning is widespread throughout the legal system, and it comes as no surprise that many commentators have sought to explain the mechanism by which lawyers use analogies in making arguments and judges use analogies in justifying their decisions.[15] And although the use of analogy in legal argument may not differ fundamentally from the way in which analogies are used in everyday life, and although analogical reasoning may be as ubiquitous outside of law as within it, analogies are still so common in law that it is important to examine more closely the structure of this widespread form of legal argument.

The crux of an analogical argument is the claim that some act or event or thing that we encounter now is similar to something we have encountered previously. In law, the typical use of analogy involves an argument by a lawyer or a justification of a result by a judge that the current case is similar to another case in the past. But then we must confront the fact that any two things are in some respects similar and in others different. My blue 2004 Subaru Legacy station wagon is similar to your blue 2004 Subaru Legacy station wagon in that they are both blue, both the same make and model, and both from the same model year. But they are different in that one is mine and one is yours, and they almost certainly differ in the number of miles they have been driven and in at least some aspects of their mechanical condition. Likewise, there are obvious differences among black cats, black widow spiders, and black ink, but they are similar in all being black.

If any and every two things are in some respects similar and in others different, then how can we say that one thing is analogous to something else? Isn't one thing analogous to everything else and nothing else just because it is similar in some respects to (almost) everything else and different in some respects from absolutely everything else? So is it not therefore true that any current case is similar in some respects to vast numbers of previous cases and different in some respects from every one of them?

15. See, e.g., Levi, *supra* note 1; Weinreb, *supra* note 1; Scott Brewer, "Exemplary Reasoning: Semantics, Pragmatics, and the Rational Force of Legal Argument," 109 *Harv. L. Rev.* 923 (1996); Cass R. Sunstein, "On Analogical Reasoning," 106 *Harv. L. Rev.* 741 (1993).

And if this is so, then how can an argument from analogy even get off the ground?

Let us return to the example we used in discussing precedent in Chapter 3. Suppose (reversing the actual chronology) that it were to have been argued in *MacPherson v. Buick Motor Company*[16] that the (hypothetically) previously decided English case of *Donoghue v. Stevenson*[17] was analogous to the situation presented in *MacPherson,* and thus that the New York Court of Appeals should decide *MacPherson* in the same way that the House of Lords had decided *Donoghue.* Obviously this is not a case of binding precedential constraint. No one would dare suggest that the New York court should decide a case in the same way that the English court decided the same issue because of some mysterious authoritative status of an English case. Simply put, the *MacPherson* court would have been under no obligation at all to treat *Donoghue* as binding or in any other way authoritative. But the lawyer for MacPherson might still have argued that the New York court should be guided by the English court's analogous (he would have said) decision in favor of Donoghue.

In order to make the argument, however, MacPherson's lawyer would have had to demonstrate that the two cases were in some way similar, and Buick's lawyer would have argued in response that they were different. MacPherson's lawyer might have claimed, for example, that both *Donoghue* and the case before the New York court involved consumer transactions, that both involved products whose defects could not easily have been identified by the consumer, and that both involved manufacturers whose ultimate aim was to sell products to consumers, albeit through an intermediate retailer. Because of these similarities, MacPherson's lawyer would have argued, the New York court should follow the lead of the English court's decision in *Donoghue.* In response, Buick's lawyer would then have pointed out that the Buick dealer could have inspected the car before selling it in a way that the retailer of a closed opaque beverage container could not have, that occasional defects in automobiles are to be expected in ways that decomposed snails in ginger beer bottles are not, and that the typical buyer of a car (especially in 1916) had the ability to bear the loss in a way that the typical patron at a café did not.

The most important thing to be said about this scenario is that both

16. 111 N.E. 1050 (N.Y. 1916).
17. [1932] A.C. 562.

lawyers are right. There are indeed similarities, and there are indeed differences. But not all of the similarities are relevant, and not all of the differences are relevant. In a case subsequent to *MacPherson* it would be a bad argument that an identical situation involving a Ford rather than a Buick represented a different case, although of course Fords *are* in some respects different from Buicks. And in a different subsequent case it would be implausible to argue in a breach-of-contract action by a supplier of parts against the Buick Motor Company that because the Buick Motor Company had been liable in *MacPherson*, it should similarly be held liable in this case, although the identity of the same defendant in both cases means that in at least one respect the two cases are similar.

What distinguishes the good arguments from the bad ones, therefore, is not that the good arguments are based on similarity whilst the bad ones are not, because both are based on similarity. Rather, the good arguments appear to draw on a *relevant* similarity, while the bad arguments draw on similarities that are not legally relevant at all, even if those similarities might be relevant for other purposes. So when a lawyer argues that gun dealers should be liable to anyone injured (or to the family of anyone killed) by a gun illegally sold to a minor,[18] he is likely to draw an analogy to the fact that sellers of alcoholic beverages, especially to minors, are often liable to those injured or killed as a result of the actions of an intoxicated purchaser.[19] In this case, the argument is not an argument from precedent in the conventional and strict sense, because there are sufficient differences between the two cases that no judge would be faulted on grounds of failing to follow precedent for refusing to extend the vicarious liability rule for sellers of alcohol to vicarious liability for gun dealers. Rather, the argument is based on the premise that the judge is assumed to think that vicarious liability for bars is a good idea, and that there is sufficient relevant similarity between this issue and a previous issue that the judge thinks was correctly resolved to believe (or at least hope) that the judge who is sympathetic in the alcohol case will be persuaded because of the analogy to be sympathetic in the gun case.

Yet although sellers of beer and sellers of guns may in some respects be similar, in others they are not. Beer and guns are, after all, very different, and so are the typical circumstances in which they are sold. So when

18. See, e.g., Pair v. Blakly, 388 A.2d 1026 (N.J. Super. 1978).
19. See, e.g., Petolicchio v. Santa Cruz County Fair & Rodeo Ass'n, 866 P.2d 1342 (Ariz. 1994).

there are obvious similarities and obvious differences, the lawyer who has chosen one analogy rather than some other is relying on something that makes the similarities relevantly similar. In 1978, for example, the American Nazi Party sought permission to stage a public march in the streets of Skokie, Illinois, a community disproportionately populated by survivors of the Nazi Holocaust.[20] In arguing that public demonstration cases involving Nazis were relevantly similar to the public demonstration cases involving the civil rights protesters of the 1960s,[21] the lawyers for the Nazis drew on some similarities—an unpopular group with a small membership seeking to protest against the views of the majority—while the lawyers for Skokie drew on the obvious differences between Nazis and civil rights demonstrators to argue that this was a bad analogy. Just as the lawyers for the Nazis argued that a judge who thought the civil rights demonstration cases had been rightly decided ought to rule for the Nazis because of the relevant similarities between the cases, the lawyers for Skokie argued that even a judge who thought the civil rights cases had been properly decided had ample grounds to refuse to analogize those cases to one involving Nazis because of the presence of relevant differences.

As with the argument in the Skokie case, and as in countless other cases, analogical argument in law will involve arguments about which similarities and which differences are or should be legally relevant. The lawyers for the Nazis would argue that the point of the First Amendment is to protect unpopular views and groups, and thus the unpopularity of the civil rights demonstrators and the Nazis was the relevant similarity. In response, the lawyers for Skokie would argue that in the Nazi case, but not in the civil rights cases, the marchers intended to cause emotional distress to the observers of the march, and thus the cases were relevantly different.

When these arguments about the relevance or irrelevance of various similarities and differences arise, the determination may hinge on the extent to which a previous case, especially a controlling one, has announced which similarities are relevant and which are not. Thus, the more the question of legal relevance has already been settled by a general

20. See National Socialist Party of America v. Village of Skokie, 432 U.S. 43 (1977); Collin v. Smith, 578 F.2d 1197 (7th Cir. 1978); Village of Skokie v. National Socialist Party of America, 373 N.E.2d 21 (Ill. 1977).
21. E.g., Gregory v. City of Chicago, 394 U.S. 111 (1969).

rule—as with the rule emerging from the civil rights demonstration cases that marches, parades, and demonstrations may not be restricted because of the viewpoint espoused by the demonstrators—the more an argument from analogy will turn into an argument from precedent. The Nazis won in Skokie (although the march never took place) because the Supreme Court had said in earlier cases that the viewpoint of the speaker, no matter how abhorrent, was not a legally relevant factor. But the more the determination of legal similarity and difference remains an open question, the more analogical argument in law will resemble the analogical arguments that are used in all walks of life. If the civil rights cases had been decided with a less explicit statement about which factors are relevant and which not, and if the civil rights cases had been decided by a court in another jurisdiction rather than by the Supreme Court, the question, like most questions involving dueling analogies, would have been settled by the determination of which of the analogies seemed more persuasive to the judge deciding the case. In this respect, analogical reasoning in law is important, but its importance resides in its pervasiveness and not in its distinctiveness to or in law.

5.3 The Skeptical Challenge

Although lawyers and judges use analogy all the time, and although analogical reasoning in the law has been analyzed, explained, and celebrated in numerous books and articles, there is an important challenge that needs to be considered. This challenge does not deny that analogical reasoning exists, nor does it deny that analogical reasoning is widespread in legal argument and decision-making. What the challenge does deny, however, is that there is very much of deep importance in differentiating analogical reasoning from various other forms of decision-making according to a (legal) rule or according to a policy.[22]

So consider again the analogy between dram shop liability to victims

22. See Richard A. Posner, *The Problems of Jurisprudence* 86–100 (1990); Larry Alexander, "The Banality of Legal Reasoning," 73 *Notre Dame L. Rev.* 517 (1998); Larry Alexander, "Incomplete Theorizing," 72 *Notre Dame L. Rev.* 531 91997); Larry Alexander, "Bad Beginnings," 145 *U. Pa. L. Rev.* 57 (1996); Richard A. Posner, "Reasoning by Analogy," 91 *Cornell L. Rev.* 761 (2006); Richard Warner, Note, "Three Theories of Legal Reasoning," 62 *S. Cal. L. Rev.* 1523, 1552–55 (1989).

of unlawful or negligent alcohol use and gun shop liability to victims of unlawful or negligent gun use. We have seen that there are similarities and there are differences between the two situations. And we have seen that the ability to conclude (or argue) that the latter is analogous to the former is a function of the existence of relevant similarities that are perceived to outweigh any relevant differences. But where does this determination of relevant similarity come from? According to the skeptics, it derives from a determination of relevance that can be found in one of two places. It can be found, sometimes, in a statement in the earlier case, as when the Supreme Court in the civil rights demonstration cases of the 1960s justified protecting the demonstrators under the First Amendment against state restriction on the grounds that neither the unpopularity of the group's views nor the likelihood of a violent audience reaction to those views could justify restricting those who would otherwise be exercising their First Amendment rights. The Supreme Court having said as much explicitly, there was then a rule that made the moral reprehensibility of the American Nazi Party legally irrelevant, and there was another rule that also rendered the possibility of hostile audience reaction equally irrelevant. Deciding the Skokie case involving the American Nazi Party in 1977, therefore, was simply a matter of applying the rule set forth in earlier cases to this situation.[23] There was indeed an analogy between civil rights demonstrators and the Nazis, the skeptics acknowledge, but the analogy, so the skeptics insist, did not determine the result. Rather, the analogy *reflected* or *embodied* the rule that the Supreme Court announced in the cases of the 1960s.

At times there will not be such a clear and preannounced rule, but the skeptical challenge still persists. If the Supreme Court had simply announced in the 1960s that civil rights demonstrators were protected by the First Amendment, and if the 1977 Nazi case then arose with only the civil rights cases having been decided, the Court in the Nazi case would then have had to decide for itself whether the similarities between the civil rights demonstrators and the Nazis were more important for First Amendment purposes than the plain differences. And in doing so, the

23. See Kent Greenawalt, *Law and Objectivity* 200 (1992) ("[R]easoning by analogy is not sharply divided from reasoning in terms of general propositions."); Peter Westen, "On 'Confusing Ideas': Reply," 91 *Yale L.J.* 1153, 1163 (1982) ("One can never declare A to be legally similar to B without first formulating the legal rule of treatment by which they are rendered relevantly identical.").

Court would not have been able to say simply that the two cases should be decided in the same way (which was in fact the outcome) because the Nazis were relevantly similar to the civil rights demonstrators, because that was exactly the matter at issue. Rather, the Court would have had to come up with a rule or principle that determined what was relevant and what not. And in coming up with this rule, the Court would not have been engaged in analogical reasoning, but would instead have been simply deciding what, as in any other case, on the basis of policy, principle, or something else, the rule ought to be.[24]

A principal motivation for the skeptical challenge is a worry on the part of the skeptics that often the court in the second case is pretending that the analogy preexists the rule that determines relevance, when it is in fact the other way around. The rule determines the analogy, but the analogy does not determine the rule. And pretending that the analogy is doing the work—that the analogy itself without the rule drives the result—masks the fact that the second court is *choosing* the rule that determines relevance. To the skeptics, the problem is that the second court is making a choice but acting as if some natural and deep similarity is dictating the result. The impetus for the skeptics, therefore, is that too much of the praise of analogical reasoning in law is a disingenuous celebration of what is in reality a quite creative exercise on the part of the second court. And although it may be too late in the day to object to widespread judicial creativity, and although there may be nothing at all wrong with judicial creativity, it may not be too late in the day to complain about the disingenuousness of using the language of analogy both to avoid stating what the rule of relevance actually is and to disguise the second court's creative choice with the language of seeming compulsion.

There are a variety of responses to the skeptics, but all in one way or another accuse the skeptics of engaging in psychological reductionism. Drawing an analogy is not just another deductive process, so it is said, and not just a matter of applying a preexisting rule or even a newly created rule. Rather, the ability to go from one particular to another without the existence of a generalization joining the two is a common form of human reasoning, and it should come as no surprise that it exists in law as well. Consider the case of *Adams v. New Jersey Steamboat Company,*[25]

24. See Melvin Aron Eisenberg, *The Nature of the Common Law* 83 (1988) ("Reasoning by analogy differs from reasoning from precedent and principle only in form.").

25. 45 N.E. 369 (N.Y. 1896).

a New York case frequently discussed in the literature on analogical reasoning in law.[26] In *Adams,* the question was the nature of the responsibility of the owner of a steamboat with sleeping compartments to an overnight passenger whose money had been stolen when, allegedly through the company's negligence, a burglar broke into the plaintiff's sleeping compartment. What makes the case interesting is that two divergent bodies of law were both potentially applicable. If the law pertaining to open sleeping compartments in railroad cars was applicable, then the company would not have been liable, but if the law pertaining to innkeepers applied, then the plaintiff would have been able to recover. The question was then whether the steamboat with closed passenger cabins was more like a railroad sleeping car or more like a hotel. The court in fact decided that the law of inns and not the law of railroads should control, but the skeptics would not see this as an example of analogical reasoning. They would imagine that the judge had in mind a rule—even if it stayed in the judge's mind and never appeared in print—that would have established the similarity between the steamboat compartments and the rooms in an inn. But in deciding that the steamboat was more like a hotel than a railroad sleeping car, the response to the skeptical challenge would go, the court did not first imagine what, on the basis of policy or principle, the best rule would be and then determine similarity on that basis. Rather, it looked at the two possibilities and simply "saw" more of a similarity in one direction than another. This might in theory have been reducible to some rule, but the rule did not consciously exist in the minds of the judges at the time they identified the similarity, so in fact for the judges the identification of similarity was a primary mental activity. And the nonskeptics insist that the judges were doing something that people do all the time in professional and nonprofessional decision-making settings, as the very title of a leading book on analogy, *Mental Leaps,*[27] makes clear.

Ultimately, the debate between the skeptics and the traditionalists, if we can call them that, is one to be determined in part with the assistance of cognitive scientists and not solely by lawyers or legal philosophers. It is a debate about how people think, and thus the debate is one about whether people always start with something general and then apply it to the particular, as the skeptical challenge at times appears to suggest, or whether people often start with more particular insights or intuitions and

26. See Weinreb, *Legal Reason, supra* note 1.
27. Holyoak & Thagard, *Mental Leaps, supra* note 6.

then seek to explain them thereafter. If much of human reasoning involves this kind of intuitive and nondeliberative leap from particular to particular, then it is important to identify analogy as the way in which this kind of thinking and reasoning frequently manifests in legal argument. But if what some view as an intuitive leap from particular to particular is actually mediated by constructing a generalization at some level of consciousness, then much of the celebration of analogical reasoning in law will turn out to be on psychological thin ice. And not only will the claim be psychologically shaky, it will also represent still another chapter in the long history of lawyers and judges denying the degree of genuine creativity and lawmaking that pervades legal decision-making, at least in common-law jurisdictions.

Even if the skeptical challenge is in the final analysis sound, it is not a challenge to the fact of analogical reasoning in law. It is a challenge only to claims of analogical reasoning's distinctiveness. And in the end this debate, like many others, may not be one that has clear winners and losers. By understanding the debate, however, we may be able to understand not only the central importance of a relevance-determining rule in making the analogical process work, but also the importance of knowing when that rule preexists the drawing of the analogy and when, at least in the eyes of the decision-makers, it does not.

5.4 Analogy and the Speed of Legal Change

Apart from the questions of whether analogical reasoning is distinct from precedential constraint and whether analogies are truly distinctive or merely something else in disguise, there is the normative question of whether analogical reasoning, especially by judges, should be embraced or avoided. In particular, it is sometimes argued that analogical reasoning is by its nature incremental, and thus that analogical reasoning is the vehicle of slow rather than speedy legal change, of proceeding by small steps rather than in large chunks, and of making legal changes against the background of leaving most of law, and even most of the law on that topic, unchanged.[28]

This variety of incremental change is often described in terms of case-

---

28. See, e.g., Cass R. Sunstein, *One Case at a Time: Judicial Minimalism on the Supreme Court* (1999); Cass R. Sunstein, *Legal Reasoning and Political Conflict* (1996).

by-case decision-making, the message being that change should be made only when there is a concrete dispute before some court presenting the opportunity for that change, and only insofar as is necessary to resolve that dispute correctly. And because reasoning by analogy requires that the current decision be connected in some way with the previous decision or decisions, operating analogically is of necessity a way of proceeding incrementally, and thus of proceeding more slowly.

It is of course not always a good thing to proceed slowly, but the question of when it is desirable to proceed slowly and when it is not involves the full scope of normative political, moral, and legal theory. But assuming that it is at times desirable for the law to proceed slowly, there remains the question of how analogical reasoning relates to achieving that end.

As we saw in the preceding section, what is an analogy is not a question that can be answered strictly as a matter of logic, because any two items, events, acts, or decisions are similar in some respects and different in others. And as long as this is so, then there is no a priori or logical reason to believe that analogical leaps must be small rather than large. Strictly as a matter of logic, *MacPherson v. Buick Motor Company* could be found analogous to any case against the Buick Motor Company, any case involving cars, or any case involving sale of products to consumers. So too could *Raffles v. Wichelhaus*[29] be understood as the source for any of a number of analogies about ships, about cotton, or about mistakes of any kind. And *Rylands v. Fletcher*[30] might be analogous to any case involving water, flooding, land, or dangerous conditions.

In practice, of course, this is simply not so. To take *MacPherson* as analogous or as a stepping stone to a decision holding all manufacturers of consumer products strictly liable for all injuries caused to all consumers of those products would strike us as implausible, and that would be so even if we could construct an analogy in which the move from the result in *MacPherson* to blanket strict liability for all manufacturers of consumer products was as logically impeccable as the move from *MacPherson* to a case like *Donoghue v. Stevenson*. The analogies that are in fact persuasive—and analogies are usually designed to persuade—strike us as somewhat more deeply connected, as dealing with things that seem more deeply similar. Whether this is so because of the way people think or be-

29. 2 H. & C. 906, 159 Eng. Rep. 375 (Ex. 1864).
30. L.R. 1 Exch. 265 (1866).

cause of the way in which parts of the world just happen to have been constructed is a question more psychological than philosophical, but it is at least possible that to think analogically is to think in ways that build on what we perceive as preexisting similarity. To the extent that this is so, proceeding analogically may turn out to be a more incremental and deliberate approach to legal change than some number of alternatives, but it might be important to bear in mind that this may be far more a matter of patterns of thinking that could be otherwise than of a strictly logical necessity.

6

THE IDEA OF THE COMMON LAW

6.1 Some History and a Comparison

A popular conception imagines law as a collection of rules written down in a master rulebook. In many ways this image is highly misleading, and especially in that the rulebook picture of law is a particularly inapt rendering of the typical common-law legal system. These systems, all of which owe their origins to the England of the Middle Ages, now include those of Great Britain, the United States, Australia, New Zealand, Canada (with the exception of the provincial legal system of the province of Quebec), India, Israel, South Africa (although with a considerable Dutch influence), Ireland, Ghana, Malaysia, Bermuda, and most of the other nations that during crucial periods in their history were in some form under English colonial rule. Together these systems comprise the common-law legal family, a family whose shared ancestor is the law of England as it existed from the time of Magna Carta onward.[1] It is also a family whose methods and structures, as we will see, differ from those of any other legal family. When people speak of the common law, or of a common-law legal system, they are referring to the overall approach of the legal systems in these countries and aim to distinguish the common-law approach from that of the civil law as it exists in countries that owe

---

1. Leading works on the historical origins of the common law include J. H. Baker, *An Introduction to English Legal History* (4th ed., 2002); S. F. C. Milsom, *A Natural History of the Common Law* (2003); S. F. C. Milson, *Historical Foundations of the Common Law* (2d ed., 1981); Theodore F. T. Plucknett, *A Concise History of the Common Law* (5th ed., 1956); Gerald J. Postema, "Classical Common Law Jurisprudence," 2 *Oxford Commonwealth L.J.* 155 (2003), 3 *Oxford Commonwealth J.J.* 1 (2003).

their legal traditions to Roman law and the French Napoleonic Code, as well as from Islamic law, Chinese law, socialist law, and the legal systems of several additional legal families.

The characteristic feature of the common law in its purest form—the archetype, but not the reality—is the absence of a master code of laws. The countries of the common-law world have inherited from England a legal system in which written-down rules are less important than the popular rulebook image of law has it, and in which judge-made law—law created in the process of deciding particular disputes—occupies central stage. In the pure common-law system, one that exists far more as caricature than as an accurate depiction of any actual legal system, judges are expected to adjudicate particular disputes, and to do so without reference to statutes or any other kind of written rule. The judges make their decisions on the basis of their own sense of fairness, reasonableness, custom, and good policy and then provide reasons for their decisions. By virtue of the operation of a system of precedent and law reporting, future courts then learn about what earlier courts have done, and over time areas of law develop without there ever having been a code, statute, or regulation. The law is made by the judges. Thus, when people refer to case-by-case lawmaking, they are referring largely to the central method of the common law, one in which law is created incrementally in the process of adjudicating particular disputes and in which there may never have been a crisp and canonical formulation of a specific legal rule. To speak of a rule of the common law, therefore, is to refer to a rule that is extracted from a collection of judicial opinions. "It is the merit of the common law," Oliver Wendell Holmes observed, "that it decides the case first and determines the principle afterwards."[2]

Not only are common-law rules created in the process of deciding specific cases, but they are also *defeasible*.[3] That is, any common-law rule

2. Oliver Wendell Holmes, "Codes, and the Arrangement of the Law," 5 *Am. L. Rev.* 1 (1870).

3. See H. L. A. Hart, *The Concept of Law* 136 (Penelope A. Bulloch & Joseph Raz eds., 2d ed., 1994). For further explication, see G. P. Baker, "Defeasibility and Meaning," *in Law, Morality, and Society: Essays in Honour of H. L. A. Hart* 26 (P. M. S. Hacker & J. Raz eds., 1977); Bruce Chapman, "Defeasible Rules and Revisable Rationality," 17 *L. & Phil.* 443 (1998). For the view that defeasibility is an important feature of the common law but not, *contra* Hart, of law itself or necessarily of legal rules, see Frederick Schauer, "On the Supposed Defeasibility of Legal Rules," *in Current Legal Problems* 223 (M. D. A. Freeman ed., 1998).

is tentative, remaining continuously open to defeat in a particular case or subject to modification as new situations arise. It is characteristic of common-law method that judges have the power to change the rules in the very act of applying them, typically in the context of a hitherto unforeseen situation in which the existing rule would produce a poor outcome. Thus, H. L. A. Hart maintained that a rule that ends with an "unless" clause is still a rule,[4] and stressed that it was an important feature of the common law that the list of possible "unlesses" could not ever be exhaustively set out in advance. Judge Posner expressed the same idea in arguing that legal rules are always and necessarily subject to "ad hoc exceptions."[5]

The way in which common-law rules are continuously revisable enables judges to shape and reshape the rules to a changing reality and to adjust the rules to make them better as new situations present opportunities for continuing refinement.[6] The common law "works itself pure," said Lord Mansfield,[7] in a phrase subsequently made famous by the American legal theorist Lon Fuller,[8] and these words aptly capture the belief that the common law, in being fluid and always improvable at the hands of common-law judges, gradually approaches a perfection in which the rules almost never generate suboptimal outcomes.

This image of the common law has no real-world instantiations. Even from the earliest days of the English common law, statutes with fixed verbal formulations had a large role to play. And nowadays, industrialized common-law countries increasingly rely heavily on precise, detailed, complex, and often very lengthy statutes. Even the briefest examination of statutes like the Clean Air Act Amendments of 1990 and the Securities Act of 1933, for example, or even the most cursory glance at the Code of Federal Regulations, will establish beyond doubt that the image of judges making law from nothing, even if it were an apt description of a common-law system, hardly represents what the law looks like

4. H. L. A. Hart, *supra* note 3, at 110.

5. Richard A. Posner, "A Jurisprudence of Skepticism," 86 *Mich. L. Rev.* 827, 834–35 (1988).

6. See Melvin Aron Eisenberg, *The Nature of the Common Law* (1988).

7. "[T]he common law, *that works itself pure* by rules drawn from the fountain of justice, is for this reason superior to an act of parliament." Omychund v. Barker, 26 Eng. Rep. 15, 23 (Ch. 1744) (Mansfield, L. J.).

8. "The common law works itself pure and adapts itself to the needs of a new day." Lon L. Fuller, *The Law in Quest of Itself* 140 (1940).

in modern industrialized common-law countries. Moreover, even apart from statutes and regulations, as common-law doctrines persist over time, they become ever more entrenched and ossified. Their contours become widely understood and substantially less malleable. This crystallization of common-law doctrines makes them more easily knowable, to be sure, but also less able to deal with the unexpected exigencies of particular cases.

Yet although the image of an entirely judge-made common law is a caricature, it captures important features of adjudication in common-law countries. The judge is indeed a central figure in the common law, and judicial decisions, by virtue of a system of precedent, are a common touchstone for common-law legal argument. Even in interpreting detailed statutes, the common-law mindset typically persists, and judicial interpretations of statutes become as important as the statutes themselves.[9] Indeed, the spirit of the common law is very much a spirit of judge-centered incrementalism, in which the necessity of adjudicating concrete disputes informs the gradual and experience-based development of the law.[10]

The caricature of the common law as entirely judge-made law is usefully contrasted with the standard caricature of civil law, the legal family

9. See Guido Calabresi, *A Common Law for the Age of Statutes* (1982).

10. There is an important literature, primarily from an economics perspective, on the extent to which the *evolution* of the common law systematically tends toward improvement and on the extent to which factors such as the selection effect (see section 2.2) and other forms of litigant incentives bias the evolution of the common law in one way or another. Among the more noteworthy contributions, some supporting a view about the general efficiency of the common-law method and others criticizing, are Richard A. Epstein, "The Social Consequences of Common Law Rules," 95 *Harv. L. Rev.* 1717 (1982); Richard A. Epstein, "The Static Conception of the Common Law," 9 *J. Legal Stud.* 253 (1980); Gillian K. Hadfield, "Bias in the Evolution of Legal Rules," 80 *Geo. L.J.* 583 (1992); Ronald A. Heiner, "Imperfect Decisions and the Law: On the Evolution of Legal Precedent and Rules," 15 *J. Legal Stud.* 227 (1986); Herbert Hovencamp, "Evolutionary Models in Jurisprudence," 64 *Texas L. Rev.* 645 (1985); William M. Landes & Richard A. Posner, "Adjudication as a Private Good," 8 *J. Legal Stud.* 235 (1979); George L. Priest, "The Common Law Process and the Selection of Efficient Rules," 6 *J. Legal Stud.* 65 (1977); Mark J. Roe, "Chaos and Evolution in Law & Economics," 109 *Harv. L. Rev.* 641 (1996); Paul H. Rubin, "Common Law and Statute Law," 11 *J. Legal Stud.* 205 (1982); Paul H. Rubin, "Why Is the Common Law Efficient?," 6 *J. Legal Stud.* 51 (1977); Douglas Glen Whitman, "Evolution of the Common Law and the Emergence of Compromise," 29 *J. Legal Stud.* 753 (2000).

existing in continental Europe, Central and South America, and those countries elsewhere in the world whose legal systems were formed during the time when they were colonies of or under the control or influence of France, Spain, Portugal, the Netherlands, and, less commonly, Germany and Italy. According to this caricature, all of the law is contained in one or a series of canonical books of rules, typically referred to as a code. The codes in civil-law countries owe their origins, loosely, to Roman law and the Code of Justinian, and often, and slightly less loosely, to the Napoleonic Code imposed upon much of Europe during Napoleon's period of domination at the outset of the nineteenth century. So just as the location of the common law is explained by patterns of English colonial domination, so too is the presence of the civil law, whether in Quebec, Argentina, Brazil, or Indonesia,[11] primarily a function of the successes of the French, Spanish, Portuguese, and Dutch navies.

The standard image of the civil law is one in which law is made only by the legislature and not by judges, and in which the code is a comprehensive and internally consistent regulation of virtually all human activity. Although civil-law judges have a role to play in interpreting and enforcing the code, the judges called upon to interpret the code in hard cases continuously draw their guidance from the code itself, treating the earlier decisions of other judges as, at best, mildly illuminating examples of how others have dealt with the same problems. Precedent is thus a far less important idea in a pure civil-law system, where most of the law is to be found not in a haphazard array of judicial opinions but in detailed, comprehensive, and internally coherent codes.[12]

Like the standard image of the common law, this image of the civil law is far more cartoon than reality. Civil-law countries recognize that a code which determines in advance the outcomes for all transactions is a "noble dream,"[13] and it is a dream nowhere existing in real life. In actual

---

11. And still to a significant extent in the state law of Louisiana, owing to its French origins.

12. For more thorough introductions to the civil law, see James G. Apple & Robert P. Deyling, *A Primer on the Civil-Law System* (1997); H. Patrick Glenn, *Legal Traditions of the World* (3d ed., 2007); Arthur T. von Mehren & James R. Gordley, *The Civil Law System: An Introduction to the Comparative Study of Law* (1977); John H. Merryman & Rogelio Pérez-Perdomo, *The Civil Law Tradition: An Introduction to the Legal Systems of Europe and Latin America* (3d ed., 2007).

13. See H. L. A. Hart, "American Jurisprudence through English Eyes: The Nightmare and the Noble Dream," 11 *Ga. L. Rev.* 969 (1977).

civil-law countries, judges (as well as influential and authoritative academic commentators) have considerably more power as well as discretion, precedent is a more widely accepted idea, and the belief that the judiciary has some role to play not only in interpreting the law but also in making it is becoming more prevalent. Indeed, sophisticated comparativists routinely talk about the phenomenon of convergence, pursuant to which elements of the common law, such as precedent, are growing in civil-law countries just as elements of the civil law—the use of detailed statutes, especially—are becoming pervasive in common-law countries.[14] Although the convergence between common law and civil law is still well short of congruence, the typical convergence claim insists that we are approaching the point at which the similarities between common-law and civil-law legal systems are more important than the differences, and at which the differences among legal systems and legal families are far more likely to be a function of modern political and economic needs and developments than of the country that happened to be the colonizing power several centuries ago.

Although convergence is the sophisticated position these days, it is wise not to be too sophisticated. In style, tone, attitude, and even to some extent formal structure, common-law legal systems genuinely do differ from civil-law legal systems. Judges remain substantially more central legal figures in common-law countries than in their civil-law counterparts, and treating the code rather than the case as the touchstone for legal argumentation remains the pervasive feature of the civil-law consciousness. Although there is much overlap and considerable convergence between common and civil law, there is still more than a touch of reality in the observation that the civil law is substantially code-centered while the common law continues to be substantially judge-centered.

6.2 On the Nature of the Common Law

Against the background of this basic contrast between common law and civil law, and with some history to guide us, it is time to explore in greater depth the fundamental features of common-law reasoning. And foremost among these ideas is the judge-centered and case-centered na-

14. E.g., John Henry Merryman, *The Civil Law Tradition* 24–25 (1969); Katharina Pistor, "The Standardization of Law and Its Effect on Developing Economies," 50 *Am. J. Comp. L.* 97 (2002).

ture of common-law lawmaking. The typical American law school case-book is so familiar as to make the centrality of the judicial opinion appear natural and obvious, but it is worthwhile pausing over the fact that American law students are initially exposed to what the law is through the use of books containing a series of decisions by judges. Indeed, although modern casebooks contain numerous statutory and regulatory provisions as well as questions, comments, excerpts from books and articles, and at times even cartoons and photographs, it is important to bear in mind that the traditional casebook is just that—a collection of cases or, more accurately, a collection of edited judicial opinions. In the traditional casebook, what comes after a case is not a series of questions or problems or comments but the next case, and then the next case and the next case after that. And traditionally, and still to a substantial extent, students are expected to learn the law by reading judicial opinions.

Although the judicial opinion occupies center stage in the common law, we should not forget that the appellate opinion is only the final stage in a process that starts with a particular dispute. Whether it be Miss Donoghue's startling experience in the café,[15] Mr. MacPherson's unfortunate automobile accident,[16] the confusion that arose out of the coincidence of there being two Liverpool-based ships named *Peerless*,[17] the bizarre series of occurrences that produced an injury to Mrs. Palgraf,[18] or the rising water level on Mr. Rylands's property,[19] it is central to understanding the common law that we recognize the extent to which the law is made, developed, and changed in the context of particular disputes between particular parties.

The common law has for generations been committed to the view that creating legal rules in the so-called crucible of experience is a good way to make and develop the law. In earlier times, of course, such a casual reference to common-law judges "making" law would typically have produced a vehement objection. Common-law judges did not make law, so it was often said; rather, they "found" it, and they used concrete cases to find a preexisting law whose preexistence was in human reason, God-given natural law, or something else equally mysterious. When Holmes

15. Donoghue v. Stevenson, [1932] A.C. 562.
16. MacPherson v. Buick Motor Company, 111 N.E. 1050 (N.Y. 1916).
17. Raffles v. Wichelhaus, 2 H. & C. 906, 159 Eng. Rep. 375 (Ex. 1864).
18. Palsgraf v. Long Island Railroad Co., 162 N.E. 99 (N.Y. 1928).
19. Rylands v. Fletcher, 2 L.R. 3 H.L. 330 (1868).

mockingly referred to the common law as some "brooding omnipresence in the sky,"[20] the target of his scorn was the traditional common-law conceit that judges used particular disputes not to make law but to locate a fixed law that was there all along.

Even in the early years of the common law, many judges and commentators had a considerably more realistic view of it. They recognized that it was created and not discovered by judges, but they believed that fashioning law in the context of deciding particular disputes was still far and away the best way of making law. Unlike the civil law, which relied on abstract speculation about the acts, events, and controversies to which the law would be applied, the common law made law only, or at least primarily, by seeing real disputes between real people and then deciding how those disputes ought to be resolved. The artificial reason that Coke celebrated[21] would help the judges decide those disputes, and over time the decisions would be increasingly guided by previous decisions and the concept of precedent, but the core idea was still one of judges making law on the platform of concrete controversies.

It is not entirely clear that the psychological assumptions of common-law lawmaking are entirely sound. Having the litigants in a particular dispute argue their controversy may well be the best way for *that* dispute to be resolved, but if we are to understand the common-law method as being in part based on the premise that seeing a particular concrete controversy is a reliable way for making the law that will affect other and future cases, then implicit in the common-law method is the belief that the case before the court may be representative of cases of that type. When the deciding court comes up with the best resolution of that particular case, therefore, it has in the process located the best resolution for the type of case in which the particular case before it is an example. Or so the common law appears to believe.

What the common law appears to believe, however, may not actually be so. In recent years psychologists have explored what is sometimes called the *availability heuristic,* according to which people commonly take what is most visible, apparent, or proximate to them as representative of some larger range of events, and they do so even when that most

20. Southern Pacific Co. v. Jensen, 244 U.S. 205, 222 (1917) (Holmes, J., dissenting).
21. See Chapter 1, *supra.*

available example is not in reality especially representative.[22] If there was a hurricane last week, for example, people will tend to think that hurricanes are more likely to occur than they actually are, and if someone meets a brain surgeon at a party, he may think that there are more brain surgeons in the world, or in the population of physicians, than is truly the case.

If the availability heuristic is a genuine problem, and if as a consequence people in general take proximate events as unrealistically representative, then it is at least possible that a judge who sees before her all of the details of a real dispute between real people will not be ideally situated to make law for some larger category of disputes. The very process of seeing and having to decide a concrete dispute may well lead the judge to overestimate the representativeness of this dispute within the array of disputes of this type—to think that other cases within some broad category are like this one when in fact they are not. To the extent that a judge making law is making law for the category of cases of which the case before her is a member, therefore, proceeding from the starting point of a particular and vivid controversy in a concrete case may produce less ideal circumstances for making law than some of the typical celebrations of the common-law method appear to believe.[23]

Yet even though this caution about the unrepresentativeness of a particular dispute is worth bearing in mind, it should not distract us too much from recognizing the basic common-law idea as one in which law is made, developed, and changed in the context of real litigated controversies. Nor should we ignore what may well be the common law's response to the unrepresentativeness objection. The common law operates one case at a time, so it is said,[24] and thus possesses the ability to see not only the first case on some topic but all of the subsequent cases.

22. The original insight is in Amos Tversky & Daniel Kahneman, "Judgment under Uncertainty: Heuristics and Biases," 185 *Science* 1124, 1127 (1974). See also Scott Plous, *The Psychology of Judgment and Decision Making* 125–26, 178–80 (1993); Robert M. Reyes, William C. Thompson, & Gordon H. Bower, "Judgmental Biases Resulting from Differing Availabilities of Arguments," 39 *J. Personality & Social Psych.* 2 (1980).

23. For a lengthier version of this point, see Frederick Schauer, "Do Cases Make Bad Law?," 73 *U. Chi. L. Rev.* 883 (2006).

24. See Cass R. Sunstein, *One Case at a Time: Judicial Minimalism on the Supreme Court* (2000).

If the first decision was correct for the litigants in that dispute but was supported by reasons or an opinion that might produce a less desirable outcome in some subsequent case, then a court in the subsequent case can at the time make the necessary changes. When Lord Mansfield provided the metaphor of the common law "working itself pure," he was simultaneously celebrating the common-law approach and offering a realistic understanding of the fact that the common law does not necessarily get things right the first (or even the second or third) time around. But the common law is self-correcting, Mansfield believed. Although there were no cameras in Mansfield's time, the best analogy may be that of focusing a camera. When the photographer looks through the viewfinder and sees a blurry, out-of-focus image, he moves the focusing control in one direction and typically goes too far in that direction. Then he will focus back in the other direction, going too far in the opposite direction but not as far in that direction as he went in the other direction. And then he goes back, and back again, and continuously back and forth, each time narrowing the gap between where he has focused and the optimal point of more or less perfect focus. Similarly, Lord Mansfield and his successors believed, the common law corrects its mistakes continuously, progressively substituting smaller mistakes for larger ones as it approaches perfection and thus works itself pure.

6.3 How Does the Common Law Change?

The classic image of the common law is not only one in which the common law contains within its methods the ability to correct its own previous mistakes. It is also one in which the common law is able flexibly to adapt to changing social conditions. Justice Cardozo's opinion in *MacPherson v. Buick Motor Company* is an icon of the American common law in part because there were no automobiles and few large-scale consumer transactions at the time that the doctrine of privity of contract first developed, long before *MacPherson*. Yet although the doctrine of privity was first developed in economically, technologically, and culturally different times, neither the invention of the automobile nor substantial changes in the way that consumers purchased what they needed were beyond the adaptive capacities of the common law, so the argument goes. Judge Cardozo recognized this, it is said, and that is why *MacPherson* exemplifies the common law's ability to evolve in response to changing circumstances, just as *Henningsen v. Bloomfield Motors, Inc.*[25] did with respect to economic changes in the consumer-retailer relationship, just as the development of strict liability did with dangerous products,[26] and just as the doctrines of quiet enjoyment, constructive eviction, and implied warranty of habitability did with the rise of the modern era and modern sensibilities about landlord-tenant transactions.[27] In all of these instances and countless others, the beauty and majesty of the common law, so its celebrants declare, resides largely in its capacity to change in response to a changing world.

But how does the common law do this?[28] The principal vehicle for common-law change is the ability of the common law to modify its rules as they are being applied. Prior to *Henningsen v. Bloomfield Motors,* the pertinent common-law rule in New Jersey, as elsewhere, was that parties were bound by the terms of their written agreements except in cases of fraud or contractual incapacity. This is somewhat of an oversimplification, but it does capture the general idea that prior to *Henningsen* there *was* a black-letter legal rule, and the aspiring New Jersey lawyer who did not know the rule could expect to have difficulty on the New Jersey bar examination. Unlike many other cases that have contributed to the development of particular areas of law, this was not one where there was no law, or where the law was vague or ambiguous, or where two equally applicable legal rules were in opposition. There was a rule, and it was moderately clear for most situations.[29] Most importantly, the rule was clear with respect to the result that it indicated for the dispute at issue— Mr. Henningsen signed a waiver of warranty, and because he signed the waiver, he would be bound by its terms.

Obviously, this is not what actually transpired. When the case reached

25. 161 A.2d 69 (N.J. 1960). *See also* Williams v. Walker Thomas Furniture Co., 350 F.2d 445 (D.C. Cir. 1965).

26. See, e.g., West v. Caterpillar Tractor Co., 336 So. 2d 80 (Fla. 1976); Sovada v. White Motor Co., 210 N.E.2d 182 (Ill. 1965); Restatement (Second) of Torts §402A (1965).

27. See, e.g., Javins v. First National Realty Corp., 428 F.2d 1071 (D.C. Cir. 1970); Park West Management Corp. v. Mitchell, 391 N.E.2d 1288 (N.Y. 1979); Johnson v. Pemberton, 97 N.Y. Supp. 2d 153 (Bronx Mun. Ct. 1950).

28. For the economics perspective on the incentives and dynamics of common-law change, see the various contributions cited in note 9, *supra*.

29. As the New Jersey Supreme Court well recognized, citing Fivey v. Pennsylvania R.R., 52 A. 472 (N.J. 1902), for the proposition.

the New Jersey Supreme Court, that court concluded that application of the existing rule to these facts would be unfair, and so it changed the rule in the very process of applying it. Although the preexisting rule would have denied recovery to Henningsen, the rule as modified in that very case now contained an exception for unconscionable consumer contracts imposed upon consumers under circumstances of unequal bargaining power, and so Henningsen prevailed under the new rule created for and in his case even though he would not have prevailed under the law as it existed prior to his case.

A similar story can be told about most of the other prominent examples of common-law change. The rule that existed in New York prior to *MacPherson* would have denied liability on the basis of the lack of privity between MacPherson and the Buick Motor Company, just as New York's rule about inheritance prior to *Riggs v. Palmer*[30] would seemingly have allowed beneficiaries to inherit even if they had murdered the testator. As these and many other cases demonstrate, it is characteristic of common-law change that preexisting rules will be changed in the very process of their application.

That common-law rules are sometimes changed as they are applied presents a range of curious implications. One is the problem of retroactivity. That is, not only is the rule changed in a particular case, but the changed rule is applied to the parties in that very case, even if they had planned their activities on the basis of the old rule. The Buick Motor Company had presumably relied on its nonliability to consumers in various ways, perhaps including the drafting of disclaimers of liability and in deciding how much of a reserve to set aside for future liability or how much and what type of insurance to have. But then not only did the New York Court of Appeals change the rule, but it changed the rule retroactively. Buick became liable not only to purchasers of its cars from dealerships in the future, but also to Mr. MacPherson now, even though the new rule was of course not in existence when MacPherson bought his Buick. How can this be fair?

It is precisely this feature of common-law change that has led the legal philosopher Ronald Dworkin to insist that cases like *MacPherson, Riggs,* and *Henningsen* are not really cases of legal change at all.[31] Yes, there ex-

30. 22 N.E. 188 (N.Y. 1889).
31. Ronald Dworkin, *Taking Rights Seriously* (1977). See also Ronald Dworkin, *Law's Empire* (1986).

isted what looked like legal rules in place when those cases first arose, he argues, but there were also broader principles, such as the principle, as it was expressed in the nineteenth century, that no man should profit from his own wrong. So when in *Riggs v. Palmer* the New York Court of Appeals decided against Elmer Palmer, the heir who murdered his grandfather in order to be able to inherit under his grandfather's will, it did so on the basis of the "no man should profit from his own wrong" *principle,* a feature of the case that leads Dworkin to conclude that the law did not really change at all. The principle was part of the law all along, he insists. What may have looked like a change in the law, he maintains, was in fact an example of a court digging deeply to uncover a preexisting right answer rather than creating a new answer.

Dworkin's claims have been the subject of long and valuable debate,[32] but the jurisprudential controversies need not much concern us here. For our purposes, what is important is only to note the difficult issue of retroactivity, for when the common law changes its rules on the basis of larger principles, as it did in *Riggs,* or even when it changes them on the basis of the court's understanding of changing social conditions, as arguably it did in cases like *Henningsen,* it is a noteworthy feature of the common law that courts will sometimes perceive in the context of a particular case that the preexisting rule is in need of large-scale change or small-scale modification. And when a common-law court so believes that a change is necessary, the change it then makes is applied not only in the future but in that very case.

Dworkin sees *Riggs* as involving no legal change at all, but such a conclusion would have been surprising to Elmer Palmer, who in theory might well have planned his activities under what he reasonably thought to be the existing law, only to see the rug pulled out from under him by the New York Court of Appeals. And even if it is difficult to have much sympathy for Elmer, it may be easier to sympathize when the change in the common law is based on the court's view that a rule needs changing simply because some change in the world has made the policy argu-

---

32. For an important response to Dworkin on retroactivity, see Kenneth Kress, "Legal Reasoning and Coherence Theories: Dworkin's Rights Thesis, Retroactivity, and the Linear Order of Decisions," 72 *Calif. L. Rev.* 369 (1984). On Dworkin's "one right answer" claim, some of the better and earlier responses are in *Ronald Dworkin and Contemporary Jurisprudence* (Marshall Cohen ed., 1984), and "Symposium," 5 *Social Theory and Practice* 267 (1980).

ments for one rule obsolete and those for a new rule compelling. A large part of what the New Jersey Supreme Court did in *Henningsen,* for example, was premised on that court's determination that the economic nature of consumer transactions had shifted drastically and that this shift in social and economic conditions necessitated a change in the rules regarding the disclaimer of warranties. Similarly, we can imagine a court believing that the determination of whether a cabin on a steamboat was to be governed by the laws regulating railroad sleeping cars or by the more lodger-friendly laws regulating innkeepers was a determination that might change over time as overnight travel by steamboat became more common and even more necessary.[33]

In the traditional explanations of the common law, such examples of policy-based change were often cloaked in the mysterious language of *reason* and sometimes in the equally mysterious idea of *custom.*[34] The common law has always been thought of as being based on custom, but what is "custom," and whose custom are we talking about? It is rarely clear whether custom is the common law itself—customary law as opposed to statute law—or whether the common law sees its task as, in part, reflecting the changing customs of the society of which it is a part, or whether the custom that the common law embodies is a judge-made legal custom, as opposed to the custom of the society at large. But regardless of whether it is custom or reason, and regardless of whose custom customary law is about, it is hard to deny that it is a central feature of the common law that common-law courts will look to the society in which they sit, and not simply to previous cases, in deciding when what appears to be an existing common-law rule is in need of change. Indeed, this adaptive and incremental process is often thought to be the singular beauty of the common law, because the common law contains within its characteristic methodology the devices necessary for it to change in response to the problems and challenges thrown up by particular issues arising in particular cases. It is this very process that enables the common law to change, and it is this very process that led Lord Mans-

33. See Adams v. New Jersey Steamboat Co., 45 N.E. 369 (N.Y. 1896), discussed in Chapter 5.

34. For a series of helpful essays on the role of reason and custom in common-law decision-making, see *The Nature of Customary Law: Legal, Historical and Philosophical Perspectives* (Amanda Perreau-Saussine & James Bernard Murphy eds., 2007).

field and his successors to believe that the common law works itself pure. That common-law change is systematically improving and refining rather than systematically worsening and degenerating, or simply random, is of course an optimistic view, but it is an optimism that has pervaded the common law since its inception.

6.4 Is the Common Law Law?

Jeremy Bentham, history's most famous critic of the common law, notoriously referred to the common law as "dog law":

> When your dog does anything you want to break him of, you wait till he does it, and then beat him for it. This is the way you make laws for your dog: and this is the way judges make laws for you and me.[35]

As was typical of his style, Bentham was being somewhat hyperbolic. His basic point was simply that the characteristic approach of the common law was one in which there were few known rules in advance, thus compelling the common law to apply punishment (and liability) only after the fact, and then to people who may not have known in advance what they were expected to do or not to do. But as we have seen, the common law does have rules, and thus it seems more than a bit extreme to understand it as being the entirely rule-free and essentially arbitrary enterprise that Bentham caricatured. Nevertheless, there is a germ of truth in what Bentham feared, and it is worth exploring his concern in more depth.

We have seen that common-law rules—and there *are* common-law rules, Bentham's suspicions notwithstanding—are susceptible to being changed in the process of application. In its simplest form, therefore, the common law appears resistant to erroneous results. If a preexisting common-law rule seems to produce a bad result in a particular case, then it must be because the preexisting rule is not yet as "pure" as it could and should be and thus stands in need of modification. And the impetus for this modification will be a court's determination that a result is "bad" in light of the full range of considerations of principle and policy that the

35. Jeremy Bentham, "Truth v. Ashhurst; or Law as It Is, Contrasted with What It Is Said to Be," *in 5 Works of Jeremy Bentham* 231, 235 (J. Bowring ed., 1962) (1823).

court would otherwise use to evaluate the wisdom of outcomes or decisions, or to make decisions under circumstances in which there were no rules at all or in which the particular case was at the fringe and not the center of an existing rule.

That is exactly the problem. If the determination that a result is bad or in some way suboptimal is based on the full range of considerations of policy and principle that the court or anyone else would use without the rule, then what work is the rule itself doing? If our ability to perceive that a rule has generated the wrong result necessarily requires a sense of what the right result would be, and if that determination cannot be made by referring to the very rule whose soundness is now in question, then the common-law judge is deciding what the right result would be under a different rule or under no rule. And if every case in which the existing rule generates a result other than the one that appears correct in a rule-free evaluation is one that occasions a change in the rule, then why do we not just dispense with the rules entirely? If the purchase for changing a rule is a perception of what the optimal result would be in the absence of the rule, and if every case in which the rule generates a suboptimal result is understood to be one in which the rule should be changed so that it no longer produces these suboptimal results, then it appears as if the rules are not operating as rules at all and that all of the work is being done by the rule-free determination of the optimal result. This would suggest that maybe Bentham was right after all.

Whether Bentham was right, however, depends on whether the existing rule, true to the very idea of a rule,[36] is entrenched firmly enough to resist or tolerate at least some suboptimal results. On the one hand, it is correct to point out that if every suboptimal result is a sufficient condition for modifying the rule to ensure that it produces the optimal result, then the rule is not working as a rule at all. But if, on the other hand, the existing rule carries with it some weight or some gravitational force, to use Dworkin's felicitous phrase,[37] then not every suboptimal result will be the occasion for modifying the rule. When gravitational force or a weighted presumption gives the existing rule some degree of resistance to modification, at least some suboptimal results will be accepted, in spite of their suboptimality, in the service of the very values that rules are sup-

36. See Frederick Schauer, *Playing by the Rules: A Philosophical Examination of Rule-Based Decision-Making in Law and in Life* 38–111 (1991).
37. Ronald Dworkin, *Law's Empire* 111 (1986).

posed to be for. If common-law rules will be modified when they produce *very* bad or *substantially* suboptimal results, but not when they produce only somewhat or slightly suboptimal results, then the rules will operate as rules do, even if they allow at times some number of somewhat or slightly bad or moderately suboptimal results.

The issue therefore turns on the magnitude of the weight or presumption in favor of existing common-law rules, and therefore on the weight that existing precedents have as well. If it is in the nature of the common law that no common-law rule and no precedent will be permitted to produce what the court in a particular case believes to be the ideal rule-free and precedent-free outcome, then there is a real question as to whether the common law is law at all, at least if we assume that rules have at least something to do with law.[38] But if the common law treats its rules as rules and treats its precedents as rules as well, even if not absolutely so, then common-law rules, even if developed incrementally and by accretion over time rather than being laid down at a particular moment by a legislature, will still function as rules, and the common law will still accurately be able to be characterized as law.

6.5 A Short Tour of the Realm of Equity

The relationship and tension between rules and doing the right thing is hardly a modern invention. Indeed, the question of the relationship between rules and rightness goes back as far as Aristotle, and maybe even further. Consider the biblical story of Solomon, and the wisdom we attribute to Solomon, who, when faced with the conflicting stories of two women both claiming to be the mother of a newborn baby, suggested cutting the baby in half, not as a real solution but as a way—a successful one, according to the Bible—of determining which of the two women was the real mother.[39]

Although we celebrate Solomon for his wisdom, we do so not because

38. See Frederick Schauer, "Is the Common Law Law?," 77 *Calif. L. Rev.* 455 (1989). For Justice Scalia, rules may have *everything* to do with law. See Antonin Scalia, "The Rule of Law as the Law of Rules," 56 *U. Chi. L. Rev.* 1175 (1989). But although real legal systems are a great deal about rules, it is surely mistaken to think that they are only about rules. See Frederick Schauer, "Rules and the Rule of Law," 14 *Harv. J.L. & Pub. Pol.* 645 (1991).

39. 1 Kings 3: 16–28.

Solomon looked the matter up in some law book and found the rule telling him as a judge how to deal with cases of contested motherhood. Rather, we praise Solomon because he came up with the best solution to this particular and unique problem without reference to any preexisting rule. Solomon did not follow any rules. He simply did the right thing. Doing the right thing—making the correct decision—without reference to rules, and perhaps even in avoidance of rules, is the idea subsequently developed by Aristotle under the name of what we now call *equity*. Aristotle recognized that rules (what he called "law") are necessarily general, and he recognized as well that, as generalizations, rules might, as we explored in Chapter 2, generate poor results on specific occasions. For Aristotle, equity was "a rectification of law in so far as law is defective on account of its generality."[40] Indeed, it is worth quoting Aristotle at some length:

> [A]ll law is universal, [but] in cases where it is necessary to make a general pronouncement, but impossible to do so rightly, the law takes account of the majority of cases, though not unaware that in this way errors are made. And the law is none the less right; because the error lies not in the law nor in the legislator, but in the nature of the case; for the raw material of human behaviour is essentially of this kind. So when the law states a general rule, and a case arises under it that is exceptional, then it is right, where the legislator owing to the generality of his language has erred in not covering the case, to correct the omission by a ruling such as the legislator himself would have given if he had been present there, and as he would have enacted if he had been aware of the circumstances . . .
>
> This is why equity . . . is not better than absolute justice—only than the error due to generalization.[41]

Aristotle gave us the idea of equity and our name for it, but he had little to say about how a legal system should actually deal with the cases in which general rules of law produced bad outcomes even when faithfully followed. For the more systemic perspective we are indebted to Cicero, and then even more to the Romans who, drawing on Cicero, developed

40. Aristotle, *Nicomachean Ethics* 1137b (J. A. K. Thomson trans., 1977).
41. *Id.* at 1137a–b.

the idea and institutions of *aequitas* in Roman Law.[42] Because Roman law was highly formal and extremely precise, with even the slightest deviations from rigid and technical legal requirements proving fatal to an otherwise worthy claimant, *aequitas* was developed to soften the inflexibility of Roman law. As so developed, the Roman magistrates—the *praetors*—were given a special jurisdiction to correct the wrongs done by the rigid application of the written law, and in doing so they had the power both to add remedies when the formal law created none and to refuse to grant the remedies of the formal law when doing so would create injustice.

Similar ideas informed the original development of equity in English law. From the thirteenth to the sixteenth century, the king's chief minister—the chancellor—exercised the power to give relief to those who could not find it in the formal written law. Originally equity was developed simply because the common law was highly incomplete in its early years, and equity was the method by which the chancellor could grant a remedy when the intrinsic merits of some controversy demanded it but as to which no remedy yet existed in the common law. Over time, however, the chancellor's equity power came to resemble the ideas that Aristotle had first developed, and the chancellor was understood to have the power to do individual justice even when the law could not or had not.[43]

Eventually the equitable power of the chancellor developed into the Court of Chancery, and thus Christopher St. German observed in *Doctor and Student* at the beginning of the sixteenth century that

> [i]n some cases it is necessary to leave the words of the law, and to follow what reason and justice requireth . . . that is to say, *to temper and mitigate the rigor of the law.*[44]

But although equity in English law was first understood as exactly this flexible and non-rule-governed power of the chancellor and then the Court of Chancery to do justice in the particular case, this Aristotelian

42. See Bruce W. Frier, *The Rise of the Roman Jurists: Studies in Cicero's* Pro Caecina (1985).

43. See generally Jill E. Martin, Hanbury & Martin, *Modern Equity* 6 (16th ed., 2001).

44. Christopher St. German, *Doctor and Student*, dialogue 1, chap. 16 (T. F. T. Plucknett & J. L. Barton eds., 1974).

conception of equity gradually disappeared. Equity began as an open-ended authority to do what the law could not, but over time it became simply a body of law (often with separate courts) charged with adjudicating those subjects and remedies—injunctions, specific performance, and restitution, for example—that emerged from the Chancery Court's historic jurisdiction. Thus, by 1941 a leading commentator on the law of equity was able to observe that

> [i]t is very certain that no court of chancery jurisdiction would at the present day consciously and intentionally attempt to correct the rigor of the law or to supply its defects, by deciding contrary to settled rules, in any manner, to any extent, or under any circumstances beyond the already settled principles of equity jurisprudence. . . . Nor would a chancellor at the present day assume to decide the facts of a controversy according to his own standard of right and justice, independently of fixed rules, . . . he is governed in his judicial functions by doctrines and rules embodied in precedents, and does not in this respect possess any greater liberty than the law judges.[45]

The de-equitization of equity, as it were, became even more complete with the demise of separate courts of equity in most of the states, and with the merger of the procedural rules of law with those of equity. But although equity is by and large no longer institutionally, procedurally, or jurisdictionally distinct, and although the areas of law governed by equity have now become as rule-based as those traditionally thought of as residing on the law side of the law-equity divide, the hold of the idea of equity has by no means been lost. When we celebrate the flexibility of the common law and its capacity to adapt to changing circumstances, when we permit courts some freedom in creating new remedies, and when we give to all courts, as we will see in Chapter 8, some power to round off the sharp edges of even the most precise of statutes, we recognize that equity in the broadest sense has its place in a legal system, even as we recognize, with Bentham, that a system based entirely on the idea of equity would fail to serve the Rule of Law values of certainty, predictability, and settlement, which are often as important as the values of direct substantive justice. As long ago as the sixteenth century, Lord Selden observed

45. Spencer W. Symons, *Pomeroy's Equity Jurisprudence* 61–62 (5th ed., 1941).

that "equity is a roguish thing. For law we have a measure. . . . Equity is according to the conscience of him that is Chancellor, and as that is longer or narrower so is equity. 'Tis all one as if they should make the standard for the measure [of a linear foot] a Chancellor's foot."[46]

Selden's concerns about the variability of the chancellor's foot have hardly disappeared, and although most courts and most judges still retain some power to *do* equity in the traditional sense, so too do we now understand the limits on that power.[47] Neither life nor law is necessarily better when there is too much choice, and just as people recoil against being given a choice among 250 varieties of mustard or 100 types of olive oil, to take two examples from recent psychological studies of the "tyranny of choice,"[48] so too do the larger society, the legal system, and even the judges themselves back away when unlimited decisional freedom is the prevailing approach. Just as the common law becomes lawlike when its rules have some degree of resistance against continuous modification in the service of optimization, and just as equity has become more lawlike in having lost its pretense to unconstrained discretion, so too are the largest goals of a legal system, including a common-law legal system, often served by striking a balance between flexibility and rigidity, between adaptability and certainty, and between getting the right answer as opposed to getting *an* answer, even if imperfect, upon which people as well as judges can rely.

46. *Table Talk of John Selden* (Frederick Pollock ed., 1927), as quoted in William Holdsworth, 1 *History of English Law* 467–468 (1903).

47. See John Tasioulas, "The Paradox of Equity," [1996] *Camb. L.J.* 456.

48. See Sheena S. Iyengar & Mark R. Lepper, "When Choice Is Demotivating: Can One Desire Too Much of a Good Thing?," 79 *J. Personality & Social Psych.* 995 (2000); Sheena S. Iyengar & Mark R. Lepper, "Rethinking the Value of Choice: Considering Cultural, Individual and Situational Mediators of Intrinsic Motivation," 76 *J. Personality & Social Psych* 349 (1999). See also Barry Schwartz, *The Paradox of Choice: Why More Is Less* (2004).

7

THE CHALLENGE OF LEGAL REALISM

7.1 Do Rules and Precedents Decide Cases?

But is it all a sham? We have spent six chapters exploring the fundamental devices of legal reasoning, but does legal reasoning genuinely decide cases? Even if as a theoretical matter we can understand the methods of legal argument and legal reasoning, and even if we can identify real examples of their use in actual cases, how representative are those examples? In other words, how much does legal reasoning actually matter in most of the arguments that lawyers make, and how often (and how much) does legal reasoning make a difference in the real decisions of real judges?

These are the principal questions posed by the skeptical perspective commonly known as Legal Realism, or, acknowledging the standpoint and location of its principal founders, American Legal Realism.[1] Although we can find traces of related ideas in the German *Freirechtsschule*

1. The common label also serves to distinguish American Legal Realism from Scandinavian Legal Realism, the latter being a mid-twentieth-century school of legal theory led by scholars such as Alf Ross, Karl Olivecrona, Axel Hägerström, and A. Vilhelm Lundstedt, which embodied the view that all the important features of law could be described through use of the empirical social sciences. For useful overviews and critiques, see Michael Martin, *Scandinavian and American Legal Realism* (1997); Gregory S. Alexander, "Comparing the Two Legal Realisms—American and Scandinavian," 50 *Am. J. Comp. L.* 131 (2002); Jes Bjarup, "The Philosophy of Scandinavian Legal Realism," 18 *Ratio Juris* 1 (2005); H. L. A. Hart, "Scandinavian Realism," 17 *Camb. L.J.* 233 (1959). The Scandinavian Realists paid little attention to the characteristics of legal reasoning and legal argument, however, and thus their perspective is largely unconnected with the focus of this book.

(Free Law School) in the late nineteenth and early twentieth centuries[2] and in the contemporaneous work of the French theorist François Geny,[3] American Legal Realism has its most important roots in the extrajudicial writings of Justice Oliver Wendell Holmes. When Holmes said, famously, that "the life of the law has not been logic; it has been experience,"[4] he posed a concrete and potentially radical challenge to the then conventional wisdom about the way in which the common law develops. When Holmes wrote, and even more so earlier, most lawyers, judges, and commentators understood common-law change to be a process of discovery rather than creation.[5] For them, the development of law not only involved locating the law that was there all along rather than making new law, but could also be characterized as a largely logical and deductive march from one case to the next.[6] But Holmes was not convinced. Although he certainly subscribed to the then conventional view that legal doctrine typically determined legal outcomes, and although he believed as well that uniquely legal categories were genuinely important in predicting legal consequences,[7] he had concluded that changes in legal doctrine were largely a function of an experience-based and empirical determination by judges who, when changing the law, were undoubtedly making policy choices dictated neither by logic nor by preexisting law.

Viewed in hindsight, Holmes's views seem scarcely remarkable, let alone radical. Nowadays it would be hard to find very many dissenters from the view that when judges change the law, they base their decisions on a mix of policy and principle that can hardly be thought of as a deductive or logical exercise. In thus anticipating what most legal insiders and

2. See Herman Kantorowicz, *The Definition of Law* (Arthur Goodhart ed., 1958) (1917); Albert S. Foulkes, "On the German Free Law School (Freirechtsschule)," 55 *Archiv für Rechts- und Sozialphilosophie* 367 (1969).

3. See François Geny, *Science of Legal Method* (4 vols., 1914–1924).

4. Oliver W. Holmes, Jr., *The Common Law* 1 (1881).

5. "There is, in fact, no such thing as judge-made law, for the judges do not make the law, although they frequently have to apply existing law to circumstances as to which it has not previously been authoritatively laid down that such law is applicable." Willis v. Baddeley, 2 Q.B. 324, 326 (C.A. 1892). "The orthodox Blackstonian view, however, is that judges do not make law, but only declare what has always been the law." R. W. M. Dias, Jurisprudence 151 (5th ed., 1985).

6. E.g., Eugene Wambaugh, *The Study of Cases* (2d ed., 1894); John M. Zane, "German Legal Philosophy," 16 *Mich. L. Rev.* 287 (1918).

7. Oliver Wendell Holmes, "The Path of the Law," 10 *Harv. L. Rev.* 457, 475 (1897).

commentators now take to be commonplace, Holmes, like Roscoe Pound and Judge Cardozo shortly thereafter,[8] was ahead of his time. In other ways, however, his views about legal reasoning remained steadfastly conventional. He believed that legal doctrine, as doctrine, was the principal determinant of legal outcomes, and it is this belief, more than any other, that has served to frame Holmes as more a forebear of Realism than a Realist himself.[9] Recourse to knowledge of the empirical facts about the world may have been necessary to change the common law, Holmes recognized, but the common law itself had elements of stability as well as change. And for Holmes, this stability was chiefly a function of legal doctrine as more or less conventionally understood. Unlike the Realists who admired and succeeded him, Holmes subscribed wholeheartedly to the belief that the relative specific legal principles contained in the language of reported judicial opinions were the principal determinants of how judges decided cases and how lawyers argued them. When Holmes insisted that the most important standpoint from which to view law was that of the "bad man,"[10] the one who was interested exclusively in what the law could do for him and, more specifically, what the law could do *to* him, Holmes was arguing that the essence of law was the *prediction* of judicial reaction to some set of factual circumstances. For Holmes, the

8. See Benjamin Cardozo, *The Nature of the Judicial Process* (1921); Roscoe Pound, "Mechanical Jurisprudence," 8 *Colum. L. Rev.* 605 (1908). Both Cardozo and Pound also decried the excess reliance on logic in law and urged, following Holmes, recognition of the importance of public policy in the wise development of the law.

9. Holmes did believe that "[g]eneral propositions do not decide concrete cases," Lochner v. New York, 198 U.S. 45, 76 (1905) (Holmes, J., dissenting), but he believed as well that propositions sufficiently concrete to decide cases were mostly *legal* propositions, and not propositions of policy, philosophy, or psychology.

10. "If you want to know the law and nothing else, you must look at it as a bad man, who cares only for the material consequences, of which such knowledge enables him to predict not as a good one, who finds his reasons for conduct, whether inside the law or outside of it, in the vaguer sanctions of conscience." "The Path of the Law," 10 *Harv. L. Rev.* at 459. The phrase has generated voluminous commentary. See, e.g., Sanford Levinson & J. M. Balkin, "The 'Bad Man,' the Good, and the Self-Reliant," 78 *B.U.L. Rev.* 885 (1998); William Twining, "Other People's Power: The Bad Man and English Positivism," *1897–1997, 63 Brook. L. Rev.* 189 (1997); William Twining, "The Bad Man Revisited," 58 *Cornell L. Rev.* 275 (1973).

focus of legal analysis must be on what the "courts are likely to do in fact."[11]

Holmes was ahead of his time in focusing on prediction and in seeming to recognize the logical possibility that what the "courts are likely to do in fact" would differ from what the formal doctrine might suggest, but he was not very far ahead. When it came to delineating the factors that the good lawyer would use to predict what judges would do, Holmes was very much the traditionalist in believing that legal doctrine remained foremost among those factors. Indeed, the very reason that Holmes made sport of the apocryphal Vermont justice of the peace who believed that "churn" was a legally relevant category was that for Holmes the legally relevant categories—the ones that would enable the "master of the law" accurately to predict what judges would actually do—were things like dangerous instrumentality, bailment, felony murder, mutual mistake, assumption of the risk, and business affected with a public interest.[12] These were the classifications of the law, these were the relatively concrete boxes into which sophisticated lawyers could place the events of the world, and these were the categories that would enable good lawyers to do exactly what Holmes and the bad man wanted them to do—predict future legal reactions to the full span of human behavior.

But what if it turned out that legal categories and legal doctrines were not especially effective predictors of judicial decision-making? What if factors other than legal doctrine played the major role in determining what judges would in reality actually do? These questions frame the challenge that lies at the core of Legal Realism, and it is a challenge that departs substantially from Holmes's rather conventional view about the role of legal doctrine in predicting legal outcomes. To see Legal Realism at its fullest, therefore, we must take our leave from Holmes and look instead, at least initially, at a group of commentators who flourished primarily in the 1930s, almost exclusively in the United States.

The most visible of these early Realists was Jerome Frank, who in 1930 was a prominent New York lawyer and later became a distinguished federal judge. Frank was preceded in his Realist pronouncements by a number of others, but he quickly became among Realism's

11. "The Path of the Law," 10 *Harv. L. Rev.* at 461.

12. *Id.* at 474–75. The full tale is quoted above, at p. 48. For a fuller analysis of the story and its connections with Holmes's thought, see Frederick Schauer, "Prediction and Particularity," 78 *B.U. L. Rev.* 773 (1998).

most prominent voices. His key claim, echoing one that had been made a year earlier on the pages of the *Cornell Law Journal* by a Texas judge named Joseph Hutcheson,[13] was that judges did not initially or primarily look to the law in order to determine how to decide a case.[14] The then conventional view was that judges determined what the facts were and then consulted the statutes, cases, and other legal materials to find out what response the law dictated for those facts or that situation. But for Hutcheson and Frank, this standard picture reversed the order of things. Rather than first looking to the law and then deciding how to rule, Hutcheson and Frank maintained that judges first decided—or intuited; hence Hutcheson's reference to the judicial "hunch"—how they wanted to rule and only then consulted the law. Like a lawyer who starts with her client's position and then searches for legal support to buttress it, Hutcheson and Frank believed that judges started, after determining the facts, with a view of the correct outcome and then looked for cases and statutes and other legal materials to provide an after-the-fact justification—a rationalization—for what they had already decided.

In itself, this claim is not a very radical idea either. Hutcheson referred to the initial determination by the judge as a "hunch," and simply describing it as a hunch, or as "intuitive," is not inconsistent with legal doctrine playing a substantial, even if less conscious, role in determining the judge's initial reaction. A hunch or an intuition, after all, might well be a legally informed hunch or an intuition based on knowledge of the law. Baseball umpires, for example, rarely engage in very much conscious thinking before calling a pitch a ball or a strike, but they nevertheless make their quick judgments on the basis of having internalized the rules about what makes some pitches balls and others strikes. The chess master who can play thirty games simultaneously against thirty different opponents does not have much time for contemplation, but his seemingly instinctive moves are still the moves of a chess expert. Similarly, a judge might have so internalized the rules of law that even though she had a quick hunch or intuition about how the case ought to be decided, it would be a hunch born of a deep knowledge of legal rules and legal doctrine. And there is nothing particularly radical or skeptical about that position.

---

13. Joseph C. Hutcheson, Jr., "The Judgment Intuitive: The Function of the 'Hunch' in Judicial Decision," 14 *Cornell L.J.* 274 (1929).

14. Jerome Frank, *Law and the Modern Mind* (1930).

But Hutcheson and Frank went further than this. Hutcheson, and to a much greater extent Frank, believed that the initial judgment—the hunch—was based less on cases, statutes, and legal principles than on a host of other factors that the law officially refused to recognize but that Frank especially thought actually played a large role. Frank is frequently caricatured as having believed that judicial decisions were a matter of "what the judge had for breakfast,"[15] but his claim is in reality far more sophisticated and nuanced. For Frank, the personal attributes of the judge did matter, and Frank would not have denied that the judge being in a bad mood because of poor ventilation in the courtroom on a hot day or even because of a bad breakfast could have an effect on legal outcomes. But the "what the judge had for breakfast" caricature is unfair to Frank, because he believed that a large number of other less frivolous but still nonlegal factors typically determined judicial decisions. These might include, for example, the judge's political preferences, his views about litigants of certain races or religions or appearances, his views about the lawyers, his overall sense of which outcome would be fairer under the circumstances, and, perhaps most of all, the makeup of his personality.[16] But although Frank believed that far more than what the judge had for breakfast determined legal outcomes, he believed as well that most of what determined legal outcomes consisted of factors that legal doctrine

15. It is not entirely clear whether Frank ever said anything like this at all. At times he said things that might have been so understood. See Jerome Frank, *Courts on Trial* 161–62 (1949); Jerome Frank, "Are Judges Human?," 80 *U. Penn. L. Rev.* 17, 24 (1931). It has also been claimed that Frank once made the breakfast remark as an offhand oral quip. Morton J. Horwitz, *The Transformation of American Law 1870–1960*, at 176 (1992). But it is more likely that Frank, because of his views, is saddled with having said something actually said in jest by Roscoe Pound (see Charles M. Yablon, "Justifying the Judge's Hunch: An Essay on Discretion," 41 *Hastings L.J.* 231, 236 n.16 [1990]) or by Supreme Court Justice Owen J. Roberts sometime in the late 1930s (see Richard D. Friedman, "Switching Time and Other Thought Experiments: The Hughes Court and Constitutional Transformation," 142 *U Pa. L. Rev.* 1891, 1896 n.11 [1994]). Nevertheless, the remark has taken on a life of its own as a common caricature of the Realist view about the sources of judicial decision. See Alex Kozinski, "What I Ate for Breakfast and Other Mysteries of Judicial Decision Making," 26 *Loy. L.A.L. Rev.* 993 (1993).

16. In thinking that the judge's personality and psychological makeup had something or much to do with his or her decisions, Frank was preceded by Theodore Schroeder, "The Psychologic Study of Judicial Opinion," 6 *Cal. L. Rev.* 89 (1918).

did not recognize. He also believed that most of these factors were highly particular, relating to aspects of this case on this occasion. In ways that seem remarkably modern at times, Frank doubted the ability of people, including but not limited to judges, to make decisions based on rules or principles or general categories, but believed instead that judges would base their decisions primarily on a host of factors peculiar to the particular case, many of which were technically legally irrelevant but which he believed might nevertheless actually be causally significant in determining (and thus predicting) legal outcomes.

In addition to being saddled with the "what the judge had for breakfast" caricature, Frank is also often dismissed these days because his first and most important book, *Law and the Modern Mind,* is infused with the consequences of his recent psychoanalysis. Indeed, a more telling caricature of Frank than one based on the view that law was what the judge had for breakfast would have been one based on the opinion that legal judgments were determined by the judge's relationship to his mother,[17] for Frank's crude and largely uncritical indoctrination into psychiatry and psychoanalysis led him to place far more weight on the judge's personality and psychic makeup than on a panoply of other factors that might also influence the judge's prelegal views about how a case ought to be decided.[18] But the more than occasional rhetorical excesses and psychological silliness in Frank's work should not blind us to the importance and arguable soundness of his major insight, the one he shared with

17. Or father, for in *Law and the Modern Mind* Frank accused those who continued to believe in the sanctity of legal doctrine of seeing law as a "father figure."

18. It is worth noting that Frank's belief that judicial opinions were highly particular and his belief that the judge's personality made a big difference are two separate claims. One could believe that personality mattered but that personalities came in types, and that personality types would react to the same factual situations in the same way. Someone might believe, for example, that judges who are short in stature would routinely side with the underdog in litigation, and if that was the case, the judge who behaved in this way would be a judge whose decisions were driven by the judge's personality but whose decisions were systematic and thus highly predictable. Indeed, much the same could even be said about the view, even if Frank did not hold it, that judicial decisions are determined by what the judge had for breakfast. If some judge were to decide for the plaintiff more often when he had oatmeal for breakfast than when he had eggs, what the judge had for breakfast could be a component of the ability to predict judicial decisions, showing again that the existence of extralegal determinants such as breakfast are fully compatible with predictability.

Hutcheson. By insisting that the outcome preceded the law rather than vice versa, Frank offered an account of judging with which few sitting judges, then and now, would disagree.[19] There might be disagreement about the motivations for the outcome, and there will certainly be disagreements about the extent to which legal doctrine disciplines and constrains these prelegal or extralegal determinations of the judge's preferred outcome, but in arguing that a judge's prelegal or extralegal view of the desired result preceded a result-independent consultation of the law, Frank, along with Hutcheson, can rightfully claim to have established the basic framework of the Realist position.[20]

At about the same time that Frank was insisting that judging was based not very much on legal doctrine and a great deal on various legally irrelevant characteristics of the judge and the litigants, his contemporary Karl Llewellyn was describing legal rules as "pretty playthings." In *The Bramble Bush,* a book initially targeted to first-year students at Columbia Law School,[21] Llewellyn sided with Frank in believing that formal legal rules—the "paper rules," as Llewellyn called them—had little effect on what judges actually *did,* but Llewellyn was far less of a particularist than Frank or Hutcheson. Judges might very well be applying general rules, he believed, but rarely were they the rules that one could find in a lawbook. A judge might, for example, believe that in cases involving mining companies the mining company should win just because it was a mining company, whether the case was brought by the company seeking an injunction against a miners' union or was brought against the com-

19. As Chief Justice Charles Evans Hughes is reported by Justice William O. Douglas to have said, "At the constitutional level where we work, ninety percent of any decision is emotional. The rational part of us supplies the reasons for supporting our predilections." William O. Douglas, *The Court Years: 1939–1975,* at 8 (1974).

20. The most powerful defense of this view comes not from any Realist but from a legal philosopher who was also trained in law: Richard A. Wasserstrom, *The Judicial Decision: Toward a Theory of Legal Justification* (1961). In distinguishing between the logic of decision and the logic of justification, Wasserstrom recognized that even the most legally persuasive of judicial opinions did not purport to explain chronologically or historically how the judge came to the conclusion she did, but instead offered the best legal justification for a decision that might well have been reached for other reasons.

21. Karl N. Llewellyn, *The Bramble Bush: On Our Law and Its Study* (1930). The 1960 edition contains an illuminating and clarifying foreword by Llewellyn, one that largely recants the "pretty playthings" observation.

pany by an adjacent landowner claiming nuisance or damage to property.[22] If the judge in both cases believed that the mining company should prevail just because it was a mining company, the judge would be applying a rule—the mining company should win—and it would be a rule that transcended, in theory, the particular facts of particular cases. It might even be a rule based on carefully thought-out moral or political or policy grounds. But it would not be a rule found in the cases or in the statutes.

Thus, although some commentators claim that the Realists are characterized by their attention to the facts of a case rather than to legal rules,[23] this way of looking at Realism is based on a false dichotomy. Even the Realists' opponents thought it important to pay close attention to the facts of a case, because otherwise there would be no way to decide which legal rule would determine the outcome. Someone believing that the outcome dictated by a statute was the outcome that a judge would invariably reach would still accept that judges would have to be concerned with the facts of the case in order to come to a decision. The real dispute is thus not between those who think judges look at facts and those who think judges look at rules, but between those who think that judges look to formal legal rules to determine both which facts are legally relevant and what outcome is indicated by those facts, on the one hand, and those who think that judges look to rules, norms, and factors other than the ones in the lawbooks to determine which facts are relevant and what should be done on the basis of those facts, on the other hand.

Thus, in order to determine how judges were actually deciding cases, Llewellyn urged empirical research aimed at identifying what Holmes called the "true basis for prophecy."[24] What were the rules and principles

22. One of the early Realists was William O. Douglas, then a young commissioner of the newly created Securities and Exchange Commission, subsequently a professor at Columbia Law School, and from 1939 until shortly before his death in 1975 an Associate Justice of the Supreme Court of the United States. Douglas had a particular interest in tax cases, and the claim that in tax cases Douglas in his later years almost always sided with the taxpayer against the Internal Revenue Service (see Bernard Wolfman et al., *Dissent without Opinion: The Behavior of Justice William O. Douglas in Tax Cases* [1975]) regardless of the actually applicable statutes, regulations, and previous cases is a vivid example of just this kind of Realist claim.

23. E.g., Brian Leiter, "Positivism, Formalism, Realism," 99 *Colum. L. Rev.* 1138, 1148 (1999); Brian Leiter, "Legal Realism," *in A Companion to the Philosophy of Law and Legal Theory* 261 (Dennis Patterson ed., 1996).

24. "The Path of the Law," 10 *Harv. L. Rev.* at 475.

that judges actually employed? Were they rules like "the mining company should win" or "the taxpayer should win," or instead were they principle-based or policy-focused rules of substantially greater sophistication, such as "maximize efficiency" or "make the decision that will produce the best long-run economic consequences" or "decide for the less- well-off party in all civil cases unless doing so would reward inappropriate conduct"? In determining whether rules such as these rather than the formal rules contained in the law books were actually producing judicial outcomes, Llewellyn urged empirical research that would reveal the real rules of the legal system and not just the "paper rules" that masqueraded as rules but in fact had little effect on legal outcomes. Among those who took up Llewellyn's call was Underhill Moore, another early Realist and a professor at Yale Law School. Moore set out to engage in the kind of empirical research that Llewellyn had urged, and thus he sought to determine, among other things, whether parking enforcement in New Haven, Connecticut, was based primarily on the official legal parking rules or instead on factors such as time of day, type of car, street, and the like.[25] Moore's methods now strike some commentators as crude, but social science in the 1930s was less well developed than it is today. The controlled field experiments that Moore employed were unsophisticated by late-twentieth-century and twenty-first-century standards, but in focusing on isolating and identifying the actual variables in the application of law, Moore well understood the basic principles of social science research.[26] In applying those basic principles, Moore recognized that which factors actually influenced legal outcomes could not be determined simply by a formal recitation of the legal doctrine. Only if that doctrine made a large difference in determining outcomes was it worth taking seriously, and with his fellow Realists, Moore recognized not only that this was an empirical question, but also that there was at least some empirical evidence supporting the view that legal doctrine played considerably less of a role than the traditional picture supposed.

25. Underhill Moore & Charles C. Callahan, "Law and Learning Theory: A Study in Legal Control," 43 *Yale L.J.* 1 (1943). See John Henry Schlegel, "American Legal Realism and Empirical Social Science: The Singular Case of Underhill Moore," 29 *Buff. L. Rev.* 195, 264–303 (1980). See also John Henry Schlegel, "American Legal Realism and Empirical Social Science: From the Yale Experience," 28 *Buff. L. Rev.* 459 (1979).

26. See Donald O. Green & Alan S. Gerber, "The Underprovision of Experiments in Political Science," 59 *Annals* 94 (2003).

As seen through the eyes of Llewellyn, Moore, and contemporaries such as Herman Oliphant, Hessel Yntema, Max Radin, Felix Cohen, Thurman Arnold, Joseph Bingham, Walter Wheeler Cook, Wesley Sturges, and Leon Green, Legal Realism is thus far more than the vulgar "what the judge had for breakfast" caricature and far more than the unsophisticated empiricism that may have marked some of their methods. At the core of the Realist claim is the view that judicial decisions are predictable but that the key to prediction of legal outcomes lies neither in the consultation of formal legal authorities nor in the internal understanding or self-reports of judges themselves. Rather, predicting legal outcomes is best accomplished through the enterprise of discovering through systematic empirical (and external) study just what makes a difference in deciding cases.[27] Frank thought that it was the personal attributes of the judge and the particular context of the particular case that made the biggest difference, while Llewellyn and most of the other Realists thought it was the application of general but nonlegal norms, but these differences should not distract us from understanding the basic claim. In looking at law externally, the Realists believed that we could discover how law actually worked and that we could treat the relationship between legal doctrine and legal outcomes as a relationship that could and should be subject to rigorous empirical testing. The Realists believed this relationship to be a weak one, but even more important was their belief that the hypothesized existence of such a relationship should be tested rather than simply taken on faith.

7.2 Does Doctrine Constrain Even If It Does Not Direct?

Let us recapitulate the structure of the central Legal Realist claim. According to the Realists, judges typically make decisions on the basis of something other than, or in addition to, existing legal doctrine. This nonlegal reason for a decision could be a nonlegal hunch, a judgment based on personal characteristics of the litigants or judge, an all-things-considered judgment about who as a matter of fairness ought to win the case, or a policy judgment about which ruling would have the best conse-

27. See William Twining, *Karl Llewellyn and the Realist Movement* (1973); Karl N. Llewellyn, "Some Realism about Realism—Responding to Dean Pound," 44 *Harv. L. Rev.* 1222 (1931); Karl N. Llewellyn, "A Realistic Jurisprudence: The Next Step," 30 *Colum. L. Rev.* 431 (1930).

quences. But rarely would a legal outcome be determined by the application of the existing stock of cases, statutes, and other legal authorities. When Llewellyn quipped that "[i]f rules were results there would be little need for lawyers," he was suggesting that the most important parts of law involve the differences between what a rule appears to *say* and the outcome actually produced by a court.

The Realists understood, however, that judges could not, professionally or culturally, explain their prelegal or extralegal judgments in terms of hunches, personal characteristics, abstract appeals to justice, or even straightforward policy analyses. Even if the Realists would have preferred it to be otherwise, they knew that the norms of the legal system required judges to justify their rulings in traditional legal terms, whatever the actual motivation for those rulings might have been. A professionally acceptable legal judgment would thus have to be couched in the language of cases, statutes, regulations, legal rules, legal principles, and accepted legal secondary authorities—in other words, in the language of the traditional sources of law.

Because the Realists recognized that decisions made on nonlegal grounds needed to be justified in traditional legal terms, it was a keystone of the Realist position that such traditional legal justifications were almost always available to justify outcomes reached for other reasons, regardless of what those outcomes might be. If it were otherwise—if most outcomes reached on nonlegal grounds could not be justified by reference to traditional legal sources—then the Realist claim would be trivial. Even the traditionalists against whom the Realists reacted acknowledged that judges would often want to reach results that the doctrine would not support. So for the Realist challenge to be a genuine challenge, it needed to insist that legal doctrine was not nearly as constraining as the traditionalists believed, and that doctrinal justifications for virtually any outcome that a judge wanted to reach for virtually any reason could be supported by traditional legal sources.

The Realist position thus rests on the claim that there are cases, statutes, maxims, principles, canons, authorities, or statements in learned legal treatises available to justify decisions in favor of *both* parties in all or at least most litigated cases. If a decision for the plaintiff can be justified by reference to standard legal sources, and if a decision for the defendant can also be justified by reference to standard (albeit different) legal sources, then the law is not actually resolving the dispute. And this was precisely what the Realists maintained, although they recognized that the

question was an empirical one: just how often are there legal rules, principles, and sources available to justify both of two mutually exclusive
outcomes? The Realists believed that roughly equivalent respectable legal
authority on both sides of most litigated questions was the overwhelming
characteristic of legal decision-making—but were they correct in so believing?

In considering this question, we can start with Llewellyn's classic
1950 article on the canons of statutory interpretation.[28] These canons, to
which we will return in Chapter 8, purport to instruct judges and other
legal interpreters in how to interpret vague or ambiguous statutes. The
rule of lenity, for example, is a canon requiring that vague or ambiguous
criminal statutes be interpreted in favor of the defendant. But in examining the canons, Llewellyn came to the conclusion that for every canon of
interpretation that said one thing, there was a "dueling" canon that said
just the opposite. One canon, for example, provides that extrinsic aids to
interpretation, such as legislative history, are irrelevant when the language of the statute is clear on its face. But another canon dictates that
even the plain language of a statute should not be applied literally if such
an application would produce a result divergent from what the legislature intended. Similarly, the canon known by the Latin *in pari materia*
mandates that statutes dealing with the same subject be interpreted so as
to be consistent with each other, but another provides that later statutes
supersede earlier ones. And so on. The beauty and charm of Llewellyn's
article is captured not just by these examples but by the way in which
for almost every canon of statutory construction he located and listed,
there was another that appeared to point in just the opposite direction.
Llewellyn called this the "thrust" and "parry" of dueling canons, and he
employed this language of fencing to demonstrate that the availability of
traditional legal support for mutually exclusive legal outcomes was a
ubiquitous feature of law. And thus he concluded that the presence of legal authority on both sides of most contested legal questions meant that
the actual decision—the tiebreaker, if you will—was to be found in something other than the law as traditionally understood.

28. Karl N. Llewellyn, "Remarks on the Theory of Appellate Decision and the
Rules or Canons about How Statutes Are to Be Construed," 3 *Vand. L. Rev.* 395
(1950), and in revised form in Karl N. Llewellyn, *The Common Law Tradition:
Deciding Appeals* 521–35 (1960).

Llewellyn's claim was less extreme than it may appear.[29] As early as 1930, in *The Bramble Bush,* Llewellyn was at pains to limit his claims to the class of cases that were worth fighting over. Anticipating important law and economics insights about the so-called selection effect that were not to come until some fifty years later,[30] Llewellyn recognized that the straightforward cases in which the law is all on one side rarely generate litigation. Indeed, they rarely generate legal disputes at all. Many Americans would prefer to pay their taxes on a date somewhat later than the April 15 deadline, but the implausibility of finding legal support for that position means that the question whether "April 15" in the Internal Revenue Code means April 15 will rarely be disputed, even more rarely be litigated, and more rarely yet wind up in an appellate court. Similarly, in the normal course of things, bills get paid, police officers obtain warrants, contracts are honored, and insurance companies whose insureds cause accidents make payments to the victims. Law abounds with such straightforward applications—we can call them "easy cases"—and the set of cases that winds up in court, and even more the smaller set that winds up in an appellate court, consists pretty much only of those cases in which both sides think that they have a colorable enough legal argument that it is worth spending time and money to go to court and then, for the losing party, worth the time and money of pursuing an appeal. Because the vast majority of applications of law are not ones in which parties holding mutually exclusive positions both reasonably think they might win, the ones that are exist overwhelmingly at the fuzzy edges of the law, and even more so for the yet smaller set that represents the universe of appellate cases decided on the merits and with full opinions.

29. Whether Llewellyn was actually right about the canons is not entirely clear. See Michael Sinclair, "'Only a Sith Thinks Like That': Llewellyn's 'Dueling Canons,' One to Seven," 50 *N.Y.L. Sch. L. Rev.* 919 (2006); Michael Sinclair, "'Only a Sith Thinks Like That': Llewellyn's 'Dueling Canons,' Eight to Twelve," 51 *N.Y.L. Sch. L. Rev.* 1002 (2007).

30. See Richard A. Posner, *Economic Analysis of Law* §21 (3d ed., 1986); George L. Priest & Benjamin Klein, "The Selection of Disputes for Litigation," 13 *J. Legal Stud.* 1 (1984). See also Samuel P. Jordan, "Early Panel Announcement, Settlement, and Adjudication," 2007 *B.Y.U.L. Rev.* 55 (2007); Leandra Lederman, "Which Cases Go to Trial?: An Empirical Study of Predictions of Failure to Settle," 49 *Case West. Res. L. Rev.* 315 (1998). And see the more extensive discussion in section 2.2, *supra*.

Llewellyn recognized the selection phenomenon, and the consequent unrepresentativeness of the appellate cases that were his concern. His claim is best understood, therefore, as a claim about the decision of hard appellate cases and not so much as a claim about the general indeterminacy of law. And much the same applies to Legal Realism generally. For the unrepresentative set of legal events that constitute the population of appellate cases, however, Llewellyn and the other Realists insisted that the judge was typically far less constrained by formal law than the traditional picture had it, and was far less constrained than judges in their opinions pretended to be. The extent of constraint, however, would be largely a function of the extent to which there was *not* a plausible legal argument available to justify either outcome. Llewellyn's "thrust and parry" is thus not merely about the canons of statutory construction and not merely about statutory construction. It is, for Llewellyn, an example of the overwhelming fact about law in hard cases that there is usually a respectable and defensible legal justification available for a wide range of possible outcomes (but decidedly not for all possible outcomes)[31] in the cases that wind up in appellate courts. As a result, he argued, the formal rules of law not only rarely dictated results, but also exercised little constraint on outcomes selected on the basis of other considerations.

7.3 An Empirical Claim

The basic Realist position about judicial decision-making is thus a two-part hypothesis. The first part is the claim that most judges have a preferred outcome—whether preferred on the basis of litigant characteristics, judge characteristics, conceptions of justice, ideology, or assessments of wise policy—that precedes consultation of the formal law. Judges, that is, typically sense an outcome first and look for a legal justification afterward. The second component of the hypothesis is the claim that in looking for a legal justification for an outcome selected on other grounds, judges in complex, messy common-law systems will rarely (but not never) be disappointed. There may occasionally be a preferred outcome that just "won't write," but these will be rare, and more often than not the experience of judging, the Realists claimed, is the experience not of being frus-

---

31. Thus, Llewellyn made plain that in his view the range of *defensible* legal justifications was often quite limited. *The Bramble Bush,* at 73.

trated but rather of finding some plausible legal justification for a non-legally selected outcome.

Both of these components of the Realist position are ultimately empirical ones, as is the question of what, if not formal law, is the principal determinant of the prelegal or extralegal judicial preferences. And because the claims of Realism are empirical, there is no reason to suppose that the empirical conclusions will be the same for all times, for all places, for all judges, and, perhaps most importantly, for all issues and for all courts. At one extreme of legal indeterminacy, therefore, it is not surprising that we find the Supreme Court of the United States. For some years now, political scientists have used sophisticated techniques of multiple regression to determine what really does influence case outcomes in the Supreme Court. Researchers have examined a range of factors and concluded that ideology, more than personal characteristics of the judge, legal variables of text and precedent, or anything else, is the leading predictor of Supreme Court outcomes.[32] The results produced by these researchers— sometimes call "attitudinalists" because of their research-based conclusions that judicial attitudes make far more difference than the law— should not be surprising. The Supreme Court controls its own docket, and these days typically decides, with full arguments and full opinions, barely more than seventy cases a year, those seventy being selected from the more than nine thousand in which one of the parties has requested Supreme Court review. On occasion the Court will accept and decide a relatively easy case with respect to which a court below has inexplicably blundered or as to which the Supreme Court thinks it important to make a statement, but far more common is a case that has gotten as far as it has

32. See, e.g., Larry Baum, *The Puzzle of Judicial Behavior* (1997); Saul Brenner & Harold J. Spaeth, *Stare Indecisis: The Alteration of Precedent on the Supreme Court, 1946–1992* (1995); Jeffrey J. Segal & Harold J. Spaeth, *The Supreme Court and the Attitudinal Model Revisited* (2004); Jeffrey J. Segal & Harold J. Spaeth, *Majority Rule or Minority Will: Adherence to Precedent on the United States Supreme Court* (2001); Jeffrey J. Segal & Harold J. Spaeth, *The Supreme Court and the Attitudinal Model* (1993); Jeffrey J. Segal & Harold J. Spaeth, "The Influence of Stare Decisis on the Votes of Supreme Court Justices," 40 *Amer. Pol. Sci.* 971 (1996). Somewhat more qualified views can be found in Lee Epstein & Joseph F. Kobylka, *The Supreme Court and Legal Change: Abortion and the Death Penalty* (1992); Thomas G. Hansford & James G. Spriggs II, *The Politics of Precedent in the U.S. Supreme Court* (2006); Paul J. Wahlbeck, "The Life of the Law: Judicial Politics and Legal Change," 59 *J. Politics* 778 (1997).

precisely either because there is no law on the subject or because there are equally good legal arguments on both sides. Moreover, given the nature of what the Supreme Court does, these will largely be cases involving issues about which people, not excluding Supreme Court Justices, have strong prelegal or extralegal views. Few judges care very much about technical issues in the interpretation of the Federal Insecticide, Fungicide, and Rodenticide Act (FIFRA), about the application of the Employee Retirement Income Security Act (ERISA), about highly obscure questions in the law of trusts, or about the law of bailments in general, so in such cases it may well be that judges or Justices have no impetus to reach a conclusion prior to consulting the law. But when the issues involved are abortion, affirmative action, pornography, financial assistance to public schools, capital punishment, and the powers of the president with respect to national security, for example, it is close to impossible to imagine a Justice of the Supreme Court having no moral, political, social, or ideological position on the matter. This being so, it is hardly surprising that the Supreme Court's combination of a small, self-selected caseload at the pinnacle of the judicial pyramid and issues on which the Justices likely have strong personal views will produce the domain in which the Realist position is most borne out by serious empirical research.[33]

It would be a mistake to assume, however, that what is true for the Supreme Court is true for other courts and other issues. There has been somewhat less research focused on state courts and lower federal courts than there has been on the Supreme Court, but the body of that research is still considerable. And when we look at the conclusions of that research, we see that legal doctrine appears to play a considerably larger role in judicial decision-making than the more extreme of the Realists supposed.[34] Although the self-reporting of judges probably exaggerates

33. See Richard A. Posner, "The Supreme Court, 2004 Term—Foreword: A Political Court," 119 *Harv. L. Rev.* 31 (2005). Judge Posner's conception of "political," however, although broadly consistent with the Realist perspective at least for the Supreme Court, is not limited to "political" in the partisan or even narrow ideological sense. See Richard A. Posner, *How Judges Think* (2008).

34. Among the studies are Sara C. Benesh, *The U.S. Courts of Appeals and the Law of Confessions* (2002); David E. Klein, *Making Law in the United States Courts of Appeals* (2002); Paul Brace & Melinda Gann Hall, "Studying Courts Comparatively: The View from the American States," 48 *Pol. Res. Q.* 5 (1993); Frank B. Cross, "Decisionmaking in the U.S. Circuit Courts of Appeals," 91 *Calif. L. Rev.* 1457 (2003); Tracey E. George, "Developing a Positive Theory of Deci-

the effect of formal law on their decisions, the admittedly oversimplified conclusion that emerges from the research is that even in lower courts a range of nonlegal factors plays a larger role than the traditional model supposes, but that legal factors explain considerably more of lower court than of Supreme Court decision-making. And although little of the existing research breaks down the question in just this way, it would be plausible to hypothesize that Realist explanations are more often true for ideologically charged issues than otherwise, more often true in high appellate courts than in trial courts, and more often true for the messier common law than for the interpretation of statutes.

Although the empirical analysis of Supreme Court decision-making has become increasingly technical and sophisticated, the empirical claims of the Realists are essentially agnostic as to method. Some of the Realists urged research that employed what were at the time the cutting-edge methods of the social scientists, and would thus likely have been sympathetic to what are now the more sophisticated methodologies. But others believed that the careful perceptions of experienced lawyers would be sufficient to identify the "real" determinants of judicial outcomes and the real divisions or categories of the law. So although if Holmes had written a torts casebook it would probably have been divided into sections such as negligence, intentional torts, strict liability, and causation, the Realist Leon Green produced one divided along just the lines that Holmes had ridiculed in "The Path of the Law." Holmes said that categories like "shipping" and "telegraphs" could not provide the basis for accurate predictions of the law because these were not categories that actually determined judicial outcomes,[35] but Green's empirical assumption was just the opposite. Implicit in Green's division of his book into sections entitled "Transportation" and "Animals," for example, was Green's prototypically Realist belief that these were the categories that would not only

---

sionmaking on U.S. Courts of Appeals," 58 *Ohio St. L.J.* 1635 (1998); Richard L. Revesz, "Congressional Influence on Judicial Behavior?: An Empirical examination of Challenges to Agency Action in the D.C. Circuit," 76 *N.Y.U.L. Rev.* 1100 (2001); Richard L. Revesz, "Ideology, Collegiality, and the D.C. Circuit: A Reply to Chief Judge Harry Edwards," 85 *Va. L. Rev.* 805 (1999); Richard L. Revesz, "Environmental Regulation, Ideology, and the D.C. Circuit," 83 *Va. L. Rev.* 1717 (1997); Donald R. Songer & Sue Davis, "The Impact of Party and Region on Voting Decisions in the United States Courts of Appeals," 43 *W. Pol. Q.* 317 (1990).

35. "The Path of the Law," 10 *Harv. L. Rev.* at 475.

enable students to understand torts best and help lawyers to predict judicial outcomes best, but would also explain the factors that genuinely influenced judicial behavior best. Perhaps Green would have done an even better job with modern tools of multiple regression, but the basic point is that as a Realist he wanted to examine empirically the actual determinants of judicial decisions, determinants that he believed had little to do with the legal justifications that judges gave in their opinions.

It is worthwhile repeating, however, that the empirical assessment that the Realists have urged may in fact turn out for some courts and some issues and some types of law to be less inconsistent with the traditional view of law than most of the early Realists imagined. It may well be, for example, that the principal determinant of judicial decisions on questions of statutory interpretation is the ordinary meaning of the words of the relevant statute, and that the chief determinant on questions of contract law in appellate cases is the traditional rules and principles and doctrines of contract law as found in conventional contracts casebooks and in treatises like Corbin and Williston. Such outcomes would have surprised the Realists, but such traditional legal explanations for judicial outcomes may well be sound for some or many domains, and the very fact of taking this to be an empirical question is, in the largest sense, perhaps the most important feature and legacy of the Realist program.[36]

7.4 Realism and the Role of the Lawyer

Let us not leave Holmes too far behind, however. It is true that his commitment to the importance of characteristically legal categories was decidedly anti-Realist, but his original insight about prediction and the "bad man" was most assuredly not. The standpoint of the bad man is of course not the only perspective with which to look at the law.[37] And the "bad man" characterization is unfortunate, because most people who want or need to know what the law will do to them or for them are not "bad" in any standard sense of that word. A newspaper that wishes to

36. See Thomas J. Miles & Cass R. Sunstein, "The New Legal Realism," 75 *U. Chi. L. Rev.* 831 (2008).

37. See William Twining, "Talk about Realism," 60 *N.Y.U.L. Rev.* 329 (1985); William Twining, "The Bad Man Revisited," 58 *Cornell L. Rev.* 275 (1973). See also Michael Steven Green, "Legal Realism as Theory of Law," 46 *Wm. & Mary L. Rev.* 1915 (2005).

predict the likely legal reaction to its publication of something unflattering about a politician hardly deserves to be labeled "bad." Nor does the ordinary citizen who wants to know how much she should pay in taxes, how fast she should drive, and what she needs to do in order to ensure that upon her death all of her assets will go to her children. In all of these cases it is important to predict the reaction of the legal system to various courses of conduct, and Holmes was right to stress this crucial dimension of the law. So too were the Realists, who understood that the typical citizen in these types of circumstances is interested in what the law will do much more than what the law says. If the law will do something other than what the law in writing says—if you can drive without fear of apprehension at 60 or even 64 even though the sign says SPEED LIMIT 55—then this is something that most citizens, bad or good, would rationally want to know.

But what does this say to the lawyer who is arguing a case? Although no Realist himself, Chief Justice Charles Evans Hughes notoriously observed earlier in his career that "[t]he Constitution is what the judges say it is,"[38] and this quotation stands as one of the icons of the Realist perspective. But even if it is true from the perspective of the misnamed bad man that the Constitution is what the Supreme Court says it is, a lawyer can hardly stand before the Supreme Court and say to the Court that the law is what the Court says it is. That observation may from one standpoint be true, but what the Court wants to know is why it should say that the Constitution says one thing rather than another, and on this question the point that the Constitution says what the Supreme Court says it is will be stunningly unhelpful. It may be important for lawyers and their clients to predict judicial decisions, but a lawyer arguing to a court can hardly adopt the posture that the law is the prediction of that court's decisions.

Yet although a court wants to know more than that its decision will establish the law, what Realism tells the lawyer is that the court, at some level of consciousness, may want to know rather more or rather less than what the legal doctrine says. If the principal determinant of Supreme Court decision-making is ideology, broadly speaking, as the attitudinalist

38. "We are under a Constitution, but the Constitution is what the judges say it is." Charles Evans Hughes, Governor of New York, speech before the Elmira Chamber of Commerce (May 3, 1907), *in Addresses of Charles Evans Hughes, 1906–1916,* at 179, 185 (2d ed., 1916).

political scientists and others maintain, then the effective Supreme Court advocate will try to persuade a majority of the Justices that a ruling in her client's favor will further their particular ideology. The lawyer may not articulate it in so explicit or transparent a way, but the good lawyer will nevertheless frame an argument to appeal to the actual bases for judicial decision-making. Similarly, if some judge is known systematically to be more likely to agree with whatever argument he heard last (and a well-known but no longer living United States district judge in New England was believed in the 1970s to behave in just this way), the good lawyer will try to arrange to speak last. If a judge is known to be a stickler about appearance, and if there is evidence that appearance is actually a determinant of his decisions, even if not the only determinant, then the good lawyer will make sure that his appearance and that of his client will not antagonize the judge. And if some other judge is concerned more about fairness than about the letter of the law, the lawyer arguing before that judge will try to ensure that much of her argument, whether in a trial, in a written brief, or in an appellate argument, will provide the judge with sufficient factual detail, even if some of it is technically legally irrelevant, for the judge to have the information on which to conclude that a ruling for her client will be a fair one.

None of this is to say that good lawyers will or should ignore the law, because, as we have seen, it is the rare judge who does not think it important to justify on traditional legal grounds a decision reached for other reasons. The Realist-influenced lawyer will not only argue the case in terms that will appeal to some judge's actual basis for decision, but will also provide the judge with the legal doctrine—a "hook," as it were—on which to hang and justify the decision. Even the judge who decides a case on the basis of law-free equity or justice or policy, for example, will need such a doctrinal hook or frame, and nothing in the Realist perspective would discourage the good lawyer from furnishing one to the judge, even as the lawyer is properly focusing her argument on other things.

7.5 Critical Legal Studies and Realism in Modern Dress

Although most of the pioneers of Legal Realism flourished from the 1920s to the 1940s, the Realist perspective still thrives. A common saying is that "we are all Realists now," but that is almost certainly false. Not only is the "all" an egregious exaggeration, but the form of Realism that survives turns out to be a highly domesticated one. Beliefs in the total determinacy of legal doctrine may have withered, but torts casebooks

144

look less like Leon Green's than might have been predicted half a century ago, with the typical modern book relying heavily on the traditional legal categories of tort doctrine. Constitutional law is still largely discussed, argued, and organized in substantial disregard of what the attitudinalists have rather firmly established, and any student who thinks that a strong Realist perspective will be rewarded on law school examinations is in for a nasty shock.

There are (at least) four explanations for what appears to be this still-conventional state of affairs. One would be that the strong empirical claims at the foundation of Realism are false. Even if it is true that something other than legal doctrine is at the heart of Supreme Court decision-making about abortion, affirmative action, and presidential power, it might be argued, once we leave this rarefied climate and look at lower court cases on less ideologically charged issues, to say nothing of non-litigated law, Realism is elevating an occasional feature of legal decision-making into something more than it is. In being an empirical response to an empirical claim, this explanation engages Realism on its own terms, and so little can be said here other than that if Realism is empirically correct for much of law, then the fact that Realism may now be substantially disregarded is surprising and disturbing. But if the centrals claims of the Realists are more false than true and more exaggerated than sound, then we should not be surprised that its import has turned out to be relatively insignificant.

The second explanation would be that Realism in fact thrives, but in different clothing. Insofar as Law and Economics explains much of legal decision-making in terms of efficiency maximization, for example, it would properly be understood as carrying on a Llewellynesque, policy-oriented approach to studying what judges actually do. And various other approaches—the "law in action" focus of the Law and Society perspective, for example—might also be seen as heirs to the legacy of Realism. Indeed, the fact that hearings on the nominations of Supreme Court Justices have begun routinely to focus on the nominee's extralegal political beliefs is an especially visible manifestation of an increasing Realist consciousness. The success of Realism, it might thus be said, is evidenced not by the number of diehard Realists there are but by the presence of Realist perspectives everywhere we look.

Third, it may be that law schools seek to teach their students more about the language of legal justification than about the determinants of judicial decision. Even if judges do base their decisions substantially on broad notions of equity and justice, or on policy considerations, or even

145

on the personal characteristics of the judge and the litigants, what lawyers need to know, and what law schools are uniquely positioned to teach, it might be argued, is the language of the law, the words and the categories and the concepts in which law talk takes place, even if beneath the talk something else entirely is going on. Lawyers can afford to be Realists, perhaps, but they will succeed only if they understand the non-Realist language and categories with which the legal system actually functions.

Fourth, perhaps Realism has been marginalized because it is too threatening. That would be the view of many members of the Critical Legal Studies Movement, some of whom seek or have sought explicitly to carry on the Realist program. Parts of Critical Legal Studies, a movement that rose to prominence in the late 1960s and may have had its greatest influence in the 1970s and 1980s, have little to do with Realism, for at least one of the important claims of Critical Legal Studies was that legal doctrine could best be understood as a reflection of contingent political and ideological decisions. Insofar as one of the important Critical Legal Studies claims was that legal doctrine reflected an existing power structure or served the interests of certain classes or segments of society, then its claims are only loosely connected with Realism and only loosely connected with this book's focus on questions of legal reasoning and legal argument.

In other respects, however, Critical Legal Studies was explicitly Realist. Some Critical Legal Studies scholars emphasized the indeterminacy of legal doctrine, arguing, as had Llewellyn in different language, that legal decision-makers typically had far more choices doctrinally open to them than the traditional view of law would have had it.[39] In light of this indeterminacy of legal doctrine, so the argument goes, it is important to understand the real bases of judicial decision-making. So when Duncan Kennedy argued, for example, that judges always had available to them sufficient "moves" to enable them with professional respectability to avoid even the clearest indications of the clearest legal rules,[40] he was

---

39. See, e.g., Joseph William Singer, "Legal Realism Now," 76 *Cal. L. Rev.* 467 (1988) (book review). See also Joseph William Singer, "The Player and the Cards: Nihilism and Legal Theory," 94 *Yale L.J.* 1 (1984).

40. Duncan Kennedy, "Freedom and Constraint in Adjudication: A Critical Phenomenology of Judging," 36 *J. Legal Educ.* 518 (1986); Duncan Kennedy, "Legal Formality," 1 *J. Legal Stud.* (1972).

making an empirical claim entirely consistent with the central core of Realism. And when Mark Tushnet insisted that political ideology was the principal determinant of much of constitutional decision-making,[41] he not only offered an explanation of American constitutional law that was consistent with those of the attitudinalist political scientists, but also offered the type of explanation that Llewellyn, even if not Jerome Frank, would have found congenial. It is true that Tushnet and others emphasized ideology rather than policy, politics rather than personality, and broad social influences rather than the equities of the particular case, but seen through a Realist lens, these differences seem comparatively minor. Although there may now be different versions of which extralegal factors in fact drive judicial decision-making and legal argument, the insistence on what traditionally would have been thought of as nonlegal connects Critical Legal Studies with the central claims of 1930s Realism.

Just as Legal Realism included perspectives on law other than those represented in the legal-reasoning focus of Hutcheson, Frank, Green, and Llewellyn, for example, so too, to repeat, Critical Legal Studies has elements unconnected with Legal Realism and indeed unconnected with the questions of legal reasoning, legal argument, and judicial decision-making. But insofar as parts of Critical Legal Studies were explicitly concerned with these topics, much of these scholars' work is best seen as carrying on the Realist program. As a set of empirical claims, the Realist program can hardly now be condemned as largely false or celebrated as largely true. The truth of Realism is itself domain-specific, and the extent to which the traditional tools and devices of legal reasoning actually determine legal outcomes will remain a continuing topic for serious research, the outcome of which will continue to vary with the subject, level, and location of judicial decision-making.

41. Mark V. Tushnet, "Following the Rules Laid Down: A Critique of Interpretivism and Neutral Principles," 96 *Harv. L. Rev.* 781 (1981).

8

THE INTERPRETATION OF STATUTES

8.1 Statutory Interpretation in the Regulatory State

The methods of the common law have their origins in the Middle Ages, were well refined by the sixteenth century, and persist even today. And because those steeped in the common-law tradition recognize that judges have the capacity to create entire bodies of law, as they did in the early days of tort, contract, and even criminal law, it is not unheard of even now for judges to be asked to take on similar tasks. Judges created much of American antitrust law on a blank slate, for example, when they were forced to interpret the Sherman Antitrust Act of 1890, a statute whose main operative provision simply prohibits "[e]very contract, combination, . . . or conspiracy, in restraint of trade or commerce."[1] In enacting such a law, Congress's use of imprecise language was not a matter of carelessness in drafting. Congress plainly knew what it was doing, and it knew how to use narrow and precise language when it wanted to. In writing the Sherman Act in broad and indeterminate language, therefore, and in thus intentionally avoiding concrete language and easily understood rules, Congress was instructing the courts to create, in common-law fashion, pretty much the entire body of antitrust law. A similar approach is exemplified in the principal antifraud provision of the Securities Exchange Act of 1934, Section 10b, which authorizes the Securities and Exchange Commission to adopt regulations prohibiting "any manipulative or deceptive device."[2] And although the commission could have fulfilled its charge from Congress by promulgating detailed regulations governing securities fraud, it instead adopted a regulation—Rule

1. 15 U.S.C. §1 (2006).
2. 15 U.S.C. §78j (2006).

10b-5—that simply barred any "device, scheme, or artifice to defraud."[3] The commission deliberately left it to the courts to fashion, again in the style of the common law, most of the law of securities fraud, including most of the law dealing with insider trading. Much of American constitutional adjudication is similar. Judicial interpretation of phrases like "life, liberty or property," "due process of law," "equal protection of the laws," "unreasonable searches and seizures," "cruel and unusual punishments," and "commerce among the several states," for example, does not look very much like interpretation at all. The broad phrases in the constitutional text—Justice Robert Jackson once called them "majestic generalities"[4]—are best understood as initiating a process of common-law development that is largely unconstrained by the words in the document.[5]

In the modern United States, however, as in most other developed common-law countries, examples such as these are very much the exception rather than the rule. Far more typical in contemporary America is the Occupational Safety and Health Act of 1970,[6] whose twenty-nine detailed sections occupy forty-four pages in the United States Code and are supplemented by another eighty-eight pages of regulations in the Code of Federal Regulations. This is hardly unusual. The Clean Air Act of 1970, with its subsequent amendments, is 464 pages long, and such familiar laws as the Securities Act of 1933, the Civil Rights Act of 1964, and, of course, the Internal Revenue Code are highly detailed statutes typically augmented by even more detailed arrays of administrative regulations, official commentary, and interpretive rulings. In these and countless other instances, the aim of a statutory scheme is the comprehensive and precise regulation of a large swath of individual, governmental, and corporate activity.

Such complex statutory regulation would have pleased someone like Jeremy Bentham, who was committed to the belief that precise and comprehensive legislation would make judicial intervention extremely rare. If citizens and officials knew exactly what was required of them, Bentham

3. 17 C.F.R. §240.10b-5 (2006).
4. W. Va. Bd. of Educ. v. Barnette, 319 U.S. 624, 639 (1943).
5. See David A. Strauss, "Common Law Constitutional Interpretation," 63 U. Chi. L. Rev. 877 (1996). See also David A. Strauss, "Common Law, Common Ground, and Jefferson's Principle," 112 Yale L.J. 1712 (2003).
6. 29 U.S.C. §§ 651 et seq. (2006).

and others have argued over the years, there would be little need for the judicial interpretation, construction, and creativity that Bentham and his followers have found so frightening. Judges might on occasion be required to enforce the law, or to interpret it in highly unusual cases, but in the ordinary course of things, Bentham believed, neither lawyers nor judges would be able to obstruct the operation of precise, publicly accessible, and largely self-enforcing statutory codes.[7]

We know now just how wrong Bentham was. Although detailed statutes are ubiquitous in the modern regulatory state, so too is what is sometimes called statutory interpretation or statutory construction. Perhaps because of poor drafting (recall *United States v. Locke,*[8] discussed in Chapters 1 and 2, in which the only plausible explanation for a "prior to December 31" filing deadline rather than "on or prior to December 31" is a drafting error), perhaps because Congress or another legislative body has found it politically safer to pass off a difficult decision to the judiciary, and mostly because even the most precise statute cannot come close to anticipating the complexities and fluidity of modern life, detailed statutes have increased rather than decreased the frequency of judicial intervention, in ways that Bentham could not have anticipated and in ways that would have appalled him if he had. Courts are constantly called upon to resolve contested interpretations of statutory language, and the prevalence of intricate statutory schemes, far from making statutory interpretation largely irrelevant, has instead produced a state of affairs in which debates about statutory interpretation loom large in contemporary discussions of legal argument, legal reasoning, and judicial decision-making.[9]

7. See Jeremy Bentham, "A General View of a Complete Code of Laws," *in* 3 *The Works of Jeremy Bentham* (John Bowring ed., 1843) (1962). Indeed, Bentham believed that lawyers were so complicit in making the law more complex for their own self-interested reasons that he proposed in 1808 that the system of lawyers' fees be abolished, with lawyers being paid by the state in fixed salaries. This reform, he believed, would eliminate the incentive for lawyers and judges ("Judge and Co." to Bentham) to make the law increasingly less understandable and thus increasingly more dependent on fee-greedy lawyers. Jeremy Bentham, "Scotch Reform," in 5 *The Works of Jeremy Bentham* 1 (John Bowring ed., 1843) (1962).

8. 471 U.S. 84 (1985).

9. For more in-depth treatments of the issues and a sample of the debates in a massive literature, see, e.g., Aharon Barak, *Purposive Interpretation in Law* 339–69 (2005); William N. Eskridge, Jr., *Dynamic Statutory Interpretation* (1994); Wil-

Questions of statutory interpretation do not arise solely in the context of legislatively enacted statutes. The same issues surround the judicial interpretation of administrative regulations, municipal ordinances, and rules of all kinds. Indeed, the kinds of questions that pervade the interpretation of statutes also infuse much of constitutional law. It may be that judicial interpretation of the equal protection and due process clauses of the Constitution is less interpretation than textually untethered common-law development, but the same cannot be said about interpretation of the more detailed provisions of the Constitution. Interpreting the provisions setting out the procedures for legislation,[10] for example, or the word "confrontation" in the Sixth Amendment,[11] is not unlike interpreting statutes enacted by Congress or the state legislatures.

8.2 The Role of the Text

The practice of statutory interpretation typically begins with the enacted words of the statute itself—the marks on the printed page. And this view is largely reflected in the academic commentary on that practice. But although it is widely accepted that the words are the starting point, the question of whether they are the ending point as well is at the center of most of the controversies about statutory interpretation. Moreover, although it seems straightforward to commence the interpretive task with determining what the words of a statute *mean,* what it means for a word or phrase or sentence in a statute or regulation to mean something is just the question to be answered, and it is hardly an easy one. Nor is it a question restricted to the issue of statutory interpretation. What it is for the

---

liam N. Eskridge, Jr., Philip Frickey, & Elizabeth Garrett, *Legislation and Statutory Interpretation* (2d ed., 2006); D. Neil MacCormick & Robert S. Summers, eds., *Interpreting Precedents: A Comparative Study* (1997); Antonin Scalia, *A Matter of Interpretation: Federal Courts and the Law* (1997); Adrian Vermeule, *Judging under Uncertainty: An Institutional Theory of Legal Interpretation* (2006); Stephen Breyer, "On the Uses of Legislative History in Interpreting Statutes," 65 *S. Cal. L. Rev.* 845 (1992); John F. Manning, "The Absurdity Doctrine," 116 *Harv. L. Rev.* 2387 (2003); Frederick Schauer, "Statutory Construction and the Coordinating Function of Plain Meaning," 1990 *Sup. Ct. Rev.* 231; Cass R. Sunstein, "Interpreting Statutes in the Regulatory State," 103 *Harv. L. Rev.* 405 (1989).

10. See, e.g., Bowsher v. Synar, 478 U.S. 714 (1986); Immigration and Naturalization Service v. Chadha, 462 U.S. 919 (1983).

11. Compare Maryland v. Craig, 497 U.S. 836 (1990), with Coy v. Iowa, 487 U.S. 1012 (1988).

words of a statute to mean something is an inquiry related in important ways to the question of what it means for a word in a contract, will, or trust to mean something. Indeed, sorting out questions about the meaning of meaning[12] is as central in law as it is in philosophy, theology, literary criticism, art, and a host of other interpretive enterprises. And as we shall see, some of the debates about statutory interpretation attempt to address the extent to which, if at all, statutory interpretation resembles the interpretation of a painting by Picasso, a play by Shakespeare, or a passage in the Bible. But that is to get ahead of ourselves. So as a start, therefore, let us return again to the enduring "vehicles in the park" example that was the centerpiece of the 1958 debate in the pages of the *Harvard Law Review* between the English legal philosopher H. L. A. Hart and his American counterpart, Lon Fuller.[13]

Hart opened the debate by offering, in his discussion of the nature of legal rules, the hypothetical example of a rule prohibiting "vehicles" from a public park.[14] Hart employed the example to point out that regulations (or statutes) such as this one invariably had a "core of settled meaning" as well as a "penumbra" of debatable applications.[15] Automo-

12. Cf. C. K. Ogden & I. A. Richards, *The Meaning of Meaning* (1923), an important early-twentieth-century work on language and interpretation by a philosopher and literary theorist.

13. Lon L. Fuller, "Positivism and Fidelity to Law—A Reply to Professor Hart," 71 *Harv. L. Rev.* 630 (1958); H. L. A. Hart, "Positivism and the Separation of Law and Morals," 71 *Harv. L. Rev.* 593 (1958). The debate was not primarily about legal interpretation but instead about the nature of law itself, with Hart defending a modern version of legal positivism, the view that the concept of law is distinct from the concept of morality, and Fuller developing his own procedural form of natural law theory, the view that law is scarcely law at all if it does not satisfy certain minimum requirements of morality. The debates between adherents of positivism and natural law have occupied center stage in the philosophy of law for generations, and unfortunately both positions have frequently been the subject of ridiculous caricatures. But although the debate between Hart and Fuller about legal interpretation was for both connected with these larger debates in jurisprudence, their interpretation debate and its central example has become sufficiently important in its own right that we can use it to illustrate valuable themes about statutory interpretation while staying well clear of the more abstract jurisprudential debates. See Frederick Schauer, "A Critical Guide to Vehicles in the Park," 83 *N.Y.U. L. Rev.* 1109 (2008).

14. 71 *Harv. L. Rev.* at 606–15. Hart uses the same example in *The Concept of Law* 125–27 (Penelope A. Bulloch & Joseph Raz eds., 2d ed., 1994).

15. The terminology of the "core" and the "penumbra" comes from Bertrand

biles would "plainly" be within the settled meaning, Hart observed, and would thus be excluded from the park, "but what about bicycles, roller skates, toy automobiles? What about airplanes?"[16] And what about baby carriages, which others have mentioned in a subsequent variation on the same example? And, these days, what about skateboards, or motorized wheelchairs? In order to determine in these penumbral cases whether bicycles or skateboards or any of the other examples would count as vehicles, the adjudicator would have to determine the purpose of the regulation and, exercising discretion, allow bicycles and baby carriages into the park (and thus exclude them from the definition of "vehicle") if the purpose of the regulation was to prohibit noise and pollution, for example, but perhaps not if the purpose motivating the rule was to secure pedestrian safety (which bicycles might endanger) or to keep narrow pathways (which baby carriages might obstruct) clear. Indeed, if the point or purpose underlying the rule was not apparent, Hart expected that the judge exercising his discretion in such penumbral cases would act very much like a legislator and take into account the same policy considerations that we would expect to see in a legislature.

Although Hart appeared to distinguish a category of clear applications of a rule from a category of unclear ones, the distinction between

---

Russell, "Vagueness," 1 *Australasian J. Psych & Phil.* 84 (1923), who distinguished the core from the "fringe." And in this article Russell took on a well-known fallacy that plagues legal as well as political argument. Lawyers all too often argue that if we cannot clearly distinguish one thing from another in all cases, then the distinction is worthless or incoherent. They may argue, for example, that the distinction between navigable and non-navigable waters for purposes of determining whether there is admiralty jurisdiction is incoherent because some waters are navigable at high tide but not low or in rainy weather but not in dry. But that is an absurd argument, and Russell sought to demonstrate it by using the example of baldness. Although there are indeed some men about whom it would be hard to say whether they are bald or not, that does not mean that there is not a usable distinction between those who are clearly bald and those who are not. Edmund Burke made the same point about night and day, pointing out that the existence of dusk does not render the distinction between broad daylight and pitch darkness incoherent. But perhaps the best example comes from John Lowenstein, a baseball player for the Baltimore Orioles, who quipped that "they ought to move first base back a step and eliminate all the close plays." *Detroit Free Press*, April 27, 1984, at F1.

16. The airplane example comes from McBoyle v. United States, 283 U.S. 25 (1931). The case, which probably inspired Hart's own example, involved the question of whether a statute prohibiting taking a stolen vehicle across state lines was violated when a stolen airplane was taken from one state to another.

the core and the penumbra is hardly a bright line. Indeed, with respect to every rule, there will not only be contested questions about how to resolve penumbral cases, but there will also be debates and uncertainty about whether some application is in the core or in the penumbra.[17] Like the penumbra around the sun during a solar eclipse, therefore, the distinction between the core and the penumbra, or between the core and the fringe, is better seen as a scale, spectrum, or continuum than as a crisp demarcation. At one pole of this continuum we will find the least controversial application—a pickup truck entering the park with its driver's family and picnic supplies is just the kind of activity that any understanding of the "no vehicles in the park" regulation would wish to exclude—and at the other end we will see the least controversial nonapplication; a pedestrian walking slowly and admiring the scenery, for example, is plainly not a vehicle. In between, however, we find not a clear category of the contested but rather a scale in which the likelihood of contestation increases as we move away from one pole or the other.

Returning to Hart's own formulation of the shape and attributes of a legal rule, we can now examine Fuller's challenge to Hart's picture. This challenge was not about what a judge was to do in the penumbra. Fuller took little issue with the need for judges to look elsewhere when the words were unclear, although where Hart saw judges exercising quasi-legislative discretion, Fuller would have had judges look for the purpose behind the statute. Still, the disagreements between the two about what judges should do in the penumbra of linguistic uncertainty were relatively minor. More serious were the disagreements about what Hart labeled the core of settled meaning, for here Fuller argued that Hart was mistaken about the idea of a core of settled meaning itself. In response to Hart's assertion that automobiles were plainly within the rule's core, Fuller asked us to consider what should happen if "some local patriots wanted to mount on a pedestal in the park a truck [in perfect working order] used in World War II, while other citizens, regarding the proposed memorial as an eyesore, support their stand by the 'no vehicle' rule?"[18] The truck would initially seem clearly be a vehicle, Fuller argued, but for him it would just as clearly be absurd to exclude it from the park for that

17. See Timothy A. O. Endicott, "Vagueness and Legal Theory," 3 *Legal Theory* 37 (1997).
18. 71 *Harv. L. Rev.* at 661.

reason. And so, Fuller insisted, the words of a legal rule could not by themselves ever present a plain case for a legal rule's application.

Fuller's hypothetical war memorial is part of a long line of cases, some hypothetical and some real, demonstrating that for any legal rule, the possibility will always exist that applying the plain meaning of the rule's words will produce a result at odds with what the rule was designed to accomplish, or even at odds with simple common sense. In the same article in which he offered the example of the truck used as a war memorial, Fuller also provided the example of a rule prohibiting sleeping in a railway station. The rule would plainly have been designed to exclude a homeless person (whom Fuller, this being 1958, referred to as a "tramp"), but Fuller asked whether the rule would apply to a tired businessman who missed his train and nodded off in the station while waiting for the next one. Such an application would be ridiculous, Fuller argued, by way of reinforcing his point that the words of a rule could *never*, by themselves and without reference to the rule's purpose, determine even a core of so-called settled meaning. To the same effect was Samuel von Pufendorf's example of the seventeenth-century decision in which a statute of Bologna prohibiting "letting blood in the streets," presumably designed to prohibit dueling, was held not to apply to a surgeon performing emergency surgery.[19] And recall from Chapter 2 *United States v. Kirby*,[20] in which the Supreme Court refused to permit the prosecution under a statute prohibiting obstructing the mail of a sheriff who had arrested a mail carrier on a charge of murder, as one further example of the frequency with which the complexities of the world frustrate the efforts of statutory language to anticipate them.

Fuller supported his argument with some clumsy philosophy, occasionally insisting that words have no meaning except in the particular context in which they are uttered. This is a mistake, because the ability of a word (or sentence) to carry meaning at all presupposes that the conventions of language attach at least some meaning to words themselves, apart from the particular context of their use. The word "dog" refers to dogs and not to cats or bats, and although the example is rudimentary, it reminds us that language can operate only if its constituent parts,

19. Samuel von Pufendorf, *De Jure Naturae et Gentium Libro Octo* (1672), as described in 1 *William Blackstone, Commentaries* *59–60.
20. 74 U.S. (7 Wall.) 482 (1868).

whether they be words or phrases or sentences, have meaning themselves, for without it they would be unable to convey the thought of the speaker to the mind of the listener. It makes perfect sense, therefore, to say that the words or text of a statute mean something, although whether what the statute means is what its text means is exactly the matter at issue.

Fuller's misguided foray into the philosophy of language, ironically, detracted from rather than supported his highly valuable central point. The war memorial made out of a functioning military truck really *was* a vehicle,[21] just as the tired businessman really was sleeping in the station, and just as the sheriff in *Kirby* really did obstruct the delivery of mail. What these and countless other examples, both real and hypothetical, show is that the application of the literal language of a rule will now and then produce an outcome that is absurd, ridiculous, or at least at odds with the principal purpose lying behind the rule. And even in less extreme cases, following the literal language of a rule will even more often indicate an outcome that is silly, inefficient, or in some other way decidedly suboptimal. It was Fuller's point that language could not, Hart's example notwithstanding, ever be sufficient to produce a core or clear case, because in at least some instances the clear application of clear language would nonetheless produce an absurd result. Only by *always* considering the purpose behind the rule, Fuller believed, could we make sense of legal rules and indeed of law itself.

There is no need (yet) to resolve the debate between Hart and Fuller, for one of the valuable features of how the debate was framed is in providing a useful framework for considering larger questions of statutory interpretation. At the heart of the framework is a distinction among three

---

21. Fuller was, of course, stuck with Hart's example, but "vehicle" may not be the best word to support Fuller's point. It is possible that a current ability to move under its own power is definitional of "vehicle," in which case the truck may have ceased being a vehicle at the point at which it was affixed to or even became part of the memorial. But this is a defect only in the example and not in the central point. Fuller could have asked the same question about an ambulance or a fire truck and his point would have remained the same. The same holds true for Fuller's example of the tired businessman, for the fact of his sleeping was a physiological fact not dependent on why or how he was sleeping. And so too with the question whether a "no dogs allowed" rule in a restaurant or store would bar guide dogs for the blind. It is almost certainly absurd to bar the guide dogs, but the fact that it would be absurd to apply the rule to guide dogs does not mean that guide dogs are not dogs.

types of cases. There are the cases in which the statutory language itself provides a plausible answer, those in which the language does not provide an answer, and those in which the language provides a bad answer—an answer that may clash with the legislative intent, with the purpose of the statute, or with some more general sense of the right result. When the language itself provides a plausible answer—the first category—that is typically the end of the matter. If the words of the law provide a sensible solution to a problem or a dispute, even if not the only sensible answer, it is rare for the literal meaning of the words not to determine the legal outcome. Indeed, such cases are unlikely to be disputed, and, if disputed, unlikely to be litigated, and, if litigated, unlikely to be appealed. Lawyers often talk of hard cases, but there are many easy cases as well.[22] When the language of a statute is clear and produces a sensible result, we have an easy case of statutory construction. In such cases, the sensible resolution provided by the words of the statute alone will normally be dispositive.

Once we move beyond the easy cases, however, the matter becomes less tractable, for at this point we encounter hard cases of two different varieties. One type of hard case arises out of linguistic indeterminacy. The words of the statute do not provide a determinate answer to the dispute before the court, either because the language is vague, as with "equal protection of the laws," "reasonable efforts," and "undue delay," or because language that is determinate for other applications is indeterminate with respect to the matter at issue, as with the question whether bicycles or baby carriages or skateboards are vehicles that should be kept out of the park. But there is another type of hard case, and this type is not a function of linguistic indeterminacy at all. Rather, it is the hard case that is hard just because a linguistically determinate result—the war memorial constructed from a vehicle, the obstruction of the mail caused by the legitimate arrest of a mail carrier in *Kirby*, the missed deadline in *Locke*—can plausibly be argued not to be the best, or even a very good, legal outcome. These are hard cases, but not because the language gives no answer. They are hard precisely because the language gives an answer, but the answer that the language gives appears to be the wrong answer.

Because virtually all litigated statutory interpretation cases present one or the other of these two types of difficulty, it will be useful to con-

22. See Frederick Schauer, "Easy Cases," 58 *S. Cal. L. Rev.* 399 (1985). And see the discussion in section 2.2, *supra*.

sider them separately. We will look first at the cases that are hard because of linguistic indeterminacy, and then take up the ones that are hard because of a seemingly erroneous linguistic determinacy.

8.3 When the Text Provides No Answer

Implicit in the foregoing framing of the question of statutory interpretation is a reinforcement of a central point not only about statutory interpretation, but also about statutes in general. Statutes—the actual language of the law itself—are important not because they are *evidence* of what the legislature was thinking or intended, but because of what they *are*. Just as *Macbeth* is not only evidence of what was on Shakespeare's mind, and just as the *Mona Lisa*'s importance is not simply a matter of what it tells us about Leonardo da Vinci, so too is a statute important in its own right. It is a primary legal item—part of the stuff of law itself—whose status is not a function of what it may reveal about something else.[23]

Because a statute *is* law and not just an indicator of where we might find the law, it comes as no surprise that its actual language looms so large in legal reasoning. The lawyer who talks too soon or too much about intentions and inferences and broader principles of justice in a case involving the interpretation of a statute is likely to be quickly upbraided by a judge asking, "Yes, but what does the statute actually *say*, counselor?" As we have already seen, the language of a statute may not be the only thing considered in a case involving a statute, and what the statute says may not be the last word on the matter, but to fail to recognize that it is the first word, the starting point, is to misunderstand something very important about the nature of law itself.

Although the words of a statute are almost always the starting point, often those words do not provide a clear answer to a particular question. Sometimes this is because the statute uses vague words, like "reasonable" or "excessive" or "under the circumstances," and in such cases the judge

23. For a contrary view, see Ronald Dworkin, *Law's Empire* 16–17 (1986), claiming that there is a "real" rule lurking behind the formulation of a rule that we might find in some place like the United States Code. Dworkin's larger interpretive account of adjudication may well be sound, or at least partially so, but the claim that there is some sort of "real" rule that is not the rule in the books is more mysterious than helpful.

inevitably must look beyond the statutory language. It is common in such cases to say that the judge has "discretion," although just what that means is controversial. Under one view, the one that Hart adopted when he offered the example of the vehicles in the park, the judge in cases of this kind of linguistic indeterminacy is acting as if she were a legislature and may take into account the full range of policy considerations typically used in legislating in order to determine how the indeterminacies in the statute should be made more specific and how a particular dispute should be resolved. This is not to say that a vague statute offers no guidance. Even though the Sherman Antitrust Act in effect authorized the federal courts to create the body of antitrust law, both the language of the statute and its accompanying legislative history made clear that the point of the law was to prohibit collaborative anticompetitive practices, as opposed to adapting a complete laissez-faire approach. So although the courts had considerable leeway in filling out the details, they were expected to do so with a particular goal in mind.

It is somewhat controversial whether determining the statutory goal should or must draw on the legislative history—the record of what the legislature explicitly intended, typically gleaned not primarily from the statute itself (which is why this history is often called *extrinsic*) but from committee reports, records of legislative hearings, and transcripts of legislative debates. The debate about when such materials should be used, if at all, is an active one, with those who favor using such material arguing that statutes are designed to further legislative intentions so that any evidence of that intention should be usable, especially when the language gives insufficient guidance.[24] Proponents of using legislative history also argue that in cases like the ones we are discussing—cases in which the language itself does not provide an answer—it would be foolish not to attempt to use any available evidence to discover what the legislature would have wanted done in just such a case.[25]

24. For a powerful and comprehensive defense of intentionalist approaches to statutory interpretation, see Lawrence M. Solan, "Private Language, Public Laws: The Central Role of Legislative Intent in Statutory Interpretation," 93 *Geo. L.J.* 427 (2005).

25. Traditional British practice excluded consideration of records of actual parliamentary debates, even when a court was attempting to discern Parliament's intentions. The exclusionary practice was justified in part by the view that only the statute itself was authoritative (see Black-Clawson International v. Papierwerke Waldhof-Aschaffenburg, [1975] A.C. 591), in part because records of legislative

On the other side of the debate about using evidence of actual legislative intentions, opponents of the use of legislative history—sometimes called *textualists,* for their unwillingness to go beyond the text of the law—are skeptical about the evidentiary value of records of legislative history. Often different legislators have different goals in mind, so it is not so clear, they say, just whose intentions have been recorded. And sometimes material is inserted into the legislative history by some legislator just to make a point, or to capture the attention of journalists, or to pander to a legislator's constituents, even though that material in no way reflects the collective intentions (assuming that a collective body can have an intention) of the legislature as a whole. What is perhaps most important for most textualists, however, is the fact that it is only the text that was voted on by the legislature. Treating the un-voted-upon legislative history as part of the legislation, they say, is profoundly undemocratic.[26]

The debates about the permissibility (or necessity) of recourse to legislative intent when a statute is unclear should not be confused with arguments about the *purpose* of a statute. It is legislators (or their equivalents) who have intentions, but statutes can have purposes, and it is often possible to determine the purpose of a statute from the words of the statute themselves.[27] Sometimes, of course, the statute will *say* what its purpose is, a phenomenon described (and praised) by Karl Llewellyn as a

---

debates were thought to be unreliable guides to actual intentions (see Davis v. Johnson, [1979] A.C. 264 [H.L.]), and in part because of a worry that encouraging recourse to hard-to-find legislative records would increase the cost of litigation (see William Twining & David Miers, *How to Do Things with Rules* 291 [4th ed., 1999]). The exclusion of legislative materials was relaxed somewhat in Pepper v. Hart, [1993] A.C. 593 (H.L.), but British practice remains substantially less receptive to the use of such materials than is now the case in the United States.

26. The most influential contemporary textualist is Justice Scalia. In addition to Scalia, *A Matter of Interpretation,* note 9 *supra,* see, e.g., Johnson v. United States, 529 U.S. 694, 715 (2000) (Scalia, J., dissenting); Holloway v. United States, 526 U.S. 1, 19 (1999) (Scalia, J., dissenting); Bank One Chicago v. Midwest Bank & Trust Co., 516 U.S. 264 (1996) (Scalia, J., concurring); Green v. Bock Laudry Machine Co., 490 U.S. 504, 527 (1989) (Scalia, J., concurring in the judgment). See also Frank H. Easterbrook, "Textualism and the Dead Hand," 66 *Geo. Wash. L. Rev.* 1119 (1998); Frank H. Easterbrook, "Statutes' Domains," 50 *U. Chi. L. Rev.* 533 (1983); Manning, "The Absurdity Doctrine," note 9 *supra;* John F. Manning, "Textualism and the Equity of the Statute," 101 *Colum. L. Rev.* 1 (2001).

27. See Felix Frankfurter, "Some Remarks on the Reading of Statutes," 47 *Colum. L. Rev.* 527 (1947); Max Radin, "Statutory Interpretation," 43 *Harv. L. Rev.* 863 (1930). See also Richards v. United States, 369 U.S. 1, 9 (1962).

singing reason, his term for a statute that not only *has* a purpose but that also announces it loud and clear.[28] But even where the purpose of a statute is not explicitly stated in the text of the statute itself, it is often possible with considerable confidence to infer the purpose of a statute from the four corners of the statutory language alone. A rule prohibiting vehicles, musical instruments, radios, and loudspeakers from a park would almost certainly be a rule whose purpose was to prevent noise, and thus this rule might be applied to prohibit a musical calliope on wheels but not a bicycle or a baby carriage. But a rule prohibiting vehicles and cooking fires might be determined, just on the basis of these two conjoined prohibitions, to have as its purpose the alleviation of pollution, such that some marginal cases of vehicles that did not pollute—for example, skateboards and bicycles—might be permitted, while polluting marginal cases—for example, fuel-powered model ships and planes—might be barred.

The debates about the permissible sources of supplementation of indeterminate statutes are extensive. We have taken a quick look at policy, legislative intent, and statutory purpose as alternative forms of supplementation, and we could certainly add a broad sense of justice as well to the list of goals that a judge might have in deciding what to do and where to look when the words of a statute do not provide a clear answer. And for the legal philosopher Ronald Dworkin, most prominently, the judge in such cases must try to interpret the statute so that it best "fits" with other statutes, with reported cases, with the Constitution, with broad legal principles, with equally broad political and moral principles, and with all of the other components of law's seamless web.[29] But even when we add these perspectives to the list, this glance is designed simply to give

28. Karl Llewellen, *The Common Law Tradition: Deciding Appeals* 183 (1960). See also Karl N. Llewellyn, *The Bramble Bush: On Our Law and Its Study* 189 (1931). Llewellyn also saw the singing reason as a virtue of judicial opinions as well as of statutes. Karl N. Llewellyn, "The Status of the Rule of Judicial Precedent," 14 *U. Cinc. L. Rev.* 203, 217 (1940).

29. Ronald Dworkin, *Freedom's Law: The Moral Reading of the American Constitution* (1996); Ronald Dworkin, *Law's Empire* (1986); Ronald Dworkin, *Taking Rights Seriously* (1977). In fact, Dworkin insists that judges do and should look for this kind of fit even when the language of the most immediate statute seems clear, but whether he is right about this is a matter of continuing jurisprudential controversy. See Frederick Schauer, "The Limited Domain of the Law," 70 *Va. L. Rev.* 1909 (2004); Frederick Schauer, "Constitutional Invocations," 65 *Ford. L. Rev.* 1295 (1997).

a flavor of the kinds of issues that are likely to arise when statutes are unclear and the kinds of sources that judges may resort to in such cases. The point is only that statutes are often linguistically unclear, whether intentionally or accidentally, and that although there are large debates about where judges should go in such cases, there are no debates about whether judges must go somewhere, for in such cases no amount of staring at the indeterminate language of a vague or ambiguous statute will provide an answer absent some sort of supplementation from elsewhere.

Before leaving the topic of the indeterminate statute, it may be valuable to distinguish two types of indeterminacy. One type is a consequence of a vague[30] or imprecise statute that furnishes virtually no answers by itself. A statute providing that in cases of disputed child custody the child should be placed so as to further "the best interests of the child," as many state domestic relations statutes specify, is one in which the vagueness of the governing standard requires an exercise of judicial discretion or at least some recourse to purpose, intent, justice, equity, or something else. And because of the pervasive vagueness of the governing standard, this recourse to something beyond the words will be required in virtually every contested case. So too with laws regulating "hazardous" products or "dangerous" animals. We may be pretty certain that chainsaws are hazardous and rattlesnakes dangerous, but for most possible applications the words themselves will need supplementation from somewhere, just because of the linguistic imprecision of the words actually used in the law.

At other times, however, words that seem precise, and words that *are* precise for most applications, will become imprecise in the context of some particular application. Hart's assumption was that "vehicle" was a reasonably precise term, such that for most applications it would be relatively easy to conclude that they were or were not vehicles. It was only

---

30. A statute that is unclear with respect to some application is sometimes described in the legal literature as "ambiguous," but that is the wrong word for the phenomenon. A word is ambiguous when it is susceptible to two (or more) quite distinct meanings, as when we are unsure whether the word "bank" refers to the side of the river or the place where we keep our money or whether a "vessel" is something into which we put water or something that floats upon it, but this is rarely an issue in statutory interpretation. In interpreting statutes or other legal texts, the problem is usually that the words have no clear meaning rather than one or another clear meaning, and the correct word for this phenomenon is "vagueness" and not "ambiguity."

when faced with an unusual application—roller skates or bicycles or toy automobiles—that the latent vagueness of *any* term—its *open texture*[31]—would come to the surface. So although the application of the Statute of Frauds (requiring a writing for contractual validity) to transactions involving land might seem rather precise, and although it would be precise for most applications, it would be less so if the contract was one for the sale or lease of air rights or beach access. Such cases would lie at the fuzzy edges of the term "land," and here, just as with the pervasively indeterminate statute, recourse to something beyond the words themselves would be necessary to resolve the controversy.

Statutory linguistic indeterminacy, therefore, may be a function either of pervasive statutory vagueness or of cases that crop up at the vague edges of normally precise statutes. The two phenomena are different, but in either case the text alone cannot do all the work. There are disputes about what should be called upon in such cases to carry the load—legislative intent, statutory purpose, good policy, economic efficiency, moral principle, consistency with other parts of the same statute, consistency with other statutes, or the equities of the particular case, for example—but this variety of statutory interpretation is mandated simply by the inability of language to anticipate all of the possible scenarios in a world far more complex than the blunt instrument of statutory language.

8.4 When the Text Provides a Bad Answer

Although many cases of statutory interpretation arise when a statute is indeterminate—whether in general or only in the context of some particular potential application—there is another category that is importantly different. In this category the words *do* give an answer, but the answer seems unacceptable. At the extreme, the answer given by the words will simply appear absurd. This was Fuller's point with respect to the examples of the vehicle used as a war memorial and the businessman who fell

---

31. The term "open texture" was used by Hart in describing the way in which a clear statute might become indeterminate with respect to some applications, and Hart got it from Friedrich Waismann, "Verifiability," *in Logic and Language: First Series* 117 (A. G. N. Flew ed., 1951). It is worth stressing that "open texture" is not the same as vagueness, but is rather the characteristic of any language, even the most precise language, to become vague in the face of unforeseen applications. Open texture is not vagueness but is rather the omnipresent *possibility* of vagueness.

asleep while waiting for his train, just as it was Pufendorf's with respect to the surgeon arrested under the literal application of a law designed to prevent dueling, and it is the principal theme of those who have argued against the Supreme Court's decision in *Locke*.[32] It is of the essence of law that it be reasonable, so the argument goes, and for that reason, insisting on a literal application of a statute that produces an absurd or plainly unreasonable result is itself absurd. Taking the text as the be-all and end-all in such cases should be avoided just because it is profoundly inconsistent with the fundamental nature of law as the reasonable regulation of human conduct.

As the Supreme Court's decision in *Locke* shows, however, there is another side of the argument. This other side argues, in part, that even allowing the words to give way in the case of a seemingly absurd result is to set out on the road to perdition, for even absurdity can often be in the eyes of the beholder.[33] The question, from this perspective, is not whether it is absurd to deny Locke his land claim, or to prosecute Pufendorf's surgeon, or to evict Fuller's tired businessman from the station, but instead whether anyone—even a judge—should be empowered to decide whether and when some application is absurd or not. The idea of the Rule of Law counsels us to be wary of the rule of people as opposed to the rule of the formal law—the rule of law and not the rule of men, as it was traditionally described—and thus at the extremes a reluctance to trust even a court to determine what is absurd or not will suggest that following the words of a statute come what may might not itself be such an absurd idea after all.[34]

32. See Richard A. Posner, "Legal Formalism, Legal Realism, and the Interpretation of Statutes and the Constitution," 37 *Case West. Res. L. Rev.* 179 (1986).

33. See, e.g., John L. Manning, "The Absurdity Doctrine," 116 *Harv. L. Rev.* 2387 (2003); Frederick Schauer, "The Practice and Problems of Plain Meaning," 45 *Vand. L. Rev.* 715 (1992).

34. In a delightful and enduring essay entitled "The Case of the Speluncean Explorers" (62 *Harv. L. Rev.* 616 (1949)), Lon Fuller demonstrated, some years before he engaged in his debate with Hart, that there were a number of ways of dealing with the unjust results that the straightforward application of the law will occasionally yield. In Fuller's example, a stranded group of explorers in a cave face a problem similar to that of the real shipwrecked sailors in R. v. Dudley & Stephens, L.R. 14 Q.B.D. 273 (1994), and in like fashion proceed to eat one of their number so that the others might survive. Upon being prosecuted for murder after their rescue, the survivors raise a number of defenses, each of which, in Fuller's story, has an adherent on the bench. What is most interesting is that Fuller

Although being unwilling to circumvent the literal words of a statute even in cases of obvious absurdity is a plausible approach, it is not one that has carried the day. In English law there is frequent mention of the "Golden Rule" of statutory interpretation, by which it is meant that the plain meaning of the text will control except in cases of absurdity.[35] In the United States as well, even those who are most wedded to the primary importance of the text would accept, even if at times grudgingly, that so-called textualism allows for an exception in cases of obvious absurdity or readily apparent drafting error.[36]

Absurdity aside, the arguments for taking the text as (almost) always preeminent are not restricted to arguments derived from the Rule of Law value of being wary of the discretion of individual decision-makers, even if they are judges. What is perhaps even more important, as briefly noted above, is the argument from democracy itself. When a legislature enacts a statute, it enacts a set of words, and at no time does it vote on a purpose or a goal or a background justification apart from the words. It certainly does not vote on the intentions expressed in the speeches or writings of individual legislators. Indeed, at times different legislators may well have different intentions or different purposes in mind, and the words enacted may represent the point of compromise among legislators with different goals and different agendas. To take what the legislature has *said* as pre-eminent is simply to respect a legislature's democratic provenance, so it is argued. But there are things that are said on the other side as well, and it is to this that we should now turn.

The other side of the argument, and one closely connected with Fuller's side of his debate with Hart, sees statutes as manifestations of reason, as expressions of collective legislative intentions, and as legal items having a point or a purpose. And although reason, intention, and

---

recognizes that there might be several different ways to avoid an unjust outcome. One is to interpret the statute in contradiction of its plain terms. But there are others, including holding the law to have been violated but imposing a minimal sentence, holding the law to have been violated but refusing to enforce the law, and imposing a sentence while urging the executive to pardon the offenders.

35. See Grey v. Pearson, (1857) H.L. Cas. 61; William Twining & David Miers, *How to Do Things with Rules* 279–83 (4th ed., 1999); M. D. A. Freeman, "The Modern English Approach to Statutory Construction," *in Legislation and the Courts* 2 (M. D. A. Freeman ed., 1997).

36. Sometimes referred to as "scrivener's error." See City of Chicago v. Environmental Defense Fund, 511 U.S. 328 337 n.3 (1994) (Scalia, J., concurring).

purpose are three different things, they all coalesce around the view that it is the job of a judge to try to make sense out of a statute rather than just slavishly follow its words down a ridiculous path. Yes, the power to make sense out of a statute might be abused, but we should not forget Justice Story's warning in *Martin v. Hunter's Lessee:* "It is always a doubtful course, to argue against the use or existence of a power, from the possibility of its abuse."[37] So although it is possible that there are some decision-making environments in which the consequences of the occasional absurd result—allowing Kirby to be prosecuted or barring Locke from his claim—will be less than the consequences of empowering judges to determine which results are absurd and which are not, there may be even more, so the argument goes, in which there is no reason to take such a dim view of judicial power. If so, then there may be many environments in which judges can and should be authorized to interpret statutes guided by reason and allowed to determine which interpretations are unreasonable and which not. In such environments, judges will be within their authority when they attempt to divine what the legislature would have wished done in the circumstances and attempt as well to understand and thus to further the basic purposes of a statute.

Where this latter view prevails, where judges are trusted to pursue reason even if occasionally they get it wrong, it is best to understand the literal interpretation of a statute as *defeasible,* a term we encountered in exploring the common law's methods in Chapter 6. The term, which originally comes from property law and is now frequently found in jurisprudential writing,[38] suggests that there are some circumstances in which a rule or principle or legally indicated outcome might be defeated. In the context of statutory interpretation, therefore, the view would be that the literal interpretation is still the standard and still the approach in the first instance. But not only when the literal interpretation is absurd, but also when the literal interpretation yields an outcome inconsistent with common sense, or inconsistent with probable legislative intention, or inconsistent with the statute's purpose, the judge may depart from literal meaning in order to produce the most reasonable result.

---

37. Martin v. Hunter's Lessee, 14 U.S. (1 Wheat.) 304 (1816).

38. See, e.g., D. Neil MacCormick, "Defeasibility in Law and Logic," *in Informatics and the Foundation of Legal Reasoning* 99 (Zenon Bankowski, Ian White, & Ulrike Hahn eds., 1995); Richard H. S. Tur, "Defeasibilism," 21 *Ox. J. Legal Stud.* 355 (2001).

The same idea might be expressed in terms of a *presumption*. Judges typically start with the text, and they presume that what the text says is what the statute means.[39] But this presumption, like many others, is rebuttable. The presumption shifts the burden of proof, as it were, but it remains possible to argue that the text should not be followed when doing so would frustrate the statute's purpose or the legislator's intent or produce an absurd or unreasonable result. These arguments are rarely easy ones to make. To argue against the plain words of the text (and it is important to remember that we are dealing here with the situation in which it is assumed that the text does have a plain or literal meaning) is never easy and is somewhat like swimming upstream. But in many legal systems, and perhaps especially in the legal system of the United States,[40] such arguments are possible and indeed frequently prevail. And so although it would be a mistake to ignore the extent to which the straightforward meaning of the statutory text is the dominant factor in statutory interpretation, it would be a mistake as well to neglect the important fact that the text, even if it is the starting point, is often not the ending point, and that the final determination of the meaning of a statute is not always the same as the meaning of the words or phrases or sentences that the statute happens to contain.

8.5 The Canons of Statutory Construction

Typically, statutes are not as uncomplicated as the examples that have dominated this chapter. Rather than simply banning vehicles from the park or prohibiting the obstruction of the mails, modern statutes are complex affairs, with numerous sections, subsections, parts, and subparts and with definitions of terms that are often as important or more so than the so-called operative sections themselves. The Securities Act of 1933, for example, controls the process by which issuers of securities must register their offering with the Securities and Exchange Commission before offering the securities to the public. But although the operative Section 5 of the act contains the requirement of registration, almost

39. See, e.g., Crooks v. Harrelson, 282 U.S. 55, 60 (1930). On presumptions in general, see Chapter 12.

40. See Patrick S. Atiyah & Robert S. Summers, *Form and Substance in Anglo-American Law: A Comparative Study in Legal Reasoning, Legal Theory and Legal Institutions* (1987).

all of the "action" in the statute as a whole is contained in the definitions, for this is where it is determined what is a security, which offerings are exempt and which not, and when various shortcuts in the registration process are available. The lawyer who does not understand the intricate interplay of the definitions in the statute simply does not understand how the statute works at all.

The Securities Act of 1933 thus presents difficulties in interpretation simply because it is complex, and consequently requires the careful and close reading that is often associated with good legal thinking. But sometimes it is not so clear, even after very close reading, what the words of a statute mean, and not because of vagueness or ambiguity. To make sense of such a statute there has developed over the years a set of *canons* of statutory construction, designed to provide guidance in determining how the words of even a seemingly precise and clear statute should be interpreted.

The canons of statutory construction have occupied entire volumes, and it would be impossible here even to scratch the surface of what they are and how they operate. And, as we saw in Chapter 7, they have been mocked as well, especially by Karl Llewellyn. If there are so many canons of statutory construction that one is virtually always available to support any side of any contested case of interpretation, then the canons turn out to be scarcely more than supplements to arguments made on other grounds, failing totally to provide the guidance that was their original aim.

Despite all of this, however, it might be useful here just to give the briefest flavor of what the canons are all about. Consider, for example, the canon (or maxim) *expressio unius est exclusio alterius* (most of the canons have Latin names, dating back to when the liberal use of Latin was the mark of the sophisticated lawyer). This canon, translated as "the expression of one is the exclusion of the other" and meaning that omissions are to be understood as exclusions, tracks what for many people is just common sense. Consider again the example of the rule prohibiting vehicles in the park. Suppose it can be established that the purpose of the rule is to preserve a quiet environment so that people can relax without the noise or potential danger of motorized vehicles. And suppose the question then comes up whether rock concerts are to be excluded. They are certainly loud and sometimes dangerous and typically interfere with the peace and quiet of those who are not attending. But the rule only prohibits vehicles, and whatever a rock concert is, it is not a vehicle. So the argument would be that the explicit prohibition of vehicles should be understood as an almost equally explicit nonprohibition of rock concerts.

This example is fictional, but real examples abound. Because Rule 9(b) of the Federal Rules of Civil Procedure requires detailed pleading of allegations of fraud or mistake, it has been held by application of the *expressio unius* maxim that pleading of any other claim need not be detailed.[41] Similarly, the fact that Congress, acting on the authority of the commerce clause in Article I of the Constitution, sometimes explicitly preempts (precludes) state regulation of the same subject has been repeatedly held to entail that nonexplicit preemption is to be treated as the permission of parallel state regulation.[42] And because Congress created a "hardship" exemption for corporations and individuals from some aspects of the Endangered Species Act, it has been held that Congress's expressed exemptions for corporate and individual hardship were to be understood as excluding any such exemption for governmental hardships.[43]

The *expressio unius* maxim is just one of the canons of statutory construction, and there are myriad others. The *ejusdem generis* canon requires that open-ended terms in a statutory list (or its equivalent) be interpreted to include only items similar to those listed. A statutory provision requiring governmental inspection of "fruits, vegetables, grains, and other products" should under this canon be understood to include only foodstuffs, not motor vehicles or televisions, within "other products." And thus in *Circuit City Stores, Inc. v. Adams,*[44] the Supreme Court held that a provision in the Federal Arbitration Act applying a portion of that act to "seamen, railroad employees, or any other class of workers engaged in foreign or interstate commerce" should be interpreted to apply only to transportation workers and not to all nontransportation employees working in interstate or foreign commerce. Another commonly used canon is the requirement that provisions in different statutes, or different parts of the same statute, be interpreted *in pari materia*—together—in order to produce a coherent and internally consistent statutory scheme. Thus courts have interpreted the jurisdictional and procedural provisions of the antidiscrimination provisions of the Civil Rights Act of 1964, the

41. See, e.g., Leatherman v. Tarrant County Narcotics Intelligence & Coordination Unit, 507 U.S. 163, 168 (193).
42. See, e.g., Cipollone v. Liggett Group, Inc., 505 U.S. 504, 517 (1992).
43. Tennessee Valley Authority v. Hill, 437 U.S. 153, 188 (1978).
44. 532 U.S. 105 (2001).

Americans with Disabilities Act, and the Age Discrimination in Employment Act as a unified whole in order to produce, or at least attempt to produce, as much of a unitary and consistent framework of antidiscrimination statutes as the language of the individual statutes could bear.[45]

For purposes of this chapter and this book, little point would be served by cataloging the full array of canons of statutory interpretation. The ones just described give a flavor of how they operate, but Llewellyn seems close to the mark in suggesting that with so many of them typically pointing in opposite directions, it is difficult to see how they can in the final analysis be dispositive in any case. Nevertheless, the canons do in their entirety suggest that even determining the literal meaning of the statute is not always a straightforward process. But they suggest as well that whatever techniques are used, the process of statutory interpretation is typically one that begins with a close reading of the text, possibly supplemented by interpretive aids such as the canons of statutory interpretation. And so although at the extremes the interpretation of statutes may have characteristics reminiscent of pure common-law development, to ignore the way in which the actual language of a statute is the starting point for analysis of cases in which a statute is relevant is to ignore a dominant feature of modern legal systems.

45. See Jennings v. American Postal Workers Union, 672 F.2d 712 (8th Cir. 1982).

9

THE JUDICIAL OPINION

9.1 The Causes and Consequences of Judicial Opinions

It is characteristic of the common law that the judicial opinion occupies center stage. It is not all that matters, of course, but few legal arguments in common-law jurisdictions lack multiple references to the published opinions of judges, and few judicial opinions fail to refer to other judicial opinions. To think about legal reasoning in the common-law world without taking into account the written opinions of judges is scarcely conceivable.

Yet although judicial opinions are an omnipresent feature of modern common-law legal argument, and although the "reasoned elaboration" provided by written judicial opinions is often said to be one of the desirable characteristics of law,[1] it is a mistake to think that all or even most legal outcomes are accompanied by a written statement of the reasons for the decision. Jurors delivering verdicts not only are not expected to provide reasons for their decision, but are typically prohibited from doing so. The Supreme Court decides with full argument and opinion only a tiny percentage of the thousands presented to it,[2] but when it refuses to hear the remainder it typically says nothing other than "the petition for

---

1. See Henry M. Hart, Jr. & Albert M. Sacks, *The Legal Process: Basic Problems in the Making and Application of Law* 143–52 (William N. Eskridge, Jr. & Philip Frickey eds., 1994); G. Edward White, "The Evolution of Reasoned Elaboration: Jurisprudential Criticism and Social Change," 59 *Va. L. Rev.* 279 (1973).

2. For the October 2006 Term, the precise count is that the Court received 8922 petitions for certiorari and (rarely) other forms of review, and decided 73 cases with full opinions after briefing and oral argument. "The Supreme Court, 2006 Term—The Statistics," 121 *Harv. L. Rev.* 436 (2007).

certiorari is denied."[3] Increasingly, appellate courts with crowded dockets and too few judges decide many of their cases with no opinions, and many others with brief "unpublished" opinions for the benefit of the parties alone.[4] And although most legal arguments in the United States take place not in appellate courts but before single judges ruling on motions at the trial level, in the overwhelming majority of such rulings the decisions are not accompanied by reasons, written or otherwise.

Yet even though written judicial opinions occupy but a small proportion of the decisions of American judges, they are disproportionately important. Judicial opinions frame legal arguments and structure much of the law. And in a common-law country, judicial opinions play a major role in telling lawyers and their clients what the law is. The judicial opinion is thus important not only for the cases that are contested, but also in giving guidance about whether a dispute is worth litigating at all and about whether a loss at trial is worth appealing. But just what *are* judicial opinions, and how are we to understand them?

In the United States, but usually not in Great Britain, for example, the appellate opinion is an opinion of the court and represents the views of a majority of the judges hearing the case. There may at times be concurring opinions, in which a judge agrees with the majority opinion but wants to elaborate on what the majority said, and often there are dissenting opinions. And in the Supreme Court we frequently see opinions "concurring in the judgment," which means that the Justice agrees with the outcome but for different reasons from the majority, and consequently refuses to join the majority opinion. And occasionally there is no majority willing to agree on a single opinion, in which case there is no majority opinion at all, and the judgment is announced, typically, in a plurality opinion. But in the normal course of things, one finds in the United States a majority opinion, also called the opinion of the court. And this is in noteworthy contrast with British practice, where traditionally each judge hearing a

3. It is a long-standing convention that the Supreme Court's denials of certiorari are not to be understood as statements on the merits of the decision below and thus may not be cited as precedent for anything. Teague v. Lane, 489 U.S. 288, 296 (1989). The newspapers often report a denial of certiorari as "approval" of the decision below, and a denial of certiorari does have the practical effect of letting the decision below stand, but the inference of approval is, within the legal system, an impermissible one.

4. For a more extensive account and analysis of this phenomenon, see section 4.4, *supra.*

case delivers his or her own opinion, and it has been the (quite a bit harder) task of the lawyers and judges in future cases to piece together the ratio decidendi—the reasons that a majority of the judges agreed on—from the serial opinions of individual judges.

Even in the United States, however, where the typical existence of a single majority opinion makes it much easier on lawyers, the judicial opinion is a curious thing, not least because it takes no single standard form. Typically, however, the judicial opinion is the explanation by a judge of the reasoning that led him or her to some conclusion. The opinion will contain enough of the facts of the case so that the reader or a subsequent court will understand the context of the case, and if necessary be able to distinguish it from some other case. Not all of the facts will be described, and it is a fair inference that most of the facts as stated by the court will be legally material, although of course some facts—the relevant dates, the names of the parties, and so on—will simply be for context and identification without being ones that are legally relevant. Having stated the facts, the court will then describe the case's procedural posture, explaining what happened below, how the case came to be on appeal, and what issues are now being heard on appeal. And the opinion will proceed to state and explain the relevant law as the court sees it, apply the law to the particular facts of this case, and announce a conclusion.[5]

All well and good, but now the complications begin. One of the principal complications is the question of whether judicial opinions should be honest. It might seem as if the answer is obviously yes, but in fact there is a debate about judicial *candor* that addresses just this issue.[6] The arguments in favor of candor are pretty straightforward. After all, the idea that public officials—a category that includes judges—in a democracy should be honest and transparent in what they say to their constituents hardly needs much argument these days. But although honesty or candor

5. See John Leubsdorf, "The Structure of Judicial Opinions," 86 *Minn. L. Rev.* 447 (2001); John J. O'Connell, "A Dissertation on Judicial Opinions," 23 *Temple L.Q.* 13 (1949).

6. See Scott Altman, "Beyond Candor," 89 *Mich. L. Rev.* 296 (1990); Micah Schwartzman, "Judicial Sincerity," 94 *Va. L. Rev.* 1276 (2008); David Shapiro, "In Defense of Judicial Candor," 100 *Harv. L. Rev.* 731 91987); Michael L. Wells, "'Sociological Legitimacy' in Supreme Court Opinions," 64 *Wash. & Lee L. Rev.* 1011 (2007); Nicholas S. Zeppos, "Judicial Candor and Statutory Interpretation," 78 *Geo. L.J.* 353 (1989).

might be the default position, the arguments against candor are intriguing. Typically, these are not arguments that urge judges to lie. They are, however, arguments that draw a distinction between the motivation or history of a judicial outcome and its written justification. As the Legal Realists (see Chapter 7) insisted, the actual motivations for a judicial decision—how and why a judge actually came to the conclusion she reached—often diverge from how the judge subsequently explains, justifies, or rationalizes that decision.[7] Even when we put aside the vulgar "what the judge ate for breakfast" caricature of Realism, it is a central tenet of the Realist perspective that judges, arguably like most people much of the time,[8] perceive a preferred outcome in an almost intuitive and holistic way—*Gestalt* is for some people the fancy word—and then, and only then, search for a legal justification to support that outcome. Under this view, the first reaction of the judge is a flash of understanding, and most of what happens thereafter is an attempt to buttress what the flash of understanding initially produced. But even those Realists, such as Llewellyn, who believed in the decision-guiding force of rules—albeit not the "paper rules" that one would find in the lawbooks—believed that judges were conventionally required to justify their outcomes in terms of the rules that *were* to be found in collections of legal rules. From even the mildest and least radical Realist perspective, therefore, we see the view that the explanation of a judicial outcome is not so much a report of the process that led the judge to reach the conclusion she reached, but is instead an after-the-fact account of the legal rules, precedents, and other sources of legal doctrine that *support* rather than motivated the outcome. Indeed, the frequency with which seeming non-Realist judges talk about judgments that "will not write"[9] suggests that it is the mainstream rather

7. "[T]he core of Realism is [a] descriptive claim about how judges decide cases according to which judges rationalize, after-the-fact, decisions reached on other grounds." Brian Leiter, *Naturalizing Jurisprudence* 16 (2007).

8. For this point in the context of moral decision-making, see Jonathan Haidt, "The Emotional Dog and Its Rational Tail: A Social Intuitionist Approach to Moral Judgment," 108 *Psych. Rev.* 814 (2001). For a recent overview of the broader psychological literature, see Jonathan St. B. T. Evans, "Dual-Processing Accounts of Reasoning, Judgment, and Social Cognition," 59 *Ann. Rev. Psych* 255 (2008).

9. See Frank Coffin, *The Ways of a Judge: Reflections from the Federal Appellate Bench* 57 (1980); Richard A. Posner, *The Federal Courts: Crisis and Reform* 106–11 (1985); Patricia M. Wald, "The Rhetoric of Result and the Results of Rhetoric," 62 *U. Chi. L. Rev.* 1371, 1375 (1995). And see Chapter 4.

than the radical view that a sense of the right outcome precedes the judicial attempt to find formal legal support for it. In fact, the view that judicial opinions are largely about providing the strongest legal support for a decision reached on nonlegal or quasi-legal grounds is a widely held but contested opinion, but the view that judicial opinions are largely about making a decision that was the product of choice and discretion appear as if it had been compelled by earlier cases and other legal materials is far more than just a widely held opinion—it is almost certainly the conventional wisdom.[10]

Once we understand judicial opinion-writing as the practice of offering legal support for decisions often involving elements other than the formal law—justice, for example, or efficiency, or wise policy, or even mercy or pity—we can see that many, maybe even most, judicial opinions are not fully candid. They read in the language of legal or rule-based motivation or compulsion, but their goal is to provide support or justification for decisions reached for different reasons. Perhaps it would be good if this were otherwise. Perhaps judicial opinions should describe accurately how the judge reached the decision she did. But as long as the idea of a judicial opinion as the accurate report of a decision-making process remains far more an aspiration than reality, the alleged importance of judicial candor turns out to be a substantial exaggeration.

9.2 Giving Reasons

We have seen that giving (as opposed to having) reasons is less pervasive in law than often asserted. At times judges or courts do not give reasons because doing so would be inefficient or impossible as a practical matter. There is no way that the Supreme Court can be expected to provide reasons for why it does not hear each of the thousands of cases a year it declines to review. Much the same can be said about trial judges when they rule on objections to testimony during a trial, and about trial judges who must rule on large numbers of often mundane pretrial motions. The judge who simply announces "sustained" or "overruled" or "motion denied" is a ubiquitous figure in actual legal practice. If judges were required to explain the reasons for each of those decisions, even orally, the trial process would come to a standstill. And we do not require juries to

10. See S. F. C. Milsom, *A Natural History of the Common Law* 107 (2003); Richard A. Posner, *Overcoming Law* 245 (1995); Richard A. Posner, "Judges' Writing Styles (And Do They Matter?)," 62 *U. Chi. L. Rev.* 1421 (1995).

give reasons for their verdicts, not only because of the difficulty (and inefficiency) of trying to get twelve people to agree on the set of common reasons for reaching their verdict, but also because the theory of jury decision-making, just like the theory of the secret ballot in a democracy, normally (unless there are credible grounds to believe that the jury engaged in some sort of misconduct) precludes external evaluation of just why a jury decided the way it did.

With respect to the typical appellate opinion, however, and for many substantial trial court rulings, judges do give reasons for their judgments, and it is worth considering just what they are doing when they do so. We start with the observation that a reason is almost always more general—broader in scope—than the result or decision that it is a reason for. If you ask someone why he is carrying an umbrella and he responds that the forecast is for rain, the implication is that whenever the forecast is for rain he will carry an umbrella—not just today, but on all of the occasions on which the forecast is for rain. When a physician says that she prescribed a statin drug because the patient had high cholesterol, she is saying that there is a reason (which may at times be outweighed by other reasons to the contrary) to prescribe a statin drug not just in *this* case of high cholesterol but in *all* similar cases of high cholesterol.

It is very much the same with the reasons given in judicial opinions. When the Supreme Court in *Brown v. Board of Education*[11] famously justified holding racially segregated schools unconstitutional under the Fourteenth Amendment by saying that "separate but equal [schools are] inherently unequal," it was announcing not just that the separate but (superficially) equal public schools in Topeka, Kansas, were unconstitutional, but that all separate but (superficially) equal public schools were unconstitutional. Similarly, when the California Supreme Court in *Knight v. Kaiser Co.*[12] refused to allow the plaintiff to claim that the sand pile under which his son died was an "attractive nuisance," it supported its conclusion by explaining why sand piles in general—*all* sand piles, and not just the sand pile under which the plaintiff's son was asphyxiated—were not to be considered attractive nuisances.

Thus, when a court provides a reason for a decision, it gives a justification necessarily broader than that decision, and accordingly it announces what is in effect a rule (or a principle, standard, norm, or maxim) more

11. 347 U.S. 483 (1954).
12. 312 P.2d 1089 (Cal. 1957).

general than the decision itself. To provide a reason in a particular case is to transcend the very particularity of that case. And indeed, the same structure operates when a court seeks to justify a rule or principle itself. Just as providing a reason for an outcome ordinarily takes the outcome to a greater level of generality, so too does providing a reason for a reason—or a reason for a rule or a reason for a principle. When the Supreme Court in *Griswold v. Connecticut*[13] struck down the Connecticut law banning the sale of contraceptives, it struck down the particular law *because* it was an example of the larger category of laws banning contraceptives, but the reason why all laws in this larger category of restrictions on the sale of contraceptives were unconstitutional was that such laws, the Supreme Court concluded, were restrictions on privacy. Thus, for the Supreme Court, all laws restricting privacy were constitutionally suspect and needed to be justified by a compelling interest if they were to be permitted. In providing a reason for why laws banning the sale of contraceptives were unconstitutional, the Court thus gave a reason broader than the outcome in the case and broader even than the rule that the reason justified. As numerous subsequent cases demonstrated,[14] therefore, the Court's use of the right to privacy as the justification for its conclusion regarding the constitutionality of restrictions on the sale of contraceptives meant that the right to privacy was henceforth available as a legitimate reason for a conclusion in cases not involving contraception at all.

It is an important consequence of the generality of reasons that a person (or a court) who gives a reason for a decision is typically committed to that reason on future occasions. If I tell a friend that I give money to Oxfam because it helps provide food to starving children in Africa, it is not at all surprising when my friend then asks me whether I will give money to his own pet charity, which also provides food to starving children in Africa. I may at that point be able to draw a distinction—the two organizations might be different in some other respect, or I might just be out of money—but having given the reason in the first "case," I am at least presumptively committed to following it in subsequent ones. And thus, when in law a court gives a reason for a decision, it is expected to follow that reason in subsequent cases falling within the scope of the reason articulated by the court on the first occasion. To speak of a decision as "unprincipled" is typically to say that a court gave as a reason for a

13. 381 U.S. 479 (1965).
14. Most obviously Roe v. Wade, 410 U.S. 113 91973).

decision a reason it was not in fact willing to follow in subsequent cases, thus suggesting that the reason given by the court was not really a reason it took very seriously.[15] An often-discussed example of this phenomenon is the Supreme Court's decision in *Shelley v. Kraemer,*[16] which invalidated racially restrictive real estate covenants. In concluding that a racially restrictive covenant in a "private" deed was nevertheless the action of the state for the purpose of the Fourteenth Amendment's state action requirement, the Court said that private discrimination becomes state action whenever the private action is enforced by the state through its laws and in its courts. It turned out, however, that the Court was not willing to follow in subsequent cases the reason it gave in *Shelley.* For example, the Court was not, unsurprisingly, willing to find state action in every instance in which the state was called upon to enforce a will, contract, trust, or right against trespass, even though the will or contract contained a racially restrictive provision or even when the reasons for excluding a trespasser were racial animosity.[17] By contrast, however, when Justice O'Connor in *New York v. United States*[18] wrote for the Supreme Court in invalidating under the Tenth Amendment a federal law that required states to regulate radioactive waste in a certain specific way, she said that "[t]he Federal Government may not compel the States to enact or administer a federal regulatory program." In so doing, she committed the Court to the proposition that *any* law compelling the states to administer a federal regulatory program would be at least presumptively unconstitutional, and there has so far been no indication that the Court is unwilling to take seriously in subsequent cases the reason it gave in this case, and thus the commitment is made in this case.

15. See M. P. Golding, "Principled Decision-making and the Supreme Court," 63 *Colum. L. Rev.* 35 (1963); Kent Greenawalt, "The Enduring Significance of Neutral Principles," 78 *Colum. L. Rev.* 982 (1978).

16. 334 U.S. 1 (1948).

17. Thus, the Court studiously avoided mentioning *Shelley* or its reasoning in cases involving racially restrictive grants and trusts (e.g., Evans v. Newton, 382 U.S. 296 [1966]) or racially motivated calls upon state trespass laws to exclude so-called sit-in demonstrators (Bell v. Maryland, 378 U.S. 226 (1964); Griffin v. Maryland, 378 U.S. 130 (1964); Peterson v. Greenville, 373 U.S. 244 (1963)). And there is no indication that the Court was ever willing even to hear a case like Gordon v. Gordon, 124 N.E.2d 228 (Mass. 1955), in which the state courts had enforced as written a will conditioning the testator's legacy on the beneficiary's marrying someone of "the Hebrew faith."

18. 505 U.S. 144 (1992).

Thus, when a court gives a reason for its decision, it creates a commitment for that court and an expectation on the part of those who seek to be guided by judicial opinions. It is true that in subsequent cases the commitment might be attacked on the grounds that it is mere dicta (about which see section 3.4 and the following section in this chapter), but we must not ignore the extent to which what a court actually *says* makes a large difference in legal practice and legal argument. It is true that lawyers will argue that the language from a previous opinion arose in a different context and that they will strain to distinguish the cases in which the language first appeared. It is also true that under the traditional account there is nothing binding about the explicit formulations that might be found in some seemingly controlling earlier decision.[19] But in reality, the actual words that a court uses are not nearly so impotent on subsequent occasions. The existence of rulelike language in a binding judicial opinion, or a statement of a legal principle in such an opinion, at the very least shifts the burden of argument. The lawyer seeking to deny the effect of what that or some higher court has previously *said* may struggle to urge that the words are mere dicta or that the actual holding of the earlier case is other than what the earlier court's words say, but in such a case the lawyer has a burden of explanation or persuasion that the lawyer who can simply point to the pertinent language does not. Words matter, in law as well as in life, and there are few advocates who relish having to argue against what some binding or influential court, especially the court before which they are now arguing, has actually said on some previous occasion.

When a court provides a reason for a decision, therefore, it can be thought of as entering into a social practice not unlike the social practice of promising. We commonly believe that promises create commitments, because it is wrong to lead someone to rely on some proposition and then to turn around and undercut the basis for that reliance. So too with providing reasons. Giving reasons induces reasonable reliance and creates a prima facie commitment on the part of the court to decide subsequent cases in accordance with the reason that it has explicitly given on a previous occasion.

If a court is prima facie or presumptively committed in the future to the reasons it gives now, and if those reasons are, as we have seen, neces-

19. See William Twining & David Miers, *How to Do Things with Rules* 313, 339 (4th ed., 1999).

THINKING LIKE A LAWYER

sarily broader or more general than the conclusions they support, then a court giving a reason for its decision is in effect committed to the outcomes of some number of future cases whose factual detail it cannot now comprehend or accurately anticipate. When a court gives a reason for a decision, therefore, it reduces its own freedom of decision in future cases, and the broader the reason is, the more the court constricts its future freedom. Understanding this phenomenon helps us to see why we do not always require legal decision-makers to give reasons for their decisions, because the virtues of reason-giving must compete with the virtues of continuing decisional flexibility. And even for a court required by convention to provide reasons, the advantages of giving broad reasons in terms of guidance and transparency must compete again with the advantages of giving narrow and particularistic reasons that will allow the court to retain flexibility in the face of an uncertain future.[20] The practice of judicial reason-giving, therefore—a practice central to the very idea of the judicial opinion—is one in which the benefits of full explanation are not without costs. The court that is wary of providing a full explanation of what it has done and why it has done it may not always be a court that is sloppy or lazy, but often may simply be a court that understands that what it says now commits it in the future. When a court does not wish to be so committed, it may be reluctant to provide reasons any broader than what is absolutely necessary to explain what it has done in the case before it, for fear that what it does in that case will restrict it more than it will wish to be restricted when additional cases arise in the future.

9.3 Holding and Dicta Revisited

Much of the foregoing discussion connects with the traditional distinction between the holding of a case (roughly, but only roughly, equivalent to what in Great Britain is called the ratio decidendi) and the dicta that a court may also offer in the process of issuing an opinion. According to

---

20. For an influential argument that the Supreme Court should routinely give narrow reasons rather than broad ones and therefore limit the effect of its decisions on other and future cases, in the Supreme Court itself and below, see Cass R. Sunstein, *One Case at a Time: Judicial Minimalism on the Supreme Court* (1999). And for a contrary view, stressing the importance for a Court that decides so few cases of giving guidance to lower courts and officials, see Frederick Schauer, "Abandoning the Guidance Function: Morse v. Frederick," 2006 *Sup. Ct. Rev.* 378; Frederick Schauer, "Opinions as Rules," 62 *U. Chi. L. Rev.* 1455 (1995).

the traditional distinction, the holding of a case consists of what is *necessary* to support the result in that case.[21] Everything else is obiter dicta, or dicta for short, and as such is more easily dismissed in subsequent cases or by subsequent courts. As it was traditionally expressed, the holding of a previous case, or a case from a higher court, was *binding,* but everything else—the dicta—could legitimately be disregarded. The traditional view is captured by the following from a classic English introduction to law: "[*Obiter dictum*] is a mere saying by the way, a chance remark, which is not binding upon future courts, though it may be respected according to the reputation of the judge, the eminence of the court, and the circumstances in which it came to be pronounced."[22]

Lawyers and judges talk less about holding and dicta than in times past, and there appear to be two reasons for the decline. First, even so-called mere dicta often has more of a burden-shifting effect than the traditional account supposes. A statement by the Supreme Court that directly supports one side in a subsequent lower court case, or even in a subsequent Supreme Court case, immediately gives that side the upper hand in argument, and the lawyer who has to argue that the statement is mere dicta is at an argumentative disadvantage. So too for statements by other courts. Lawyers can and do argue about which part of an opinion is holding and which part is dicta, but the lawyer who can point to specific words and argue from what an authoritative or influential court has *said* already has his opponent off-balance.

Not only does dicta have this practical power, but even the theoretical distinction between holding and dicta is also open to challenge. As we have seen, both here and in Chapter 3, *any* statement by a court beyond the simple recitation of the facts and the announcement of an outcome is broader than the case at hand and is thus strictly unnecessary to the out-

---

21. See, e.g., Diaz-Rodriguez v. Pep Boys Corp., 410 F.3d 56, 60 (1st Cit. 2005); Cal. Pub. Employees Retirement Sys. v. WorldCom, Inc., 368 F.3d 86, 106 n.19 (2d Cir. 2004); United States v. Johnson, 256 F.3d 895, 919–21 (9th Cir. 2001) (en banc) (Tashima, J., concurring); Rupert Cross & J. W. Harris, *Precedent in English Law* 76 (4th ed., 1991); Eugene Wambaugh, *The Study of Cases* 18 (2d ed., 1894). For modern general discussions of the distinction between holding and dicta, see generally Michael Abramowicz & Maxwell Stearns, "Defining Dicta," 57 *Stan. L. Rev.* 953 (2005); Michael C. Dorf, "Dicta and Article III," 142 *U. Pa. L. Rev.* 1997 (2004); Note, "Implementing Brand X: What Counts as a Step One Holding?," 119 *Harv. L. Rev.* 1532 (2006).

22. Glanville Williams, *Learning the Law* 72 (10th ed., 1978).

come. Every time a court gives a reason for its decision, it necessarily opines about cases other than the one before it,[23] and thus, strictly speaking, all statements of reasons have an aura of dicta surrounding them. And even if there are some reasons that are necessary to the outcome, it is never necessary that those reasons be stated at one level of generality rather than another. Because Judge Cardozo in *MacPherson v. Buick Motor Company*[24] could have announced that the reason for the outcome in that particular case was that automobile manufacturers were liable regardless of privity to the ultimate consumers for injuries caused by defective parts in those automobiles, was his actual reason—about manufacturers and not just about automobile manufacturers—broader than necessary because it encompassed manufacturers of products other than automobiles? Even then, would it have been broader than necessary because it included manufacturers of automobiles other than Buicks? As we saw in Chapter 3, trying to identify what a case stands for without reference to the case's own statement of what it stands for is elusive at best. It may well be, therefore, that any attempt to locate the distinction between holding and dicta in an alleged difference between what is necessary for the decision and what is not will turn out to be little more than an argument in a subsequent case about which was the holding and which was the dicta, with no clear answer to that question being provided by the very case alleged to be binding. In *Parents Involved in Community Schools v. Seattle School District No. 1*,[25] for example, a 2007 Supreme Court case dealing with affirmative action and racial assignment in the public schools, both the majority and the dissent accused the other of relying on mere dicta from earlier cases, and the lesson of this may be the skeptical one that dicta is little more than a statement of a previous court that an advocate or subsequent court now wants to discount, and that a holding is the statement of a previous court upon which a lawyer or judge now wishes to rely.

This idea should not be taken too far. In *Flood v. Kuhn*,[26] the Supreme Court upheld professional baseball's historical exemption from the antitrust laws, and Justice Blackmun's majority opinion gave as the principal reason for this outcome the failure of Congress to react to two earlier Su-

23. Frederick Schauer, "Giving Reasons," 47 *Stan. L. Rev.* 633 (1995).
24. 111 N.E. 1050 (N.Y. 1916).
25. 127 S. Ct. 2738 (2007).
26. 407 U.S. 258 (1972).

preme Court decisions, *Toolson v. New York Yankees, Inc.*[27] and *Federal Baseball Club v. National League,*[28] which had reached the same conclusion. This being a statutory (and not constitutional) case, the Court reasoned, Congress's failure to eliminate a Court-announced exemption could be taken as congressional ratification of that exemption. And because this was the reason for the Court's decision, albeit a reason broader than absolutely necessary to support the outcome, it would be perfect appropriate for a lawyer in a subsequent case to rely for authority on the proposition that congressional failure to reverse a Supreme Court statutory decision could be understood as an endorsement or incorporation of that opinion. Opposing counsel could claim, again appropriately and plausibly, that this broad statement was sufficiently broader than what was necessary to support the *Flood* result that it should be taken as nonbinding dicta, and the clash of interpretations of the Court's reasoning would hardly be unusual.

But the facts of the case and the explanation of this reason were not the only things to be found in Justice Blackmun's opinion. The opinion also included a long discussion about baseball, offering for the reader of the opinion a long list of great players throughout the game's history, quotations from *Casey at the Bat* and *Tinker to Evers to Chance,* and numerous other references to the game in poetry and literature and popular culture, as well as various other amusing but not especially relevant observations about baseball in American history.[29] And there is an obvious difference between this part of the opinion—much closer to the "chance remarks" identified by Professor Williams—and the statement of a broad reason that actually did support the outcome.[30] In this respect, the former

27. 346 U.S. 353 (1953).

28. 259 U.S. 200 (1922).

29. Justice Byron White, himself a professional football player in his earlier years, joined all of the majority opinion except for this part, believing that such material was inappropriate in a Supreme Court opinion.

30. An interesting contrast with Justice Blackmun's celebration of baseball history in *Flood v. Kuhn* is Chief Justice Rehnquist's opinion in *Texas v. Johnson,* 491 U.S. 397 (1989), in which the Chief Justice dissented from the majority's ruling that burning or otherwise desecrating the American flag was protected by the First Amendment. The Chief Justice also included a great deal of history, folklore, music, and poetry about the American flag, but his point was that the flag was unique and thus entitled to be treated differently from other targets of or vehicles for political protest. From that perspective, the history was for the Chief Justice necessary to *his* conclusion, and it would be harder to dismiss it as mere dicta.

can be considered to be "real" dicta and the latter just a broad statement of the holding. To this extent, therefore, there remains some substance to the distinction between holding and dicta, but it bears emphasizing that the distinction is fragile on both theoretical and practical grounds. In reality, all statements of a previous court in a case that are in any way different from the case now before a court will be dismissed by one side as dicta, just as those very statements will, as statements, be heavily relied upon by the side that those statements favor. The distinction between holding and dicta may help the subsequent court slightly in deciding how much weight to give to the previous statements, but it is far more likely that the judge will simply label as a holding those previous statements that she wishes to follow for other reasons and will similarly dismiss as dicta those previous statements that the judge, again for other reasons, has decided that she does not wish to follow.

9.4 The Declining Frequency of Opinions

From 1986 to 2008, the number of appeals filed in the United States courts of appeals increased by 110 percent, but in that same time the number of judges on those courts increased by only 15 percent. The inference to be drawn from these figures is that on a per-judge basis, the workload of a typical federal appellate judge would have been expected almost to double during this period. Federal appellate judges might compensate for this increase in caseload by working twice as hard, but that approach would be possible only on the assumption that these judges were not working very hard in 1986. If that were the case, then a doubled workload, while not pleasant, would have been manageable. But there is no indication that federal judges were slacking off in 1986, and thus the federal courts have been faced with the problem of how to deal with twice the number of cases in approximately the same number of judge-hours.

The solutions to this problem have been threefold, and all relate to how appellate courts, especially federal courts of appeals, have dealt with so-called easy cases. Recall from Chapter 2 the discussion of the selection effect, the phenomenon by which legally straightforward disputes tend not to be litigated and legally simple trial outcomes tend not to be appealed. If I have left my car in neutral and forgotten to set the parking brake and it rolls into and damages another car, it is almost certain that I or my insurance company will make an out-of-court payment and that will be the end of it. And if for some reason the matter winds up in court and I am compelled to pay damages, in the ordinary course the damages will be paid and no appeal will be taken. And as a consequence of the rarity of such legally easy matters winding up in appellate courts, the cases that do get appealed represent the atypical corner of the law, a corner disproportionately represented by hard cases—the cases in which both sides have some reason to believe that they can win.

The selection effect is important, but a large exception to its operation (although not the only exception) is the domain consisting of criminal appeals, petitions for habeas corpus, and complaints brought to remedy what are perceived to be unconstitutionally restrictive prison conditions. This category of cases—cases in which the plaintiffs or petitioners or appellants are ordinarily incarcerated throughout the pendency of the proceedings—represents an exception to the selection effect precisely because of the different incentives under which those who are incarcerated operate. So although for a typical corporate litigant the cost of an appeal might be substantial, in the typical criminal appeal the defendant has assigned counsel at no cost to the appellant, and often the very fact of filing an appeal has advantages for someone who is incarcerated. Having an appeal pending may provide such an individual the opportunity to work in the prison library, which is often a far better way to pass the day than many of the alternatives for those who are in prison. Moreover, the prisoner may have the opportunity to leave the facility when a petition or appeal is actually being heard. And perhaps most important is the sense of hope that having a pending appeal brings, even if the likelihood of success is very small. As a consequence of all of these factors, many criminal appeals and prisoner petitions are close to frivolous under existing law and would be the kind of cases that someone paying for a lawyer with his own money or who had valuable options for his own time would not pursue. But these dimensions do not apply to most criminal appeals and prisoner petitions, and as a result the typical appellate workload consists of an unexpectedly (from the perspective of the selection effect) large number of cases that do not present very much difficulty, many of which are criminal cases.

In dealing with these easy cases, federal appellate courts started in the 1970s to issue rulings from the bench immediately after (and occasionally *during*) the oral argument. After a brief whispered consultation or passing of notes, the court would simply announce in open court that the judgment below would be allowed to stand, and that would put an

185

end to the matter. Alternatively, the court might do the same thing by post-argument written order, and the large number of cases described in the *Federal Reporter* as being in the "Table" are typically of this fashion—easy cases whose resolution neither needs nor receives an explanation.

Most common, however, is the practice of accompanying such summary decisions by a brief opinion written solely for the benefit of the parties. As discussed at greater length in section 4.4, the court in one of these opinions will typically explain its ruling in an abbreviated way and will by court rule specify that such opinions are not to have precedential effect. And until a recent change in the Federal Rules of Appellate Procedure, the courts would often have a court rule prohibiting citation to such opinions.[31] In the modern era of electronic publication, such opinions are generally available, and indeed many are now published in the *Federal Appendix,* so it is more than a little misleading to persist in the common description of such opinions as "unpublished." But the important point is that the courts that issue such brief and nonprecedential opinions wish to make clear that they are intended for the benefit of the parties only.

This practice, which is also followed in many of the larger and busier state appellate courts, has been controversial,[32] with one federal appellate panel even briefly holding that it was unconstitutional to limit the precedential effect of its own opinions on the grounds that this was an

31. See Scott E. Gant, "Missing the Forest for a Tree: Unpublished Opinions and New Federal Rule of Appellate Procedure 32.1," 47 *B.C.L. Rev.* 705 (2006).

32. In addition to the references in section 4.4, see Bob Berring, "Unprecedented Precedent: Ruminations on the Meaning of it All," 5 *Green Bag 2nd* 245 (2002); Danny J. Boggs & Brian P. Brooks, "Unpublished Opinions and the Nature of Precedent," 4 *Green Bag 2nd* 17 (2001); Richard B. Cappalli, "The Common Law's Case against Non-Precedential Opinions," 76 *S. Cal. L. Rev.* 755 (2003); Jeffrey O. Cooper, "Citability and the Nature of Precedent in the Courts of Appeals: A Response to Dean Robel," 35 *Ind. L. Rev.* 423 (2002); Dunn G. Kessler & Thomas L. Hudson, "Losing Cites: A Rule's Evolution," 42 *Ariz. Att.* 10 (2006); Frank I. Michelman, "*Anastasoff* and Remembrance," 58 *Ark. L. Rev.* 555 (2005); Bradley Scott Shannon, "May Stare Decisis Be Abrogated by Rule?," 67 *Ohio St. L.J.* 645, 648–51 (2006); J. Thomas Sullivan, "Unpublished Opinions and No Citation Rules in the Trial Courts," 47 *Ariz. L. Rev.* 419 (2005); Symposium, Anastasoff, "Unpublished Opinions, and 'No Citation' Rules," 3 *J. App. Prac. & Process* 169 (2001).

impermissible abrogation of the common-law powers of the courts.[33] Insofar as it rested on the Constitution, the decision was an aberration, but the controversial aspect of the practice persists. Should courts issue opinions upon which others may not rely? Does the practice encourage courts to disregard the responsibility of taking opinion-writing seriously? Does writing an opinion for the particular case only lead appellate courts to slight the implications of a decision for future cases?

These are all fair questions, but now that we see just how rare it is for the legal system in general to give reasons for its decisions, the practice of providing abbreviated reasons for the benefit of the parties only does not seem nearly so aberrational. Even when we focus only on appellate courts, a part of the legal system in which opinion-writing and reason-giving is the norm, we now see that doing so has its costs as well as benefits. And the benefits are not restricted to matters of efficiency and practical necessity. Once we understand that giving reasons commits, even if not absolutely, the reason-giving court to certain outcomes in other and future cases, the court that wishes to tell the parties why it decided the way it did but does not wish to commit itself can use the noncitable or no-precedential-effect opinion as a way of respecting the parties' desire for reasons while retaining maximum flexibility. As long as there is no indication that judges are using the practice to justify laziness—and there is no evidence at all of that—then it is hard to find much fault with a practice likely to increase as the workload of the courts increases as well. Moreover, there is little indication that the workload crisis in the appellate courts is likely to subside, and as a result the practices of the non-opinion, the so-called unpublished opinion, the noncitable opinion, and the no-precedential-effect opinion are probably with us to stay. The discursive appellate judicial opinion will remain a central feature of the common law, but even in the common law, law is and will continue to be far more than just judicial opinions.

33. Anastasoff v. United States, 223 F.3d 898, 899–905 (8th Cir. 2000), *vacated as moot*, 235 F.3d 1054 (2000) (en banc). Compare Hart v. Massanari, 266 F.3d 1155, 1170–74 (9th Cir. 2001) (Kozinski, J.).

10

MAKING LAW WITH RULES AND STANDARDS

10.1 The Basic Distinction

In most American states, the law instructs family court judges to make determinations about child custody and visitation rights in such a way as to further the "best interests of the child."[1] The judge is expected to take testimony about the facts, hear argument, and then make the decision that in his relatively unconstrained discretion will promote the best interests of the child, as opposed to, say, the best interests of the parents or the best interests of society. Similarly indeterminate is the Fourth Amendment to the Constitution, which provides that "[t]he right of the people to be secure . . . against unreasonable searches and seizures . . . shall not be violated." Courts applying the Fourth Amendment thus find themselves with the task of deciding what constitutes a "search," what constitutes a "seizure," and especially which searches and seizures are to be considered "unreasonable."

By way of contrast to open-ended legal terms like "best interests" and "unreasonable," consider the specificity of the regulation under the Occupational Safety and Health Act requiring that on all construction sites with "[m]ore than 20" and "fewer than 200" employees there shall be no less than "[o]ne toilet seat and one urinal per 40 employees."[2] In much the same way, a Securities and Exchange Commission rule promulgated under the Securities Act of 1933 directs registrants to file "three copies of the complete registration statement" on "good quality, unglazed, white

1. E.g., Ariz. Rev. Stat. §25–403 (2006); Cal. Fam. Code §3011 (Parker's 2001); Mass. Gen. L., ch. 119, §23 (2003); Mich. Comp. Laws Ann. 722.23 (West 2001); Wash. Rev. Code §26.10.160 (3) (1994).
2. 29 CFR §1926.65, Table D-65.2 (2002).

paper no larger than 8½ x 11 inches in size."[3] And Article III of the Constitution mandates that "[n]o Person may be Convicted of treason unless on the Testimony of two Witnesses to the same Overt Act."[4]

The difference between the former set of provisions and the latter should be obvious. The first group, including language such as "best interests" and "unreasonable," is broad, vague, general, and imprecise. The second group, with its use of terms like "more than 20" and "unglazed, white paper," is detailed, specific, concrete, and determinate. Conventionally, the difference between the two groups is described as a difference between precise *rules,* such as "more than 20," and vague *standards,* such as "unreasonable." The distinction between rules and standards appears everywhere, and no discussion of legal reasoning would be complete without a careful consideration of this centrally important distinction.[5]

Although rules such as the ones set out above are highly precise, and although the standards just described are vague in the extreme, the difference between rules and standards is actually a matter of degree. Or, to put it differently, the extreme of vagueness—"the best interests of the child" or "unreasonable"—is close to the vagueness/standards end of a spectrum, and the extreme of precision—"two witnesses," "white paper no larger than 8½ x 11 inches in size"—is close to the precision/rules end. In between these extremes there is a continuum, on which some legal directives are more at the rules end and others closer to the standards end. "Drive prudently" is pretty clearly a standard, and "Speed Limit 55" is equally clearly a rule, but "Slow Down for Children," "Yield to Oncoming Traffic," and "Lights on at Dusk" are all somewhere in between. Lo-

3. Rules and Regulations Under the Securities Act of 1933, Rules 402(a) and 403(a), 17 CFR §§230.402(a), 230.403(a) (2002).

4. U.S. Const., art. III, §3, cl. 1.

5. Among the leading analyses are Clayton P. Gillette, "Rules, Standards, and Precautions in Payment Systems," 82 *Va. L. Rev.* 181 (1996); Joseph R. Grodin, "Are Rules Really Better than Standards?," 45 *Hastings L.J.* 569 (1994); Louis Kaplow, "Rules versus Standards: An Economic Analysis," 42 *Duke L.J.* 557 (1992); Duncan M. Kennedy, "Form and Substance in Private Law Adjudication," 89 *Harv. L. Rev.* 1685 (1976); Russell B. Korobkin, "Behavioral Analysis and Legal Form: Rules vs. Standards Revisited," 79 *Or. L. Rev.* 23 (2000). See also Colin Diver, "The Optimal Precision of Administrative Rules," 93 *Yale L.J.* 65 (1983). And an influential application of the distinction to some constitutional issues is Kathleen M. Sullivan, "The Supreme Court, 1991 Term—Foreword: The Justices of Rules and Standards," 106 *Harv. L. Rev.* 22 (1992).

cated more or less midway between the Constitution's requirements of two witnesses to convict for treason and the minimum age of thirty-five to serve as president, on the one hand, and the prohibitions of cruel and unusual punishments and unreasonable searches and seizures, on the other, are the Seventh Amendment's guarantee of a jury trial in "suits at common law" and Article I's prohibition on "bill[s] of attainder." Accordingly, rather than thinking of a distinction between rules and standards, it might be better to think of a location on the vagueness-precision continuum, and "How vague?" or "How precise?" may be far more useful questions to ask than whether some directive is more like a rule or more like a standard.

10.2 Rules, Standards, and the Question of Discretion

The rules-standards continuum is important for many reasons, but foremost among them is the way in which selecting the point on the spectrum can be a highly effective device for the management of discretion. Discretion is, of course, a central concern of the law. Under what circumstances will which officials be given the freedom to exercise their own judgment and make their own choices, and under what circumstances will that freedom be constrained or even mostly eliminated? When a judge is determining which custody decision is in the best interests of the child, for example, she might be faced with a choice between a wealthy mother who can provide the child with high-quality education, housing, recreation, and culture and a less wealthy father who appears to understand the child better than the mother. Under these circumstances, some judges would prefer the mother and others the father, but the basic idea of discretion is that neither of these decisions, given the "best interests of the child" standard, would be legally incorrect. People might criticize one or the other decision for being morally wrong, psychologically ignorant, or based on erroneous factual premises, and so it would not be correct to say that the two decisions are equally right. But it would be correct to say that the two decisions are equally *legally* right, and thus that either decision would, in the ordinary course of things, be upheld on appeal. By contrast, if instead of the "best interests of the child" standard there existed a rule stating that custody was always to go to the wealthier parent, then a judge would no longer have the discretion to award custody to the less wealthy but more caring parent, and we would expect that a decision to do so would be overturned on appeal as outside of the judge's discretion.[6]

This idea of discretion has many different labels. Sometimes it is called leeway, sometimes it is seen as a variety of deference, and in European Community law and European human rights law, and sometimes elsewhere, it is referred to in terms of a *margin of appreciation,* the latitude that member states are given in making their own judgments about matters ultimately controlled by European law.[7] But regardless of the label, the idea of discretion is that some institution with the power to control or review will let stand a multiplicity of quite different decisions, including some that the controlling institution might think wrong. Just as the "no vehicles in the park" rule may permit a judge discretion about whether to include or exclude bicycles, skateboards, and baby carriages, so does any other official with discretion have the power to make any one of a number of different decisions.

Analyzing the idea of discretion is not our primary goal here. But from the perspective of the devices of legal reasoning, it is important to appreciate that a common way of granting discretion is to couch the governing law or regulation as a standard. When Montana eliminated its numerical speed limit for a few years in favor of the vague requirement—a standard—that driving be "reasonable and prudent," it gave police officers the discretion to decide what speeds under what conditions were reasonable and prudent, and it similarly gave to traffic court judges much the same discretion.[8] The Montana Supreme Court subsequently ruled that "reasonable and prudent" was too much of a standard to support a statute that provided for criminal penalties, but the basic idea here

6. "Abuse of discretion" is a very common phrase, and indeed abuse of discretion is commonly a ground for judicial invalidation of an administrative decision. See generally Charles E. Koch, "Judicial Review of Agency Discretion," 54 *Geo. Wash. L. Rev.* 469 (1986). The phrase only makes sense, however, if it is assumed that an official or judge has considerable decisional freedom, or leeway, short of abuse.

7. See Douglas Lee Donoho, "Autonomy, Self-Governance, and the Margin of Appreciation: Developing a Jurisprudence of Diversity within Universal Human Rights," 15 *Emory Int'l L. Rev.* 391 (2001).

8. Mont. Code Ann. 61–8–303 (1996), *invalidated as vague in* State v. Stanko, 974 P.2d 1132 (1998). See Robert E. King & Cass R. Sunstein, "Doing without Speed Limits," 79 *B.U.L. Rev.* 155 (1999).

should be clear. When a directive is expressed in broad and vague terms, it grants discretion to and thus empowers not only those, like police officers, who are charged with enforcing the directive, but also those, like judges, whose task it is to interpret it.

Conversely, therefore, the use of directives at the rules end of the continuum can be understood as a device for constraining or withdrawing discretion. If a filing deadline for, say, the signatures necessary to put a candidate on the ballot is 5:00 P.M., the official who decides whether to accept the filing has far less discretion than would be the case if the requirement were only that the filing be "timely" or "sufficiently prior to the election as to permit the ballots to be printed."[9] Similarly, Article 35(1) of the Constitution of South Africa provides that

> [e]veryone who is arrested for allegedly committing an offence has the right . . . to be brought before a court as soon as reasonably possible, but not later than 48 hours after the arrest; or the end of the first court day after the expiry of the 48 hours; if the 48 hours expire outside the ordinary court hours or on a day which is not an ordinary court day.

This provision is, to put it mildly, vastly more precise than the American counterparts of mandating a "speedy" trial in the Sixth Amendment and "due process of law" in the Fifth, and this should come as no surprise. Police, prosecutorial, and even judicial abuses of power were widespread in the apartheid era, which ended with the 1995 enactment of the new South African constitution, and we can thus appreciate a reluctance at the time the constitution was drafted to grant discretion to mostly the same police officers, prosecutors, and judges who had been in power during apartheid. And even after the makeup of officialdom began to change, we can still understand the residual skepticism about official discretion in the criminal justice system. This skepticism about official dis-

---

9. See the unreported Vermont case of *Hunter v. Norman*, described in Frederick Schauer, "Formalism," 97 *Yale L.J.* 509 (1988).

Insofar as administrative officials or judges believe they have some flexibility in the matter, would they be more likely to be flexible with a "5 pm" deadline than with a "5:00 P.M." deadline, and more likely to be flexible with a "5:00 P.M." deadline than with a "5:08 P.M." deadline? Are drivers more likely to exceed a posted speed limit of 55 than one of 54 or 57? The very familiarity of 55—the conventionality of round numbers—will lead drivers to expect the normal leeway, but 54 cries out, "We mean it!"

cretion would naturally lead to the choice of rules over standards, and the highly specific provisions quoted above are the consequence of just this skeptical attitude.

Skepticism about discretion is not always a function of distrust of officials. Sometimes we worry about excess discretion because we are concerned with the lack of predictability that too much discretion will bring. If I want to know how fast I can drive, being told that I must drive reasonably and prudently will not answer my question, any more than being told that I must not enter into contracts in restraint of trade will help me to know how to comply with the antitrust laws. Indeed, this is one of the reasons why the Supreme Court has traditionally created so-called per se antitrust rules, under which schemes such as price-fixing, resale price maintenance, and tying arrangements were understood to violate the Sherman Act without regard to their economic effects in the particular case.[10] Some of these per se rules have been eliminated or weakened,[11] but the basic point persists that a per se rule is likely to give far more information about likely consequences of action than a less determinate standard.

Sometimes we wish to constrain discretion simply in the service of efficiency. A food inspection official at a border customs station can make a quick determination of whether a product being carried into the country is or is not "meat," but if the same official were empowered to determine on a case-by-case basis whether a product was "unsafe" or "unhealthy," he might have far less time to watch out for drug couriers and terrorists. Not only do precise rules require officials to spend less time on routine decisions, but they also allow the designers of decision-making environments to employ people with less skill or experience. Deciding whether a certain kind and level of factory waste dumped into a river is harmful to the environment probably requires an experienced environmental expert, but deciding whether the concentration level of a certain chemical is above or below a specified number can far more easily be entrusted to a less experienced and less well trained technician.

10. E.g., Times-Picayune Publishing Co. v. United States, 345 U.S. 594 (1953) (tying arrangements); United States v. Socony-Vacuum Oil Co., 310 U.S. 150 (1940) (price-fixing); Dr. Miles Medical Co. v. John D. Park & Sons, Inc., 220 U.S. 373 (1911) (per se rule against resale price maintenance).

11. See, most recently, Leegin Creative Leather Products, Inc. v. PSKS, Inc., 127 S. Ct. 2705 (2007), eliminating the per se rule for resale price maintenance.

Although these efficiency concerns are important, the use of directives toward the rules end of the rules-standards continuum will typically be a product of a determination that making individualized judgments in each case will produce too many unacceptable errors. That was the impetus behind the Federal Sentencing Guidelines,[12] a highly precise and constraining sentencing system, since softened somewhat by the Supreme Court,[13] intended to replace a regime of sentencing discretion that had generated wide disparities in sentencing for the same crimes. The use of vaguer directives at the standards end, conversely, will typically reflect a judgment that individualized or case-by-case determination is what is most important, preferring to endure the errors of individualized judgment to the errors that will come from the over- and underinclusiveness of rigid and precise rules. Indeed, something like this goal is what led the Supreme Court to make the Federal Sentencing Guidelines somewhat less rulelike. But there is no strategy that will be best in all contexts, and thus the lesson may be that the determination of how much officials should be allowed to look at the particular context of a particular instance—how much the official should be operating under a standard rather than a rule, or vice versa—will itself be a contextual determination.

10.3 Stability and Flexibility

It is true that location on the rules-standards continuum is an important way of allocating discretion between the issuer of the directive and those who must apply it, enforce it, or interpret it. But the difference between rules and standards is also a way of allocating decision-making between the present and the future. When a legislature, agency, or court sets forth a rule, it is making a decision *now* about what is to be done in the future. And when instead it moves toward the standards end of the continuum, it holds things open for the future and allows for a flexible approach to the problems of tomorrow.

Accommodating to a future that we can at best dimly perceive is a re-

12. Pub. L. No. 98–473, 98 Stat. 1837, 2017, *codified as* 18 U.S.C. §§ 3551–3673, 28 U.S.C. §§ 991–998 (2002). For an authoritative account of the original goals, see Stephen Breyer, "The Federal Sentencing Guidelines and the Key Compromises on Which They Rest," 17 *Hofstra L. Rev.* 1 (1988).

13. See Rita v. United States, 127 S. Ct. 2456 (2007); United States v. Booker, 543 U.S. 220 (2005).

curring problem in the law, and one that is almost certainly growing. With respect to rapid changes in electronic communications, for example, any attempt to write specific laws at this time is as destined to obsolescence as were those specific rules of only a generation ago that did not and could not have anticipated widespread cell phone usage, the development and dominance of the Internet, and a density of satellite-based communication technologies that makes a list of communications media limited to radio, television, and motion pictures seem archaic. So too in many other areas. Developments with respect to cloning, genetic modification, DNA identification, and much else will almost assuredly doom to failure, or at least to predictable obsolescence, any attempt to use the scientific knowledge of today as a basis for the categories of the rules that we expect to have effect in the future.

Just as the location of the rules-standards continuum can help to allocate discretion, therefore, so too can it allocate decision-making authority between the present and the future. A communications regulation that is drafted as a highly specific rule and that therefore inevitably draws on current and not future knowledge allocates power today to determine outcomes in and for an uncertain future, while a much vaguer standard—"medium of communication," for example—would let the future make decisions for itself, but at the cost of less guidance and less precision for the present.

The allocation of decision-making authority between the present and the future thus presents the fundamental tradeoff in the question about rules and standards. Highly specific directives—rules—will maximize certainty, constraint, and predictability, but they will do so at the cost of retaining the ability to achieve exactly the correct result in some currently unanticipated case or situation. And much vaguer directives—standards—will hold open the ability of some future decision-maker to make just the right decision (assuming for the sake of argument that that decision-maker will in fact do so), but at the cost of providing very little certainty, predictability, and decision-maker constraint.

There is, to repeat, no right solution to this inevitable tradeoff. Nor can it be said that one or another approach is more or less consistent with the values of the Rule of Law, because although some Rule of Law values are served by precise, predictable, and understandable rules, others are served by relatively open-ended standards that will allow judges and other official decision-makers the discretion to do justice in the individual case. But although there is no easy or consistent answer, understanding the way in which the rules-standards continuum is a valuable tool for allocating authority among officials, allocating decisions between the present and the future, and allocating our concern between predictability and individualized justice will enable participants in the legal system to understand one of the most important devices of legal and regulatory institutional design.

10.4 Rules and Standards in Judicial Opinions

The distinction between rules and standards is central to questions of legislative control and administrative discretion, and thus it is common to think of rules and standards in terms of the degree of specificity and vagueness in a constitutional provision, in a statute, and especially in an administrative regulation. But judicial opinions can also be sources of guidance, command, and authority, and as such they are equally susceptible to analysis in terms of the extent to which the guidance offered by a judicial opinion is more or less like a rule or a standard.

Consider, almost at one extreme of the rules-standards continuum, the Supreme Court's 1966 decision in *Miranda v. Arizona*,[14] in which the Court held that the Fifth Amendment (either directly, with respect to the federal government, or through the Fourteenth Amendment, as applied to the states) mandated that a confession or other statement by a suspect subject to custodial interrogation could be used against him only if the suspect had been warned of his constitutional right to remain silent as well as his right to a lawyer. Having reached this conclusion, the Court could have announced what was in effect a standard for the lower courts to follow in evaluating subsequent claims under *Miranda*. The Court could have said, for example, that a confession or other statement will be admissible if and only if it is found that the statement had been made *voluntarily*, and it could have made clear that the determination of voluntariness was a contextual judgment that should consider all of the circumstances in which the statement had been made. Or the Court could instead have said that statements taken *unfairly* or *unjustly* or *coercively* would be inadmissible, again leaving it to lower courts in particular cases to decide in light of the circumstances whether a statement was taken unfairly, unjustly, or coercively. Had the Court proceeded in this way, by the use of these kinds of flexible, contextual, and vague requirements, we

14. 384 U.S. 436 (1966).

would have said that the Court had elected to set forth a standard to be followed by the police and lower courts alike.

As is well known to viewers of television and movies, to say nothing of lawyers and judges, the Court did not proceed this way in *Miranda*. Instead, it told police officers more or less exactly what to say: "You have the right to remain silent. Anything you say can and will be used against you in a court of law. You have the right to a lawyer. If you cannot afford a lawyer, one will be appointed for you." If the police did not say something pretty much exactly like this prior to a custodial interrogation, the Court emphasized, any statements made by the suspect to the police would be excluded from the trial. And in deciding whether the police had acted consistently with the requirements of *Miranda* and the Fifth Amendment, lower courts were charged with determining little more than whether the police has uttered something very close to these magic words.

The Supreme Court's actual approach, therefore, was very much a rulelike one. The Court told the police and the lower courts exactly what they should do, and it is remarkable that police officers now essentially read from a Supreme Court opinion when they are interrogating a suspect. The words on a so-called *Miranda card,* the text that police officers carry with them and read aloud to those they have apprehended, are almost word-for-word taken from the Supreme Court's opinion. And in so laying down exactly what police offers should do, the Court acted very much like a legislature or highway department deciding that drivers should drive no faster than a posted numerical speed limit, rather than telling drivers that they should simply drive prudently or carefully or reasonably.

It is controversial whether courts should proceed as the Supreme Court did in *Miranda,* or as the Court did in *Roe v. Wade*[15] when it set forth the precise trimester approach to the restrictions that states might permissibly place on the right of a woman to an abortion. For some critics, laying down detailed rules is for a legislature, and a court exceeds its authority and goes beyond the particular competence of a *court* when it does things that look legislative.[16] But this criticism seems odd, at least if

15. 410 U.S. 113 (1973).

16. See Robert F. Nagel, "The Formulaic Constitution," 84 *Mich. L. Rev.* 165 (1985). See also Akhil Reed Amar, "The Supreme Court, 1999 Term—Foreword: The Document and the Doctrine," 114 *Harv. L. Rev.* 26 (2000).

we assume that other courts, policymakers, and ordinary people should be guided by what the courts have done.[17] If we think that courts are only in the business of making decisions for the parties, then perhaps it is not so bad that others cannot be guided by those decisions. But especially for the Supreme Court, which these days decides so few cases, such a view of the Court's role seems as inefficient as it is unrealistic. There are rules that are addressed to courts and purport to tell courts how to decide cases, and there are rules that are addressed to the citizens and officials who wish simply to know what to *do*,[18] and judicial opinions that resemble the directives at the rules end of the rules-standards continuum are often quite plausibly focused on providing a source of guidance for citizens and nonjudicial officials alike. Especially where a judicial opinion deals with conduct that is repeated daily by numerous individuals, rulelike precision brings the virtue of providing reasonable advice to large numbers of people, and the advantages of doing so may often outweigh the disadvantages that come from relinquishing standardlike flexibility.[19]

Joining those who criticize courts when they issue rulelike directives are others who have argued that appellate courts should decide only "one case at a time,"[20] often insisting that this is what courts do best or that this is the only thing that courts legitimately ought to do.[21] The question of legitimacy may be somewhat remote from issues about legal reasoning and the rules-standards continuum, but not so for the other dimensions of the argument for deciding one case at a time—for deciding a particular controversy and not setting forth broad prescriptions for deciding others. And one argument for this approach is that making broad decisions—making decisions that in effect decide cases not before the

17. See Henry P. Monaghan, "The Supreme Court, 1974 Term—Foreword: Constitutional Common Law," 89 *Harv. L. Rev.* 1, 20–21 (1975); Frederick Schauer, "Opinions as Rules," 62 *U. Chi. L. Rev.* 1455 (1995).

18. See Stephen McG. Bundy & Einer Elhauge, "Knowledge about Legal Sanctions," 92 *Mich. L. Rev.* 261 (1993); Meir Dan-Cohen, "Decision Rules and Conduct Rules: On Acoustic Separation in Criminal Law," 97 *Harv. L. Rev.* 625 (1984).

19. See Frederick Schauer, "Abandoning the Guidance Function: *Morse v. Frederick*," 2006 *Sup. Ct. Rev.* 205.

20. See Cass R. Sunstein, *One Case at a Time: Judicial Minimalism on the Supreme Court* (1999).

21. See Edward A. Hartnett, "A Matter of Judgment, Not a Matter of Opinion," 74 *N.Y.U. L. Rev.* 123 (1999).

court—requires fact-finding capabilities that are beyond what we can expect in the appellate process. When a court decides an issue broadly—when it decides that *all* custodial interrogations by *all* police officers of *all* suspects under *all* circumstances must be preceded by a warning of the kind the Supreme Court delineated in *Miranda*—it is in effect deciding a whole bunch of cases, but in the process it is required to guess about what those other cases might look like. It is likely, for example, to assume that many of these other cases will look like the case before it, an assumption consistent with what psychologists refer to as *availability*[22]—the belief that that which is most cognitively accessible to us is representative of some larger class of acts or events or cases. But often the facts on which an appellate court must focus are not at all representative, and to that extent making broad rulings in the context of concrete cases may not be the best way to lay down broad principles of law.[23]

Once again, there is no right or wrong answer to the question of whether appellate courts should lay down broad rules in the process of deciding cases or whether instead they should focus on producing the best answer for the case at hand, leaving other cases for other occasions and other decision-makers. The decision about how much to decide, however, and thus of how much law to make—it is far too late in the day to think that courts do not make law—is much like the distinction between rules and standards. It involves the allocation of decision-making authority among potential decision-makers; it involves the assignment of decision-making responsibility between the certain present and the uncertain future; and it involves the pervasive tension between the advantages of flexibility and the competing virtue of letting citizens, officials, lawyers, and other courts know what the law is, even if the law they

22. The original insight is in Amos Tversky & Daniel Kahneman, "Judgment under Uncertainty: Heuristics and Biases," 185 *Science* 1124, 1127 (1974), and there is now a voluminous literature. See, e.g., *Heuristics and Biases: The Psychology of Intuitive Judgment* (Thomas Gilovich, Dale Griffin, & Daniel Kahneman eds., 2002); Scott Plous, *The Psychology of Judgment and Decision Making* (1993); John S. Carroll, "The Effect of Imagining an Event on Expectations for the Event: An Interpretation in Terms of the Availability Heuristic," 14 *J. Exp. Soc. Psych.* 88 (1978).

23. See Neil Devins & Alan Meese, "Judicial Review and Nongeneralizable Cases," 32 *Fla. St. L. Rev.* 323 (2005); Jeffrey J. Rachlinski, "Bottom-Up versus Top-Down Lawmaking," 73 *U. Chi. L. Rev.* 933 (2006); Frederick Schauer, "Do Cases Make Bad Law?," 73 *U. Chi. L. Rev.* 883 (2006).

know may not always be the best law that could be developed for every individual dispute and every particular act.

10.5 On the Relation between Breadth and Vagueness

We commenced this chapter by describing the conventional distinction between precise rules and vague (or indeterminate) standards, and we have moved gradually to the question of whether courts should issue broad rulings or narrow ones. This is the appropriate place to point out, therefore, that the scale of broad to narrow has little to do with the scale of precise to vague.

We can start with a simple example. Take the category of insects. It is a huge category. In the first place, there are lots of insects. Trillions of them. Lots more than there are mammals, fish, and birds combined. And there are lots of *kinds* of insects. Again, there are far more species of insects than of all the other members of the animal kingdom put together. Yet although there are lots of insects and lots of kinds of insects, the category of insects is very determinate, and so is the word "insect." Like any other word, it is not perfectly determinate, and there are certainly contexts in which we can imagine struggling with whether a toy insect or a dead insect is really an insect, just as we would struggle with whether a bicycle or a skateboard is a vehicle for the purpose of the "no vehicles in the park" rule. Yet for the category of insects, the proportion of borderline cases is very small. It is not nonexistent, but it is much smaller compared to the class of nonborderline cases than would be the case for vehicles, say, or for schools, or, to take an example made famous by the philosopher Ludwig Wittgenstein, for games.[24] What the example of in-

---

24. "Someone says to me: 'Shew the children a game.' I teach them gaming with dice, and the other says 'I didn't mean that sort of game.'" Ludwig Wittgenstein, *Philosophical Investigations* 33 (G. E. M. Anscombe trans., 3d ed., 1958). The example has been used and misused countless times and has spawned a voluminous literature, but the basic idea is that the word "game," as used in the language, refers to many different things that may have what is called a *family resemblance* among them. That is, there is no list of necessary and sufficient features that all proper applications of the word "game" share. Even so, however, there are clear cases of games—baseball, for example, or chess—and there are marginal cases— playing the stock market, perhaps—and the inability to specify the necessary and sufficient conditions for what makes the clear cases clear does not mean that such clear cases do not exist.

sects teaches us, therefore, is that broad categories can be extremely precise. And of course narrow categories can be vague. Even though there are far fewer cases of heroism than there are insects, and though most people would agree that heroism is quite rare, the term itself is highly vague, and there would be little agreement about what counts as a heroic act and what does not.

In law, the distinction between the precise and the vague is largely a question about discretion, a question about flexibility, and a question about the competing aims of predictability and individualized justice. And the distinction between the broad and the narrow is largely a question about how much courts or legislators or other rulemakers should do when they are deciding a case or laying down a rule. Both the distinction between the broad and the narrow and the distinction between the precise and the vague—and both, of course, are questions about a place on a continuum and not simply about one thing or another—are important, but they are not the same. A court concerned with not deciding too much but also concerned with giving guidance might, for example, make a decision containing a precise but narrow rule. The Supreme Court might still have specified, as in *Miranda,* close to the exact words that a warning would have to contain, but might have limited, as it did not, the cases to which those words would have to be given to a narrow class of police interrogations or to a narrow class of crimes. In such case, it would have selected an approach to rulemaking that was on the rules end of the rules-standards continuum but on the narrow end of the broad-narrow one. And in doing so, it would have done something quite different from what *was* done in *Miranda,* where the Court set forth a rule that was, like the class of insects, both broad and precise.

Conversely, the Court in a different hypothetical variation on the real *Miranda* case might have decided that flexibility was more important than guidance. It might have decided, for example, that it could not in 1966 predict all of the future possibilities for police conduct and misconduct, or that the case it had before it—an actual controversy involving the state of Arizona and a particular individual named Ernesto Miranda in the context of a particular criminal case with particular facts—did not provide sufficient information for the Court to be making broad rules for the future. It might, therefore, have chosen to prefer something more like a standard than a rule—confessions would be inadmissible if they were "uninformed," for example. But it would still have had to make a choice about the scope of application of that standard. It might again have decided that the "informed" (or "uninformed") standard would apply to all custodial interrogations, or it might have concluded that it would be best to restrict its application to a much narrower class of police actions. At times the arguments for proceeding by way of a standard will be similar to those for deciding narrowly rather than broadly—both are ways of leaving some determinations for the future, for example—but it is still the case that the question of the scope of a rule or a ruling is different from the question of its precision.

Entire books could be written about the techniques of rulemaking,[25] and indeed some of the manuals on legislative drafting come close to having this aim. But rulemaking is not just for legislatures, and once we recognize that courts as well as legislatures make law and that courts as well as administrative agencies make rules, we can begin to think of judicial rulemaking as a task worthy of far closer attention than it has received to date.

25. Surprisingly, and perhaps disturbingly, very few such books have in fact been written. Maybe it is thought that such things are self-evident, but they are not. And maybe it is thought that the techniques for rulemaking can be picked up from other places, but again there is quite a bit of evidence to the contrary.

11

LAW AND FACT

11.1 On the Idea of a Fact

Most discussions of legal reasoning and legal argument, including much of this book, tend to focus a great deal on law and not very much on facts. The standard treatments assume that the interesting issues in *Donoghue v. Stevenson*[1] are about whether Mrs. Donohue ought to be able to recover against the ginger beer bottler despite the absence of privity, and mostly ignore the question of whether it really was a decomposed snail that came out of the bottle or just how ill, if at all, the sight of the snail actually made her. We know after *Raffles v. Wichelhaus*[2] that when both of two contracting parties are fundamentally mistaken about the object of the contract, there is no contract at all, but how do we know that there were two ships named *Peerless,* and how do we know that each of the parties really was mistaken? *R. v. Dudley & Stephens*[3] is a staple of criminal law classes, but just how hungry really were the survivors, and just how close to death was the cabin boy before he was killed for the alleged survival of the others? And although the Supreme Court in *Brown v. Board of Education*[4] appeared to base its conclusion on the proposition that racially separate but physically equivalent educational facilities impaired the education of black children, how did the Court obtain that information, and was the information it obtained correct?

All of these questions are *questions of fact:* Was it a decomposed

1. [1932] A.C. 562 (H.L.).
2. 2 H. & C. 906, 159 Eng. Rep. 375 (Ex. 1864).
3. 14 Q.B.D. 273 (1994). For an engaging and important account, see A. W. B. Simpson, *Cannibalism and the Common Law* (1984).
4. 347 U.S. 483 (1954).

snail? Were there two ships named *Peerless,* or only one, or maybe even three? How close to death were the shipwrecked sailors? Do black children get a worse education in an all-black, legally segregated school whose physical facilities and teacher training are the same as those in the all-white schools? These questions are traditionally contrasted with *questions of law:* Is a manufacturer (or bottler) directly liable to the consumer when there is a decomposed snail in a ginger beer bottle? Is there a contract when the contracting parties have different beliefs about what they are contracting for? Is dire necessity a defense to a charge of murder? Does a separate but nominally equal racially segregated school system violate the Fourteenth Amendment? The typical legal decision involves an initial assessment of what happened—the question of fact—and then moves on to a determination of what the law should *do* in light of what has happened—the question of law.

The distinction between questions of law and questions of fact is not without difficulty. A controversy about how to explain the difference between law and fact has generated a substantial body of commentary,[5] even including the view that the distinction is entirely illusory.[6] Much of the debate centers on the implications of the way in which, conventionally, the jury (or a judge explicitly serving as the trier of fact) is charged with determining the facts, while the judge has the job of interpreting and (perhaps) applying the law. In reality, however, juries make many decisions that partly involve determinations of law, such as whether someone's actions were "reasonable" or whether the defendant's actions "caused" the plaintiff's injury. Conversely, judges commonly make factual determinations when they are reaching legal conclusions, sometimes just by virtue of having to make the factual determination that some rule or precedent is or is not the law, and sometimes because, especially with respect to constitutional issues, making determinations about facts is part of what we want judges to do in order to ensure that constitutional values are preserved.[7]

5. See, e.g., Richard D. Friedman, "Standards of Persuasion and the Distinction between Fact and Law," 86 *Nw. U.L. Rev.* 916 (1992); Henry P. Monaghan, "Constitutional Fact Review," 85 *Colum. L. Rev.* 229 (1985); Stephen A. Weiner, "The Civil Jury and the Law-Fact Distinction," 54 *Cal. L. Rev.* 1867 (1966).

6. Ronald J. Allen & Michael S. Pardo, "The Myth of the Law-Fact Distinction," 97 *Nw. U.L. Rev.* 1769 (2003).

7. See David Faigman, "'Normative Constitutional Fact-Finding': Exploring the Empirical Component of Constitutional Interpretation," 139 *U. Pa. L. Rev.*

Yet although the fact-law distinction in law can become muddied quite quickly, the confusion does not always stem from the lack of a fundamental distinction between fact and law, which becomes far less mysterious if we just think of it as a variation on the venerable distinctions between fact and value, is and ought, and description and prescription.[8] Rather, the confusion comes from the way in which the law has traditionally insisted that facts are for juries and the law is for judges, when in reality many of the things that juries do by way of law application involve making legal determinations, and many of the things that judges do involve making factual ones. If we accept that the distinction between law and fact does not and could not track the distinction between what judges do and what juries do, then we need not reject the basic distinction between what happened and what someone ought to do about it in order to recognize that making factual determinations is a central part of reasoning and argument at all stages of the legal system.

Thus, although legal decisions, even those made by judges and even those made in appellate courts, typically involve both factual and legal elements, discussions of legal reasoning have traditionally focused overwhelmingly on the latter only.[9] They have assumed that thinking about factual questions is for the law of evidence or that making factual determinations is not really a matter of legal reasoning at all. But given that questions of law almost always turn on determinations of fact, and given that determinations of fact are in numerous ways structured by legal rules and by characteristic ways of reasoning, to exclude questions of fact from the topic of legal reasoning seems peculiar. In this chapter, therefore, we shall take up the question of questions of fact and examine the

---

541 (1991); Monaghan, *supra* note 5; Note, "Corralling Constitutional Fact: De Novo Fact Review in the Federal Courts," 50 *Duke L.J.* 1427 (2001).

8. There are, of course, controversies about and challenges to these venerable distinctions as well, some but not all of which come from perspectives loosely labeled as "postmodern." And it is true that many purported descriptions have a normative element to them, with values being smuggled in under the cover of purported neutral description. Nevertheless, it is sufficiently implausible to insist that there is no difference between "John fired a gun whose bullet entered Mary's heart and caused her death" and "John ought to go to prison for murdering Mary" that allegedly sophisticated challenges to any of the distinctions in the text need not detain us any further here.

9. A noteworthy exception by a prominent Legal Realist is Jerome Frank, *Facts on Trial: Myth and Reality in American Justice* (1949).

reasoning processes that legal decision-makers use to determine in the first instance simply what happened.

11.2 Determining Facts at Trial—The Law of Evidence and Its Critics

In the normal course of things, determining what happened is for the trial court. Did the defendant shoot her husband? Was that the testator's authentic signature at the bottom of a document that appears to be a will? What kind of damage did the overflowing water cause in *Rylands v. Fletcher*,[10] and how much would it cost the plaintiff to repair it? These issues are normally determined at trial and not on appeal, and they are determined by the person or institution we call the "trier of fact." The classic trier of fact in common-law legal systems[11] is the jury, although it turns out that in many criminal cases and most civil ones the determination of what happened is made by the presiding judge.

If we set aside the law for a moment, we can appreciate the fact that there are multiple ways of finding out something about the world. Outside of the legal system, for example, a common method of determining what happened in the past is to go out and investigate, just as police detectives do when a crime has been committed, and just as congressional investigators do when Congress initiates an inquiry into the cause of a disaster such as the explosion of the *Challenger* space shuttle or the nuclear leaks at Three Mile Island. Investigation itself takes many forms, but all share the idea that the investigators go out into the field, ask questions, poke around, interview witnesses, examine physical evidence, and then make the decision themselves.

In other contexts, particularly in science, the way to find out about something is to conduct an experiment. Sometimes the experiment will be conducted in a laboratory, sometimes it will involve some variation on giving some people a drug and others a placebo, and sometimes scientists and others can analyze a natural experiment, the situation in which the world rather than the scientist creates the conditions in which almost ev-

10. 3 L.R.E. & I. App. 330 (H.L. 1868).
11. In general there are no juries in civil-law systems, and judges both determine the facts and apply the law. In some civil-law systems, however, judges will occasionally try cases, especially criminal cases, in conjunction with several laypeople typically known as "assessors."

erything is the same except for some consequence or symptom whose cause we wish to identify. And empirical social scientists often find out about the world by collecting and analyzing data, often in the large computerized arrays of information called data sets. They run regressions using different variables, typically in an attempt to locate the causes and consequences of various social phenomena.

There are, to be sure, other forms of discovering facts of the world, but cataloging all of them here would serve no purpose. The point of mentioning of few of the more widespread fact-finding methods, however, is to highlight the fact that the law's characteristic way of determining what happened is hardly universal and hardly the only way of finding out about things, even the things that the law would need to know for its own purposes. Indeed, the fact-finding methods that we associate with the law in the common-law world—adversarial trials in which whatever information the judge or jury has on which to base its decision is supplied by the parties—are themselves hardly universal. In France, for example, judges play an active role in managing and conducting the more serious criminal investigations,[12] and variations of this approach are seen in many other civil-law countries. In England prior to the fifteenth century, jurors were largely self-informing, expected to rely in part on their personal knowledge of the litigants, in part on their personal knowledge of the situation, and in part on what they could find out by their own investigations.[13] The idea that a jury—or the judge serving as the trier of fact—should be largely ignorant of the specific litigants and the specific facts prior to the trial itself is a relatively modern invention and hardly a universal one. But even apart from the question of the jury's prior knowledge, the view that the best way to make a factual determination is to allocate to the parties all of the burden of coming forth with evidence and then to have a group of nonexperts evaluate that evidence in an adversary mode, rather than, say, an investigative or collaborative one, and rather than relying on people who might have relevant expertise, is hardly self-evident. Nor is the common law's adversary method self-

---

12. An intriguing and instructive narrative is Bron McKillop, "Anatomy of a French Murder Case," 45 *Am. J. Comp. L.* 527 (1997).

13. See Sanjeev Anand, "The Origins, Early History and Evolution of the English Criminal Trial Jury," 43 *Alberta L. Rev.* 407 (2005); Thomas A. Green, "A Retrospective on the Criminal Trial Jury, 1200–1800," *in Twelve Good Men and True* 358 (J. S. Cockburn & Thomas A. Green eds., 1988).

evidently wrong, and indeed it has its counterparts in other decision-making environments. The Roman Catholic Church, after all, has institutionalized the concept of the devil's advocate as a way of ensuring that the initial impression of a candidate's sainthood is not accepted as final before hearing the best argument against the proposed saint's actually having been one. Thus, the determination of facts in most common-law countries is premised on the belief that adversarial procedures in which the parties have the primary responsibility for coming forth with evidence are valuable ways of determining the truth, even if they are not the only ones. Just as one argument for a system of freedom of speech is based on the assumption that a good way of finding out the truth is through the clash of opposing ideas, the adversarial process relies on similar assumptions.[14] Let the parties bring forward their evidence, let that evidence be subject to the particular form of scrutiny we call cross-examination, and then let the truth, or at least the closest approximation of it we can achieve, emerge. Or so we believe.

This is not the place to evaluate the adversary system as a method of discovering the truth, whether for the Catholic Church, for public deliberation, or for the law. But contrasting the law's methods of fact-finding with others that are or have been used in other contexts or other countries does put the law's method of fact-finding in proper perspective. Moreover, contrasting the adversary system of fact-finding with others reminds us that that jurors or even judges are not only at the mercy of the parties in terms of what evidence they can consider, but are also prone to a host of cognitive failures—bias, inattention, and countless others—that affect most human decision-makers. Indeed, a large body of social science research, mostly by psychologists, concentrates not only on how jurors—and judges, for that matter—might be subject to many of the same cognitive failures that we observe in all decision-makers,[15] but also on the

14. This is not necessarily to say that adversarial epistemology is a particularly reliable way of determining the truth, whether in public debate (see Frederick Schauer, *Free Speech: A Philosophical Enquiry* 15–34 [1982]) or even in the courtroom (see Frank, *supra* note 9, at 80–81; Leon Green, *Judge and Jury* [1930]; David Luban, *Lawyers and Justice* 68–92 [1988]; John H. Langbein, "The German Advantage in Civil Procedure," 52 *U. Chi. L. Rev.* 823 [1985]).

15. A large, growing, and highly valuable body of research focuses on the cognitive failings of juries, of judges as fact-finders, and of judges as interpreters and appliers of law. As to juries, for which the literature is by far the largest, see, e.g., Dennis J. Devine et al., "Deliberation Quality: A Preliminary Examination in

fact that even some of the law's characteristic methods are potentially more flawed than the law has traditionally assumed. Eyewitness testimony, for example, is far less reliable than many people have traditionally thought,[16] and even reliable scientific methods such as DNA identification are subject to the imperfections of the human beings whose job it is to administer the tests and analyze the results.[17]

Legal fact-finding is not only subject to the myriad problems of an adversarial approach to locating the truth, but is also framed by the odd set of rules that are called the law of evidence. Space does not permit providing here even a brief summary of the substance of evidence law, but it is nevertheless important to highlight its peculiar assumptions. In part because of the special needs of the adversary system, in part because of a

---

Criminal Juries," 4 *J. Empirical Legal Stud.* 273 (2007); R. Hastie, D. A. Schadke, & J. W. Payne, "A Study of Juror and Jury Judgments in Civil Cases: Deciding Liability for Punitive Damages," 22 *L. & Human Behavior* 287 (1998); R. J. MacCoun & N. L. Kerr, "Asymmetric Influence in Mock Jury Deliberations: Jurors' Bias for Leniency," 54 *J. Personality & Social Psych.* 21 (1988). On judges as fact-finders, see Paul H. Robinson & Barbara A. Spellman, "Sentencing Decisions: Matching the Decisionmaker to the Decision Nature," 105 *Colum. L. Rev.* 1124 (2005); Barbara A. Spellman, "On the Supposed Expertise of Judges in Evaluating Evidence," 155 *U. Penn. L. Rev. PENNumbra* (2006); Andrew J. Wistrich, Chris Guthrie, & Jeffrey J. Rachlinski, "Can Judges Ignore Inadmissible Information? The Difficulty of Deliberately Disregarding," 153 *U. Pa. L. Rev.* 1251 (2005). On judges and the law, see Chris Guthrie, Jeffrey J. Rachlinski, & Andrew J. Wistrich, "Inside the Judicial Mind," 86 *Cornell L. Rev.* 777 (2001); Frederick Schauer, "Do Cases Make Bad Law?," 73 *U. Chi. L. Rev.* 883 (2006); Dan Simon, "A Third View of the Black Box: Cognitive Coherence in Legal Decision Making," 71 *U. Chi. L. Rev.* 511 (2004); Dan Simon, "Freedom and Constraint in Adjudication: A Look Through the Lens of Cognitive Psychology," 67 *Brooklyn L. Rev.* 1097 (2002); Dan Simon, "A Psychological Model of Judicial Reasoning," 30 *Rutg. L.J.* 1 (1998).

16. See, e.g., Elizabeth F. Loftus & James Doyle, *Eyewitness Testimony: Civil and Criminal* (3d ed., 1997); Elizabeth F. Loftus & Edith Green, "Warning: Even Memory for Faces May Be Contagious," 4 *L. & Human Behavior* 323 (1980); Gary L. Wells & Elizabeth F. Loftus, "The Malleability of Eyewitness Confidence: Co-Witness and Perseverance Effects," 79 *J. Applied Psych.* 714 (1994).

17. See, e.g., Brandon L. Garrett, "Judging Innocence," 108 *Colum. L. Rev.* 55, 63, 84 n.109 (2008); Edward J. Imwinkelried, "The Debate in the DNA Cases over the Foundation for the Admission of Scientific Evidence: The Importance of Human Error as a Cause of Forensic Misanalysis," 69 *Wash. U.L.Q.* 19 (1991); William C. Thompson & Simon Ford, "DNA Typing: Acceptance and Weight of the New Genetic Identification Tests," 75 *Va. L. Rev.* 45, 66–67 (1989).

substantive concern for the rights of criminal defendants, and in very large part because finding the facts has traditionally been the province of a jury with no specialized training either in law or in factual analysis, a body of law developed whose principal function has been to keep even relevant evidence away from a frequently distrusted jury. For fear that jurors would make too much of some evidence and too little of other, the law of evidence has a host of exclusionary rules that often seem strange. Although we often give some weight to what people hear other people say, for example, the law has traditionally prevented jurors from taking such hearsay evidence into account. And despite the fact that we commonly think that what someone has done in the past might help us determine whether they have done something similar now, much of this evidence of "bad character," "prior bad acts," or even previous convictions for the same type of crime is excluded at the typical trial.

The exclusionary rules of the law of evidence generated no small amount of ire in our old friend Jeremy Bentham, who would pretty much have eliminated all of the rules of evidence in favor of what he called the "natural" (as opposed to "technical") system, which has now come to be known as a system of Free Proof.[18] Under a natural or Free Proof approach, one that Bentham thought not that different from what ordinary people do in their daily lives, evidence is not excluded at the outset by rules that exclude entire categories of evidence, such as hearsay and prior criminal convictions. Rather, virtually all relevant evidence is admitted and then sifted, weighed, and evaluated in light of other evidence in order to give each piece of evidence the weight to which it is entitled. Some evidence will seem unreliable and will be discarded, while other pieces of evidence will be given a bit of weight but discounted. The basic point is that when we are trying to find out what happened, we do not set up a system that will keep potentially relevant evidence from our fact-finding process just because it fits some category of imperfect evidence.

In objecting to a system of factual determination largely structured around a series of what Bentham thought were artificial and categorical exclusions, Bentham was joined then, and even more so since, by many others, including not a few philosophers whose concern is epistemology.[19] And in important respects Bentham and his allies have been carry-

18. Jeremy Bentham, *Rationale of Judicial Evidence* (1827).
19. E.g., Alvin I. Goldman, *Knowledge in a Social World* (1992); Larry Laudan, *Truth, Error, and the Criminal Law: An Essay in Legal Epistemology*

ing the day. Especially with the decline in the importance of the jury—juries have for all practical purposes disappeared throughout the common-law world in civil cases, except in the United States, where the Seventh Amendment and its state constitutional counterparts have rescued the civil jury from oblivion—the formal rules of evidence have been consistently relaxed. Judges sitting without juries often treat the rules of evidence casually and appear to have little hesitancy in announcing that because there is no jury, most of the exclusionary rules of evidence will simply be ignored.[20] Moreover, exclusionary rules such as the hearsay rule and the original documents rule (often called the "best evidence" rule) are increasingly subject to a host of exceptions, and various other exclusionary rules have been officially eliminated or unofficially ignored. We may still be a long way from Bentham's preferred system of Free Proof, but we are also a long way from the highly rule-based and largely exclusionary system that generated Bentham's anger in the first place.[21]

The somewhat peculiar institution of the adversary system, the even more peculiar institution of the jury, and the especially peculiar idea of rigid exclusionary rules of evidence are all of a piece with the larger themes of this book. Law does things differently, for better or for worse, and the difference between how law determines the facts of a case and how other decision-makers find out about the world around them is consistent with law's use of the unusual devices that we have considered earlier, such as stare decisis and a commitment to the sometimes suboptimal control of rules. As with some of the other tools of legal reasoning, law's methods of fact-finding are not totally unique to law. Adversary determinations can be seen in other decision-making environments, as can even exclusionary evidentiary rules. But the fact that law's methods are not unique to law does not mean that law is no different from anything else,

---

(2006); Susan Haack, "Epistemology Legalized: Or, Truth, Justice, and the American Way," 49 *Am. J. Jurisp.* 43 (2004).

20. See Frederick Schauer, "On the Supposed Jury-Dependence of Evidence Law," 155 *U. Pa. L. Rev.* 165 (2006).

21. This is especially obvious once we realize that Bentham allocated a large part of his considerable capacity for outrage to the rules of competency—the rules that made it impossible for most women, most minors, most convicted felons, and most of the litigants themselves to be witnesses at trial. In large part the rules of competency have been eliminated in the United States, and although there are still things to which witnesses may not testify, there are few blanket exclusions based on a witness's status or personal characteristics.

and thus it should come as no surprise that when it comes to facts as well as to law, it is a mistake to fail to recognize how decision-making within the legal system is, at the very least, a little bit different.

Law's commitment to its own methods of factual determination is reflected even in the structure of the legal system's decision-making about questions of law. Because law is committed to the distinction between the trier of fact and the determiner of law, findings of fact are typically separated from conclusions of law when the same trial judge takes on both tasks. More importantly, findings of fact are typically, except in the most egregious of instances, treated as sacrosanct in the appellate process. It is only slight hyperbole to say that if a jury were to find that the moon was made of green cheese, an appellate court ruling on a legal question about the moon or about green cheese would be expected to take the jury's false conclusion as true. We have seen throughout this book that questions of jurisdiction in the broad sense—what is important is not only what is decided but who has the authority to decide it—are a ubiquitous feature of legal analysis. And jurisdiction in this broad sense has much to do with determining the facts. It is the job of a jury, or the trial judge acting as the trier of fact, to determine the facts. Even if the facts which that trier of fact has found seem wrong to an appellate court, the fact-finder's seemingly erroneous factual conclusions must nevertheless be taken as true. This will seem odd at times, but it may be part of a larger and pervasive characteristic of law itself. What makes law different is that legal decision-making, whether about law or about fact, differs from the simple mandate to judges and other legal decision-makers that they simply "do the right thing." Just as rule-based and precedent-based decision-making often requires legal decision-makers to do something other than the right thing, the strong obligation to accept the fact-finder's factual finding sometimes produces the same kind of suboptimality. To some this may be a bad thing, but to others it is simply part of law's commitment to achieve the greatest good in the aggregate, even if that requires giving up the aspiration to do what particular decision-makers think is the right thing in particular cases.

11.3 Facts and the Appellate Process

At the beginning of this chapter we made reference to *Brown v. Board of Education* and the way in which the Supreme Court in that case relied on psychological studies showing that segregated African-American children suffered educationally from their exclusion from the schools attended by whites. This aspect of *Brown* generated much controversy, and for several reasons.[22] First, it was not clear that the conclusions of the studies were necessarily correct. Other psychologists had come to different conclusions, and there was a worry about whether litigation was the best way to resolve disputed questions of scientific fact.

More importantly, the Supreme Court appeared to make its *own* evaluation of the question rather than simply relying on the trial court's resolution of the factual issues. It may be, as we discussed in the previous section, that litigation and the adversary system are not the best ways to resolve some or all factual questions, but that is the way of the law, and it has been for centuries. Not so, however, for appellate courts, and for just as many centuries the assumption has been that determining the facts is for the trial court and evaluating the trial court's handling of the law is for appellate courts. If, barring blatant error or prejudice, the trial court, whether by judge or jury, has found *x*, then *x* must be accepted as true. The lawyer who tries to argue before an appellate court that *x* is not true will quickly find himself on the wrong end of a scolding from the court for trying to use the appellate courts as the forum for relitigating factual determinations that appellate courts are expected to take as final.

This is a nice model, but it may not capture fully the extent to which appellate courts are themselves engaged in determining questions of fact. *Brown v. Board of Education* may have highlighted the issue because of the prominence of the case and because of the Supreme Court's footnote reference to the relevant studies made it quite obvious what was going on, but *Brown* turns out not to be all that unusual.

Consider, for example, *New York Times Co. v. Sullivan*,[23] the 1964 case in which the Supreme Court constitutionalized and revolutionized the law of defamation throughout the United States by holding that public officials (and, later, public figures)[24] could succeed in a libel case only if they could prove with convincing clarity not only that what had been said about them was false, but also that it had been said with knowledge

22. For descriptions of the controversy, see John Monahan & Laurens Walker, *Social Science in Law: Cases and Materials* 84–99, 106 (1985); Mody Sanjay, Note, "Brown Footnote Eleven in Historical Context: Social Science and the Supreme Court's Quest for Legitimacy," 54 *Stan. L. Rev.* 703 (2002).
23. 376 U.S. 254 (1964).
24. 388 U.S. 130 (1967).

of its falsity. In other words, plaintiffs had to prove not only intentional publication, but also intentional falsity. This was a dramatic change in the common law, and the Court justified the change by concluding that criticism of public officials would be "uninhibited, robust, and wide open" only if publishers were relieved from liability for even their negligent untruths. This empirical conclusion may well be true, but it is not at all clear how the Supreme Court knew that it was true. Some might think the proposition self-evident, but once we realize that uninhibited, robust, and wide-open press criticism of public officials exists in countries with far more restrictive defamation doctrines (Australia, for example) than exist in the United States, it becomes less clear that the factual proposition that provided the linchpin for the Court's conclusion was as self-evident as the Supreme Court thought it was. Nevertheless, this factual proposition about press behavior was an essential element of the Court's conclusion. Whether the Court was right (probably) or wrong (possibly) in its assessment is not the important issue here. The important issue is the question of the extent to which a potentially contestable factual proposition—and not one that had been part of the trial proceedings at all—turned out to be central to the Court's legal conclusion. Perhaps because the Court in *Sullivan* did not cite to nonlegal sources, as it did in *Brown,* the factual link in the Court's argumentative chain was less obvious, but no less than in *Brown,* the Court in *Sullivan* rested its conclusion on a contestable factual proposition as to which there had been no finding of fact below.

Much the same was true, and with a level of controversy closer to *Brown* than *Sullivan,* with respect to the Supreme Court's conclusion in *Mapp v. Ohio*[25] that illegally obtained evidence could not be used at a subsequent criminal trial regardless of its reliability. If an illegal search, for example, actually did lead to the discovery of drugs plainly belonging to the defendant, after *Mapp* those drugs would be excluded as evidence from the trial. The Court based its conclusion on the belief that an exclusionary rule would deter the police from engaging in unconstitutional behavior, but once again this is an empirical conclusion with which reasonable people can and did disagree.[26] Maybe the police do not much

25. 367 U.S. 643 (1961).
26. See Yale Kamisar, "Does (Did) (Should) the Exclusionary Rule Rest on a 'Principled Basis' Rather than an 'Empirical Proposition'?," 16 *Creighton L. Rev.* 565 (1983).

worry about what goes on at trials and are concerned mainly with apprehending perpetrators, or maybe unconstitutional police behavior would be deterred more by threats of internal sanctions against police officers personally. But whatever the fact of the matter, the important point is that once again the Court's route to a new legal rule was one that took it through the making of a factual determination as to which most of the evidence appeared to come from the Justices' own beliefs, experiences, hunches, intuitions, and armchair sociology.

Finally, consider the plurality opinion in *Bush v. Gore*.[27] In concluding that the Supreme Court of Florida had erred in rejecting George W. Bush's equal protection challenge to the Florida vote-counting procedure, the Supreme Court found it important that the casting of invalid ballots was not in fact a historically infrequent occurrence and that many invalid presidential ballots had been cast in most previous elections. Whether this should or should not have been important to the Court is not pertinent to our discussion of factual determination, but what is germane here is the fact that on this factual proposition there was again virtually no finding below, and the Court reached its conclusion, as discussed at somewhat greater length in Chapter 4, on the basis of several newspaper articles, presumably located by the Justices (or, more likely, their law clerks) through a Nexis search.

Brown, Sullivan, Mapp, and *Bush v. Gore* are all constitutional cases in the Supreme Court, but it would be a mistake to think of the phenomenon as restricted to constitutional law. When Holmes insisted that the "life of the law has not been logic; it has been experience,"[28] he made it clear that appellate judges, in both following and creating "the path of the law," would have to rely on empirical and factual determinations, a phenomenon extensively theorized almost a century later by Melvin Eisenberg in showing how reliance on what he called "social propositions" is an essential element in common-law reasoning.[29] *Henningsen,* for example, was premised on a view about the nature of consumer transactions that came largely from the Court's own impressions, and when the New York Court of Appeals in *Adams v. New Jersey Steamboat Co.*[30] concluded that a stateroom on a steamboat was more like an inn

27. 531 U.S. 98 (2000).
28. O. W. Holmes, Jr., *The Common Law* 1 (1881).
29. Melvin A. Eisenberg, *The Nature of the Common Law* (1988).
30. 45 N.E. 369 (N.Y. 1896). The case has become a staple of discussions

than like a sleeping compartment on a train, it relied heavily on what *it* believed about contested factual propositions regarding the normal uses and expectations with respect to steamboats, inns, and trains.

But if social propositions—which are conclusions of fact, albeit about general social conditions and not about the particular facts of the particular case—play such a large role in appellate decision-making, then how is an appellate court to find out about the facts necessary to reach such conclusions? This has been a recurring issue, and it is one that Justice Breyer of the Supreme Court, more than anyone, has brought to the forefront of legal debate, especially in the context of questions about science.[31] Justice Breyer himself is hardly reticent about going far beyond the record to make factual determinations he believes necessary to resolve the cases before him, and his dissenting opinion in *Lopez v. United States*[32] is replete with scores of references to economic, sociological, and political materials directed at the question of whether the possession of weapons in the public schools has an effect on interstate commerce. Similarly, Justice Breyer's (again dissenting) opinion in the high school affirmative-action case of *Parents Involved in Community Schools v. Seattle School District No.1*[33] drew heavily not only on his own research about the factual background of *that* case[34] but also on far-reaching em-

---

about the use and misuse of analogy in legal reasoning. See Richard Posner, *How Judges Think* 169–70 (2008); Lloyd Weinreb, *Legal Reason: The Use of Analogy in Legal Argument* (2005); Scott Brewer, "Exemplary Reasoning: Semantics, Pragmatics, and the Rational Force of Legal Argument by Analogy," 109 *Harv. L. Rev.* 923 (1996). And see Chapter 5, *supra*.

31. See Stephen Breyer, "Introduction," *in Reference Manual on Scientific Evidence* (2d ed., 2000); Stephen Breyer, "The Interdependence of Science and Law," an address at the American Association for the Advancement of Science Annual Meeting and Science Innovation Exposition, Feb. 16, 1998, available at www.aaas .org/meetings/scope/breyer.htm *and in* 280 *Science* 537 (1998).

32. 514 U.S. 549 (1995).

33. 127 S. Ct. 2738 (2007).

34. This practice is both unusual and controversial. There is a traditional distinction between legislative facts and adjudicative facts, the former being the facts necessary to make or support a legal rule and the latter being the facts of a particular controversy or rule application. This is a distinction that is of some import with respect to questions of due process and the right to a hearing, because it is accepted that individuals have due-process rights to notice and hearing with respect to adjudicative facts that will produce adverse consequences to them, but not to legislative facts that will produce adverse consequences to them only in respect to which they are members of a class adversely affected by the legislative rule. See Bi-

pirical inquiry about the history, sociology, psychology, and politics of student assignment in American public schools. For Justice Breyer, managing appellate factual and scientific inquiry has been for some time a pressing question, but it may be that we are not especially close to an answer.

If what Holmes called experience and what Eisenberg calls social propositions are a pervasive and indeed necessary component of common-law *legal* decision-making, then where are appellate judges (or trial judges making legal and not factual determinations) to get the information necessary to reach their factual and empirical conclusions? Justice Breyer's opinions, the social science data in *Brown v. Board of Education,* and the newspaper reports in Justice Kennedy's opinion in *Bush v. Gore* have the virtue of displaying the sources on which the Justices were relying, but *Sullivan, Mapp, Henningsen,* and *Adams* are for just that reason more important. Even when a judge does not cite to nonlegal academic journals or newspapers or anything else, she is still, although less obviously, relying on sources of information that are importantly factual, that may very well be contested, and that wind up being part of the law in a somewhat under-the-table manner, even apart from the way in which such propositions may produce adverse consequences for one of the parties without that party having much or any opportunity to challenge those propositions by the normal adversarial processes, including but not limited to cross-examination.[35]

Metallic Investment Co. v. State Board of Equalization of Colorado, 239 U.S. 441 (1915); Londoner v. Denver, 210 U.S. 373 (1908). Related to but somewhat distinct from the notice and hearing question is the question of whether an appellate court should investigate adjudicative facts not found below or even reevaluate findings about adjudicative facts made by the trier of fact. The answer to these questions has traditionally been a clear no, and the extent to which judges may or should do research about the facts of *this* case, outside of the formal adversary processes of trial with the rules of evidence, is more controversial and far less accepted than the idea that judges can and must do their own research with respect to legislative facts.

35. It is worth noting here that traditional English practice, now softening somewhat, prohibits judges from doing their own research outside of the presence of counsel, even as to the law. Cases and statutes not cited and argued by the parties or discussed in open court might as well not even exist. This practice may seem unusual to Americans, but it is part of a tradition of *orality* that stresses that nothing should happen in litigation that is not transparent and available for argument by all parties. See Delmar Karlen, *Appellate Courts in the United States and En-*

To the extent that contested factual propositions are increasingly "flagged" by citation to nonlegal materials,[36] the issue is becoming more patent, but the deeper question is not about the materials that judges consult or cite in order to make legal, as opposed to adjudicative factual, determinations. Even with no explicit consultation and no citation, judges making law, and often just applying law, must rely on empirical conclusions that lurk scarcely beneath the surface. When the existence of such conclusions is not announced by means of, for example, citation to newspapers or nonlegal books or periodicals, there is a risk that we may ignore the extent to which such conclusions are open to contest, which may well be a function of what the judges think of as common knowledge but which others may wish to challenge. Citation to materials outside of the traditional legal canon may be for some a source of alarm, but it may as well be a way in which the empirical propositions that are necessarily a part of all judicial lawmaking and much judicial law application can be subject to argument and challenge, rather than simply being clothed in the disguise of common knowledge or what judges believe, not always correctly, and not necessarily unrelated to their own backgrounds, to be the common wisdom of humanity.

---

gland (1964); Suzanne Ehrenberg, "Embracing the Writing-Centered Legal Process," 89 *Iowa L. Rev.* 1159 (2004); Robert J. Martineau, "The Value of Appellate Oral Argument: A Challenge to the Conventional Wisdom," 72 *Iowa L. Rev.* 1 (1986); Richard A. Posner, "Judicial Autonomy in a Political Environment," 38 *Ariz. St. L. Rev.* 1, 10 (2006). The tradition can produce extraordinarily lengthy appellate arguments (which often take days, rather than the typical thirty minutes per side in American appellate courts), because the expectation is that everything on which judges rely is open to argument by both sides, and it produces a tendency to rely on only a narrow range of widely accepted legal sources. But it does forestall most objections that judges are making decisions based on information not known to or argued by both parties.

36. See the discussion in section 4.4, *supra*. See also Frederick Schauer & Virginia J. Wise, "Non-Legal Information and the Delegalization of Law," 29 *J. Legal Stud.* 495 (2000).

THE BURDEN OF PROOF AND ITS COUSINS

12.1 The Burden of Proof

Law navigates through a fog of uncertainty. In attempting to figure out what happened in the past, the legal system must deal with faulty recollections, lost documents, missing witnesses, inattentive jurors, and countless other impediments to knowing with very much confidence what actually took place months or years earlier. And even in trying to assess what law should apply to the facts so imperfectly perceived, lawyers and judges face a world of conflicting precedents, vague statutes, substantive disagreement, and a host of additional obstacles to being able to determine just what it is that the law requires.

Not only does law do its work under conditions of uncertainty, but the legal system is also a complex one in which the separation of powers, in the nontechnical (or at least non-constitutional) sense of that term, is a dominant consideration. Appellate courts must take account of the tasks assigned to trial judges and trial juries, federal courts are constitutionally required to be cognizant of the proper domains of state courts and vice versa, and courts engaged in judicial review of legislative or administrative action need to recognize the distinct responsibilities of legislatures and the specialized expertise of agencies. The question before a judge is rarely simply the question of what is right but is almost always imbued with the issue of whose job it is to determine what is right. *Jurisdiction* may be an important component of the law of civil procedure, but it is even more central to the very structure and idea of law itself, for law is characterized by its concern not only for what is decided but for whose job it is to decide it.

Under such conditions of uncertainty and divided responsibilities, the burden of proof, and its companion concepts of deference and presumption, play a huge role. These concepts tell us just how sure the legal system needs to be in order to reach a particular conclusion, and indirectly tell the system what is to happen in the event that it is not sufficiently sure. And by specifying how confident the law must be in order to produce a particular legal outcome, the burden of proof, especially, reflects deeper substantive and not just procedural values that vary depending on the consequences of that outcome.

The most familiar operation of the burden of proof is in criminal cases, where we encounter the well-known requirement that the prosecution must prove its case beyond a reasonable doubt. But what does this mean, and what values does it reflect? In order to address these questions, and also for purposes of simplicity and clarity, let us assign a rough numerical probability to the burden of proof.[1] We can thus start with the premise, say, that the prosecution must prove its case such that the jury, to convict, must be 95 percent certain of the defendant's guilt. This percentage is in some sense arbitrary, or at the very least a rough estimate, but it captures the basic idea that the beyond-a-reasonable-doubt standard requires that the jury or judge have a very high degree of confidence in the defendant's guilt in order to convict. If they are not 95 percent sure, then they must render a verdict of "not guilty."

An important feature of such a high burden of proof is that if taken seriously—and there is scant reason to believe that it is not in most criminal cases—the 95 percent "beyond a reasonable doubt" standard can be predicted systematically to let a large number of guilty people go unpunished. Suppose we have ten defendants, and suppose further that each of them is 90 percent, but only 90 percent, likely to have committed a crime. If the jury is doing its job properly, then all ten defendants will go free, because in none of these cases will the prosecution have met the requisite burden of proof of 95 percent confidence in the defendant's guilt. But because each of the ten defendants is 90 percent likely actually to have committed the crime with which he has been charged, we can expect that nine of those ten acquitted defendants will actually be guilty of that for which they are on trial, in spite of which they are now going free.

In letting so many of the guilty go free, the "proof beyond a reasonable doubt" standard may seem like a bad idea. And of course it certainly does seem so to legions of politicians who claim that the legal system

1. See Frederick Mosteller & Cleo Youtz, "Quantifying Probabilistic Assessments," 5 *Statistical Sci.* 2 (1990).

coddles criminals and lets far too many of them escape their just deserts. But William Blackstone has given us the canonical justification for the law's approach. "The law holds, that it is better that ten guilty persons escape," he wrote in 1769, "than that one innocent suffer."[2] What Blackstone understood was that if the legal system employed a lower burden of proof in criminal cases, say 60 percent, then we could expect that for every ten defendants for whom the probability of guilt was exactly 60 percent and no more, all ten would go to prison, but only six of them would be guilty.[3] No guilty people would go free, but four innocents would be punished. And that, for Blackstone and the legal system he celebrated, was just too much. It is unfortunate when guilty people go free, Blackstone thought then and we still think now, but it is far worse when innocent people are condemned. Consequently, the legal system calibrates the burden of proof in such a way that the law can serve the social interest in convicting the guilty while keeping the number of innocents that it punishes very low.[4]

Blackstone's solution—our solution—to the problem of uncertainty is far from perfect. If we really wanted never, ever to convict the innocent, we would set the burden of proof astronomically high—absolute certainty, or 99.99 percent determined by three consecutive juries, or something of that sort—and we would have solved most of the problem of convicting the innocent. We would have done so, however, at the cost of convicting far too few of the guilty. The standard that common-law legal systems have chosen is a balance, but a balance heavily weighted in favor of the social judgment that convicting the innocent is a great deal worse

2. 4 William Blackstone, *Commentaries* *358. Blackstone was not the first to express the idea, John Fortescue having written in 1471 that "I should, indeed, prefer twenty guilty men to escape through mercy, than one innocent to be condemned unjustly." Sir John Fortescue, *De Laudibus Legum Angliae* 65 (Dr. Chrimes ed., 1942) (1471). And in 1824 it was said that "it is better that ninety-nine . . . offenders shall escape than that one innocent man be condemned." Thomas Starkie, *Evidence* 756 (1824). Fortescue, Blackstone, and Starkie were all expressing the same principle, but the differences among ten to one, twenty to one, and ninety-nine to one reflect different views about the comparative harms of the two types of errors. See generally Alexander Volokh, "n Guilty Men," 146 *U. Pa. L. Rev.* 173 (1997).

3. For the statistically inclined, it is worth noting that Blackstone's ten-to-one ratio reflects an underlying burden of proof of 0.91.

4. See John Kaplan, "Decision Theory and the Factfinding Process," 20 *Stan. L. Rev.* 1075 (1968).

than freeing the guilty, but also that avoiding convicting the innocent is not the only social value there is.

Now let us compare to the criminal standard the standard that is typically used in civil cases. Here the plaintiff will prevail simply if she proves her case by a preponderance of the evidence; the British call this the "balance of probabilities." If the plaintiff proves her case by a bare preponderance—50.000001 percent, say—she will win, but if she falls below that, she will not.

This is a very different standard from that used in criminal cases, and that is because the values at stake are very different. Yes, it is regrettable when a defendant who is not actually at fault, say, is held liable in a tort action and has to pay damages. But in the eyes of the law this is no more regrettable than someone who is injured through the fault of another not being able to recover because the defendant has been mistakenly found not to be liable. Unlike in the criminal case, where we deem the mistake of imprisoning the innocent far worse than the mistake of freeing the guilty, in the civil context we consider the mistake of a wrongly uncompensated plaintiff to be no less serious than that of a defendant wrongfully held liable. The two errors being equal, the burden of proof selected reflects this underlying equality of values.[5]

Although proof beyond a reasonable doubt and proof by a preponderance of the evidence are the best-known and most widely used of law's burdens of proof, there are in fact many others. People may not be committed to mental institutions, for example, unless they have been proved by "clear and convincing" evidence to be dangerous to themselves or others, and it is generally accepted that this standard is somewhat higher than proof by a preponderance of the evidence, yet somewhat lower than proof beyond a reasonable doubt.[6] The police may obtain a search warrant only if they can establish "probable cause"—the exact words used in the Fourth Amendment—to believe that the search will yield evidence of the crime they are investigating. And although it

5. In fact the matter is somewhat more complicated than this, because the plaintiff must prove *each* element of a cause of action by a preponderance of the evidence. In other words, the plaintiff must prove *all* of the elements by a preponderance of the evidence to prevail, but the defendant will prevail if she proves only one element to such a standard. The effect of this is to place a burden on the plaintiff to actually prevail that is somewhat higher than a bare preponderance. See Ronald J. Allen, "The Nature of Juridical Proof," 13 *Cardozo L. Rev.* 373 (1991).

6. See Addington v. Texas, 441 U.S. 418, 432–33 (1979).

may be even harder to translate this standard into a number, it is well understood that this places a higher burden of proof on the police than the "reasonable suspicion" standard applicable when the police would stop and question a person but not seek to search his residence.[7]

Although the burden of proof is most visible with respect to the final determination of the outcome of a civil or criminal case, it is even more prevalent when used in conjunction with the various decisions that have to be made prior to final judgment, or when the burden is assigned to one party or another for various elements of a case. For the numerous legal and factual questions that are heard by judges leading up to the trial itself, for the procedural and evidentiary issues that arise during a trial, and for numerous different substantive issues, one party or another will have what is called the burden of persuasion. In criminal cases, for example, the defendant will have the burden of persuasion on defenses such as insanity, alibi, and self-defense. And in tort actions for trespass or battery, a defendant who claims consent must persuade the trier of fact that such consent existed, as opposed to the plaintiff having to show that there was no consent. And on most procedural issues arising at or before a trial, it will be the moving party who bears the burden of persuasion.

The burden of persuasion needs to be distinguished from the burden of production, sometimes called the burden of going forward with the evidence. Largely because one party or another is more likely to have the relevant information, the law will often assign to a particular party the burden of producing sufficient facts to put some matter at issue, and this is what is called the burden of production. Sometimes the party with the burden of production will also have the burden of persuasion, but often the two will be distinct. In contract cases to enforce a contract, for example, it is common for the defendant to have the burden of coming forward with sufficient evidence to put into issue the possibility of mutual mistake, or impossibility, or release, but once the defendant has met its burden of production, the burden of persuasion still rests with the contract-enforcing plaintiff to show the lack of release, or the lack of mutual mistake, or the lack of impossibility.[8]

Whether it is the burden of proof for the case as a whole, or the bur-

7. See Alabama v. White, 496 U.S. 325 (1990); Terry v. Ohio, 392 U.S. 1 (1968).
8. See Robert E. Scott & George C. Triantis, "Anticipating Litigation in Contract Design," 115 *Yale L.J.* 814 (2006).

den of persuasion on a particular issue, or the burden of production of evidence, it is important to bear in mind an important theme: these devices are all called "burdens" for a reason. From the point of view of an advocate, these burdens, like most other burdens, are almost by definition something that you do not want to have. The burden of proof is, for entire cases or for components parts of them, something a lawyer wishes her opponent to have, and often much of legal argument consists of attempting to persuade a judge (or jury) that your opponent has the burden of proof. It is an exaggeration to say that once you have saddled your opponent with the burden of proof on some issue, your job as an advocate is done. As we know in the criminal law, even high burdens of proof are met with great frequency. Still, the advocate who can persuade the decision-maker that the other side has the burden of proof has gone a long way toward success, and as a result, arguments about the burden of proof are as frequent in legal argument as arguments about the law and the facts themselves.

12.2 Presumptions

As we have just seen, allocating the burdens of proof, persuasion, and production is one way in which the law deals with decision-making under factual uncertainty. But it is not the only way. Often the law uses *presumptions,* which are the starting point from which factual inquiry takes off and which specify what facts will be taken to be true if the party with the burden of proof does not satisfy the burden of proof and thus overcome the presumption. Presumptions also specify what additional facts are taken to have been proved when one of the parties proves some particular fact.

In some respects, a presumption is prior to but closely related to the burden of proof, because it is a presumption that typically establishes who *has* the burden of proof, independent of just how much that party needs to demonstrate in order to satisfy it. And it is the presumption that specifies what is to happen when the party with the burden of proof on some issue does not meet it. When we say that a defendant in a criminal case is presumed innocent, for example, we are also saying that the prosecution has the burden of proof, with the failure to satisfy it resulting in the defendant's acquittal. Similarly, when it is held that a will is presumed to have been properly executed,[9] the effect is that a party claiming fraud,

9. See Slack v. Truitt, 791 A.2d 129 (Md. 2002).

duress, or lack of capacity must demonstrate that one of these defeating conditions has actually occurred, and in the absence of such a demonstration, the court will accept the validity of the will, even though the party claiming that the will was validly executed has proved nothing at all. In the same way, the common law has traditionally had a presumption of legitimacy, such that a child is presumed to be the legitimate offspring of his parents, and the burden is on someone challenging legitimacy—in the context of a dispute about inheritance, for example—to show that the presumed fact of legitimacy is not in reality so.[10] And perhaps the most familiar presumption of all is res ipsa loquitur ("the thing speaks for itself"), the effect of which, for example, is to establish that that a surgical patient does not need to prove negligence when he emerges from the surgery with a sponge or a surgical instrument in his abdomen, because negligence will be presumed from the very nature of the event.[11]

Quite often presumptions do not operate on the basis of a clean slate but require a party to prove something, by virtue of which something else will be presumed. A good example is the long-standing rule in most jurisdictions that proof that a letter has been mailed will create a presumption that it has been received.[12] The presumption of innocence may be unusual, therefore, because it is a background assumption of the legal system. But in the normal course of things, the legal system will require a party to prove A, and by virtue of A having been proved, B will be presumed. A beneficiary under an accidental death insurance policy may have to prove that the decedent died from something other than natural causes, but under what is called the "presumption against suicide," it will ordinarily be presumed that if the claimant so proves, then accident rather than suicide will be presumed. Consequently, the burden is on the insurance company to come forward and prove suicide, failing which the death will be presumed to have been caused by an accident.[13]

It is common to distinguish between rebuttable and irrebuttable

---

10. See, e.g., John M. v. Paula T., 571 A.2d 1380 (Pa. 1990); Joseph Cullen Ayer, Jr., "Legitimacy and Marriage," 16 *Harv. L. Rev.* 22 (1902).

11. See, e.g., Fla. Stat. § 766.102 (4) (2004); Armstrong v. Wallace, 47 P.2d 740 (Cal. 1939); Fink v. Bonham, 183 N.E.312 (Ind. 1932).

12. See, e.g., Hagner v. United States, 285 U.S. 427 (1932); Santana Gonzalez v. Attorney General, 506 F.3d 274, 278–79 (3rd Cir. 2007); Holt v. Mississippi Employment Security Commission, 724 So. 2d 466, 471 (Miss. Ct. App. 1998).

13. See Davison v. National Life & Accident Insurance Co., 126 S.E.2d 811 (Ga. 1962); Schelberger v. Eastern Savings Bank, 458 N.E.2d 1225 (N.Y. 1983).

(sometimes called "conclusive") presumptions. And it is the former that are most closely aligned with the burden of proof. When a defendant is presumed innocent, when a sponge is presumed to have been left in a patient's abdomen by virtue of the negligence of the nurse or physician, when a child is presumed legitimate, and when a will is presumed to have been validly executed, it remains open to the other party to prove, by the burden of proof that has been assigned to it, that the state of affairs embodied in the presumption is not in reality so in this case. The existence of a presumption of validity for a will, for example, does not prevent another party from attempting to prove that the will was made under duress, or as a result of fraud, or by someone not in full possession of her mental faculties at the time of execution. And if it is so proved, then the presumption can be said to have been *rebutted*. In this respect, the presumption is in effect an allocation of the burden of coming forward, a specification of the burden of proof to be borne by the party who has the burden of coming forward, and a statement of the facts that will be understood as having existed if the party with the burden either does not come forward or comes forward and does not meet his burden of proof.

Irrebuttable presumptions are quite different. In structure they are similar to rebuttable ones, because an irrebuttable presumption also specifies the state of affairs that the law will assume to exist (even if it does not). But because the law does not allow the other side to challenge the conclusion of an irrebuttable presumption, it remains unconnected with procedural issues such as a burden of coming forward or a burden of proof. Indeed, there is little difference, except in the form of expression, between an irrebuttable presumption and what we would simply call a rule of law. The state of Florida, for example, has, like all other states, a law prohibiting the sale and distribution of illegal drugs, including cocaine. The law imposes a much higher penalty on those who are trafficking in drugs than on those who merely possess them, and then goes on to say that anyone possessing 28 grams or more of cocaine is irrebuttably presumed to be in the business of and guilty of trafficking illegal drugs.[14] In other words, if you are found in possession of more than 28 grams of cocaine, you are presumed to be a cocaine dealer, whether you are or not. The burden of proof is not an issue, because the law simply does not permit you to try to rebut the presumption, even if it is totally false as to you.

14. Fla. Stat. §893.135(1)(b)(1) (Supp. 2002).

Such a presumption might seem unfair, and indeed this kind of pre-sumption seemed very unfair to the Supreme Court for a few years back in the 1970s.[15] But as the Supreme Court came to realize upon further re-flection,[16] an irrebuttable presumption is little different from any other legal rule. Yes, the possessor of 28 grams of cocaine might not be a drug dealer, but the person who drives at 70 miles per hour in a 55-miles-per-hour zone might not be driving unsafely, and the insider who buys and then sells shares in her own company in a less-than-six-months period may not be in possession of any inside information at all. But, as we saw in Chapter 2, rules do their work precisely by cutting off access to their background justifications, and few are surprised that exceeding the speed limit while driving very safely is still an invitation to a traffic ticket.

Once we see that rules have force even when they produce results that would not be produced by direct application of the rationales or background justifications, we can see irrebuttable presumptions in their proper light. If Florida, in order to address the problem of cocaine sell-ing (the background justification), had simply prohibited possessing 28 grams or more of cocaine, the nondealing possessor of more than 28 grams of cocaine would have no better an argument than the safe driver who is exceeding the speed limit. Just as we would say to the safe driver that he has broken the law even if he is not within the class of people the law was designed to encompass, we can say the same thing to the nondealing drug possessor. An irrebuttable presumption is thus just a different way of characterizing an omnipresent feature of all legal rules, and there is no reason to suppose that there is anything deeply wrong with that.

The category of interest, therefore, is the category of rebuttable pre-sumptions, for these are the ones that actually make a procedural dif-ference. By allocating the burdens of proof and persuasion, and by specifying what we might think of as the factual "default," rebuttable presumptions are essential elements in the structuring of litigation, not only serving substantive legal goals, but also attempting to ensure that scarce legal and judicial resources are not wasted by forcing parties to spend time and money proving what is usually but not always true.

15. See Cleveland Board of Education v. LaFleur, 414 U.S. 632 (1974); United States Department of Agriculture v. Murry, 413 U.S. 508 (1973); Vlandis v. Kline, 412 U.S. 441 (1973).

16. Weinberger v. Salfi, 422 U.S. 749 (1975).

Most presumptions arise in the context of facts. But presumptions can be legal as well as factual. Consider the structure of American equal protection doctrine, for example. It is now well settled that state classifications based on race, religion, ethnicity, and national origin are presumptively unconstitutional and will be upheld only if the state demonstrates a *compelling interest* in using such a classification, and demonstrates as well that there is no less restrictive (of equality) alternative that it can use to achieve that interest.[17] Here the question is one not of fact but of law, but we are still talking about a presumption. The law is presumed unconstitutional, but the state may rebut that presumption by satisfying a heavy burden of justification. Conversely, when a statute draws a classification within this category of "suspect" classifications, it is presumed to be constitutionally permissible and will be invalidated only if the challenger meets *its* burden of proving that the classification is irrational.

It turns out that this kind of presumption not only pervades constitutional law but may usefully characterize much of the operation of American law generally. As we have seen in various places throughout this book, it is sometimes the case in American law that judges will set aside the literal or plainest indications of formal law in order to serve the law's purpose or in order to achieve larger goals of justice. This is a fair characterization of *Riggs v. Palmer*,[18] *Church of the Holy Trinity v. United States*,[19] and *United States v. Kirby*,[20] for example, and it is a frequent occurrence on the American legal landscape. But it is also the case that the formal law often prevails even when the outcomes it produces are somewhat unjust or in other ways somewhat suboptimal. That is how we might explain *TVA v. Hill*,[21] constitutional separation-of-powers cases like *Immigration and Naturalization Service v. Chadha*[22] and *Bowsher v. Synar*,[23] the large number of cases in which unworthy beneficiaries who

17. See Palmore v. Sidoti, 466 U.S. 429 (1984); Loving v. Virginia, 388 U.S. 1 (1967). The standard in fact originated in the notorious Korematsu v. United States, 323 U.S. 214 (1944), in which the Supreme Court proceeded to conclude that internment of Americans of Japanese origin during the Second World War satisfied the "compelling interest" standard.

18. 22 N.E. 188 (N.Y. 1889).

19. 143 U.S. 457 (1892).

20. 74 U.S. (7 Wall.) 482 (1868).

21. 437 U.S. 153 (1978).

22. 462 U.S. 919 (1983).

23. 478 U.S. 714 (1986).

were in some way responsible for the death of the testator were, unlike Elmer Palmer, allowed to inherit, and possibly even *United States v. Locke*.[24] And perhaps the idea of a legal or normative presumption is the best way of at least partially reconciling these two seemingly opposed lines of cases and decisions. It may be, that is, that the best characterization of much of American law is that the formal side of law—what the rules or the precedents *say*—will be *presumed* to control, but the outcome indicated by the formal law will not be the final outcome of the case if the party burdened by the formal outcome can prove or persuade the court that the result so indicated will be *highly* unjust or in some other way not simply wrong but very wrong. In adopting this approach to the effect of rules and precedents, American law has perhaps used the idea of a presumption as a way of reconciling the stability and predictability needs that are satisfied by a formal approach to law while recognizing that formal law cannot always produce the right answer and that sometimes a wrong answer will be so wrong that it would be irresponsible and reprehensible were the legal system unable to do anything about it.

12.3 Deference and the Allocation of Decision-Making Responsibility

In the same cluster of ideas in which we find burdens of proof and presumptions, we also find the idea of *deference*. Law, perhaps even more than other institutions, is very concerned with *jurisdiction*, in both the technical and the nontechnical senses. In the technical sense, the law worries about whether and when a court has the power to make a decision and enforce a judgment against certain individuals and other entitles. Questions about *personal jurisdiction* are about whether, for example, a court can hear and decide a case against an individual with few connections to the location of the court, or at times about whether a court can exercise power over people holding certain kinds of positions.[25] And sometimes the jurisdictional question is not so much about *who* a court

24. 471 U.S. 84 (1984).

25. Marbury v. Madison, 5 U.S. (1 Cranch) 137 (1803), has achieved its fame by virtue of having established the power of judicial review, but at the time it was most controversial and raised President Thomas Jefferson's hackles for its assertion of jurisdiction over officials of the executive branch of government.

can reach as about *what* a court can adjudicate. Thus, the issue we refer to as *subject matter jurisdiction* is about whether a court can hear cases of this kind, as when, for example, a federal court must decide whether its authority to decide diversity of citizenship cases between citizens of different states includes the authority to decide a case between a citizen of a state and another state itself.[26]

But, as noted briefly above, the concept of jurisdiction looms larger in law than we might suspect if we were to focus only on the procedural questions of personal and subject matter jurisdiction. In this larger sense, jurisdiction is about who gets to decide what, and a pervasive concern of the legal mind is the question of whether some institution that made a decision had the authority to make it. It is not enough, especially for the law, that the decision was right. It must also be the case that the judge or other person making the decision, or the institution making the decision, was authorized by the system to make it. Whether it is constitutional concerns of federalism, or the question of when congressional legislation has preempted the states, or whether it is for a judge or a jury to decide questions of fact, most legal decisions involve, sometimes explicitly but usually implicitly, the question not only of whether some decision was right but of whether the right institution made it.

Many of these issues arise in the context of direct determinations of jurisdiction or decision-making authority. But sometimes they are embedded in the important question of *deference:* under what circumstances will a decision-maker respect the decisions of another body, even when the decision-maker thinks the decision of the other body is mistaken?[27] In some respects this resembles the questions of authority we took up in Chapter 4, but deference often operates in just the opposite direction. When we think of authority, we ordinarily think of it as a relationship from top to bottom. Those in authority—sergeants, parents, teachers, supreme courts—give orders or make decisions, and those below them are expected to obey even when they disagree with the decisions. To respect authority is to look up from the bottom to the top. Deference also involves respecting decisions with which the deferrer may well disagree, but by contrast, often it is from top to bottom rather than from bottom to top. Deference is the way in which those in the higher po-

26. It does not. Moor v. Alameda County, 411 U.S. 693, 717 (1973).
27. See generally Philip Soper, *The Ethics of Deference: Learning from Law's Morals* (2002).

sition in some hierarchy allow some leeway to those below them in the service of efficiency, respect, specialization, diversity, or separation of powers in the broad sense.

Thus, it is frequently the case that an appellate court will defer to the determinations of a trial judge, and in doing so it says that even though it exists above the trial judge in the hierarchy, it will accept some number of trial decisions as valid, even if it disagrees with them. So too when a judge defers to the jury, when the Supreme Court defers to Congress or an administrative agency, or when the European Court of Human Rights allows individual states a *margin of appreciation* in making their own individual rights determinations.

Deference is in important ways closely related to presumptions and burden of proof, and often the mediating idea is the idea of the *standard of review.* When an appellate court reviews the decision of a court below, or when a court reviews the actions of an administrative agency, it typically operates according to an explicit standard of review, which in a way is the mirror image of a burden of proof. It is often the case, for example, that a court will not overturn the action of an administrative agency unless it finds the action to be *arbitrary and capricious,*[28] and an appellate court will not generally overturn a trial court ruling with respect to the admission or exclusion of evidence unless it finds that there has been an *abuse of discretion.*[29] Such standards are highly deferential, because their implication is that most evidentiary and administrative decisions will remain standing, even by judges who disagree with them, unless the decisions are, say, outrageously or extremely wrong. Decisions that are perceived from above to be only somewhat wrong, or maybe even significantly wrong, will under these highly deferential standards be allowed to stand.

Similar standards apply to the review of jury verdicts, to appellate review of trial court findings of fact, and to myriad other questions. But at other times the standards of review are not nearly so deferential. When an appellate court reviews a finding *de novo*—"from the beginning"— the idea is that the appellate court will not defer to the court or agency below but will make its *own* decision, and this is frequently the standard

28. See William S. Jordan, "Ossification Revisited: Does Arbitrary and Capricious Review Significantly Interfere with Agency Ability to Achieve Regulatory Goals through Informal Rulemaking?," 94 *Nw. U. L. Rev.* 393 (2000).

29. See Old Chief v. United States, 519 U.S. 172 (1997).

explicitly or implicitly applied to review of questions of law. When an appellate court is reviewing a trial court ruling about the interpretation of a statute, for example, it will typically say or assume that its ability to interpret the law is no less than that of a trial court. There are no witnesses to observe or physical evidence to evaluate, and thus the standard reasons for appellate deference to trial decisions—apart from simple efficiency—are no longer present, and under such circumstances appellate courts become less hesitant to substitute their judicial judgment for that of another judge. So too, traditionally, for review of legal determinations by an administrative agency, where the presumed greater expertise of the agency entitles it to deference as to questions of fact and policy but not for questions of statutory interpretation.[30]

Deference, legal presumptions, and the burden of proof are thus concepts that not only work together but that are also in some respects and in some contexts different ways of saying the same thing from varying standpoints. It may be hard to understand the idea that a defendant in a criminal case is entitled to deference, and thus there may not be a corollary in the criminal law context to the fact that the prosecution bears the burden of proof. In other contexts, however, the relationship among the burden of proof, deference, and the standard of review is more apparent. It seems quite sensible, therefore, to say that because an administrative agency is presumed to have come to the correct conclusion within its domain of expertise, then it is entitled to deference, and thus that its decision may be overturned only if the challenger can meet the burden of proving that the agency decision was, say, arbitrary and capricious. There is only one relationship in the previous sentence, but deference, presumption, the burden of proof, and the standard of review are all different ways of describing that same relationship from different angles.

The relationships and concepts described in this chapter not only relate to each other, but also connect to the larger themes in this book. When a

---

30. After the Supreme Court decision in Chevron, U.S.A., Inc. v. Natural Resources Defense Council, Inc., 467 U.S. 837 (1984), reviewing courts are expected to defer to an agency even with respect to interpretations of the agency's principal governing statutes. The Court in *Chevron* justified this change on the basis of the agency's presumed expertise in understanding the ins and outs of the technical and specialized statutes with which it deals constantly, but *Chevron* might also be justified simply as a matter of conservation of scarce judicial resources.

court defers to a lower court or to an agency, or when it operates under a high standard of review, it in effect commits itself to accepting—maybe *tolerating* is the better word—some number of what it perceives as erroneous outcomes. So too with presumptions, which under conditions of uncertainty will sometimes compel factual conclusions that are simply not true. And when a party finds itself saddled with the burden of proof, it will on occasion not be able to prove something that is in fact the case. Just as the "beyond the reasonable doubt" standard in criminal law will acquit some number of people who are probably guilty, so too will any high burden of proof commit the system in which it operates to some number of mistakes, although it is to be hoped that they are, like the mistake of acquitting the guilty, mistakes of the right kind.

In accepting the inevitability and strategic or long-term desirability of some number of mistakes of mostly the right kind, the legal system's use of burdens of proof, presumptions, standards of review, and principles of deference, perhaps especially the last, resembles the system's use of rules and precedents, and resembles the legal system's at least partial commitment to formality. It may also resemble the legal system's willingness to make decisions on the basis of less than all of the best or available information. In all of these dimensions, the law, more than many other decision-making institutions, commits itself to accepting wrong or at least suboptimal answers, and it does so in the service of larger or longer-term institutional values, as well as service to the idea that the best way to get the largest number of correct decisions in the long term is often something other than attempting to make the best decision on every occasion. In operating in this way, law and legal reasoning may not be different in kind from other decision-making institutions, but they may differ in degree. At the heart of much of law's use of its characteristic reasoning devices is its acceptance of the fact that the best decision is not always the best *legal* decision. In operating in this fashion, law does not intend to be perverse. It does, however, intend to take institutional values especially seriously, and it does *that* in the hope that in the long run we may be better off with the right institutions than we are when everyone simply tries to make the best decision.